# Basic Italian

Everything you need to live the dolce vita at home

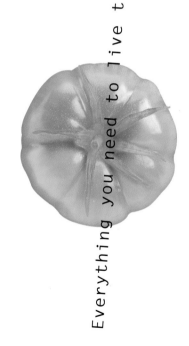

Cornelia Schinharl   Sebastian Dickhaut   Kelsey Lane

# Basic
## Italian
# Contents

Front Flap: Let's learn about the dolce vita—
   Basic Italian cooking lingo to use at home
Back Flap: Four postcards you can send

# Be Italian
## Niente più

Whenever you think of Italy, can you almost taste the basil and olive oil? When the pasta water starts to bubble and boil, do you hear the splashing of the sparkling blue Mediterranean? As the scent of garlic wafts from the pan and you roll a fine "rosso" over your tongue, can you almost reach out and touch the Tuscan hills? When you take your seat at the table and all around you is steam and laughter and the clinking of dishes, the whole world merges into a giant pasta sauce — you and your companions have become the finest ingredients of all.

Whenever you can "be Italian," everything takes on a special beauty – your food, your life and, most of all, you. Just by having a plate of spaghetti Napoli, you're suddenly on vacation, even as you huddle in your kitchenette. Just add a few drops of balsamic vinegar to the salad and you've opened the door to the "terra Italia classica." And you don't need a tour guide because cooking, eating and drinking are all the culture you'll ever need to enjoy yourself on Europe's "boot" in the Med.

After all, everybody speaks some Italian: "Pasta pizza salame, espresso?" Naturalmente! How about some "Polentina focaccia salsicce, ristretto...Non hai capito?" Don't worry, that's why there's the Basic Italian cookbook, the culinary and cultural guide for living the dolce vita at home. It gives you the history of pasta and caffè, and stories about mamma and nonna, with racy tales from Aunt Edna...all with the delectable understanding that Italy is one big lunch where the sun always, always, always shines. When you think of Italy, envision not just ruby-red tomatoes but, from now on, a few green ones, too.

So have a nice trip! And don't forget, be basic. Be Italian. Niente più. Nothing to it.

# Mercato
## Italiano
### The Italian Market

If you ask Felizitas from Frankfurt what she's going to eat, she'll say, "Italian!" If you look on Stuart's plate in Seattle, you know you'll find pizza. If you ask Penelope from Paris for the secret of French cuisine, she'll whisper something about "dei Medici." We see Italy as a sort of culinary capital of the world. But how did it get there?

```
BELLA ITALIA
International import and export.
Family-owned for thousands of years.
Our recipe for success: Recognize the best.
Take the best. Give the best.
```

Those Italians are pretty clever. When they find something good in the world, they take it home, make it into something better and sell it back to everybody again. Take this for example: The Americas once gave the Italians tomatoes and coffee and then left them to their own devices. And now people in the U.S. want nothing less than pomodori from the "boot" and prefer any coffee called "espresso." To cook in the Italian spirit means a deep connection with the ingredients...which is why we're going to describe them for you...

tomatoes

garlic

spaghetti

olives

red wine

lemon

amaretti

basil

red chile

parmesan

anchovies

pine nuts

salami

# 17 essentials for Authentic Italian cooking

olive oil

bread

sun-dried tomatoes

# Fresh Mozzarella

*[motsarElla]*
If you don't believe fresh mozzarella is cheese, you'd best go to the farm and watch the buffalo being milked. Then watch the farmers gently scald, knead and roll the milk mixture. When the little balls have barely soaked in brine, they become a little firm on the outside, and they're full of holes and a flavor that will make you cry out for tomatoes, basil and extra virgin olive oil. No time for the farm? Then ask your grocer for "mozzarella di bufala" (fresh mozzarella or buffalo mozzarella). Regular mozzarella will work for pizza and such, but it's lackluster when the tomatoes and basil come out for Caprese!
For more, see p. 16

# Tomato

*Ital. pomodoro [pomodOro}*
It's still hard to believe tomatoes are native to the Americas. They're so...Italian! No one makes canned pomodori as well as the Neapolitans—straight from the vine, bursting with ripeness and juiciness, then right into the can. It's hard to beat that taste, especially in the middle of winter. During summer, of course, there's nothing better than a naturally vine-ripe tomato—but they're hard to find. If you must grow your own, it's worth it. Or seek out a local farmers' market and try the heirloom varieties. Try some green, too. Well, we gave Italy tomatoes, but they have given us back the recipes for them—and much much more!
For more, see p. 59.

# Garlic

*Ital. aglio [Alyo]*
Wonder why we didn't choose garlic for the front cover of this book? It can be found in almost every Italian dish! But the whole world has gone garlic crazy, in almost every cuisine. That's just fine because tomatoes go excellently with garlic. So do basil, bread, olives, olive oil, Parmesan, fresh red chiles, pine nuts, red wine, anchovies, spaghetti, lemons, salami and sundried tomatoes. Bottom line: garlic goes well with almost everything on this page plus many more things on the next.

# Spaghetti

*[spagEti], thin strings*
First the earth gives wheat, then water is added to form a dough; air dries the mixture and when that's subjected to fire you get a fifth element: Spaghetti, the wise person's pasta that turns everything it touches into gold—garlic, tomatoes and bacon—as well as the annual balance sheets of Italian restaurants and cookbook publishers. Then just imagine its goldness with truffles, scampi, and olive oil—perfecto! It came to all of Italy via the Middle East, then Sicily and Naples long before Marco Polo could say the word "China."
For more, see pp. 12-13, 56.

# Olive

*Ital. oliva [olEEva]*
Who ever came up with the idea that olives are edible? It must have been an optimist. They're so bitter when raw that any thought of marinating them seems insane. Maybe nature thought of it first? One day a few ripe black olives fell into bogs next to the Mediterranean and sat under the sun until they transformed into what we know today as cured olives in brine. They went from bitter to delicious. People deemed them good and soon started marinating unripe green olives, stuffing them and spicing them up. For the purest pleasure, however, there's nothing like eating an assortment of olives that still have their pits.

# Red Wine

*Ital. vino rosso [vEEno r-r-r-r-r-rOso]*
Regardless of whether you're sitting in a merely adequate little Italian dive down the street or on a glowing golden hilltop in Tuscany, you need a glass of red wine to get that dolce vita feeling. Red wine is the best compliment to Italian spices and sunshine. Nevertheless, it's seldom used in recipes. In salad, it only occurs in the form of vinegar. In sauces, it's at most used to loosen sediment from the pan. It's rare in meat dishes because red-wine meats like beef and lamb are used sparingly in Italy. But at the table, red wine flows like water—Italians drink it all through the meal. Ahhh, the dolce vita.
For more, see p. 22.

# Lemon

*Ital. limone [limOne]*
You could press grapes into wine and let the bacteria and air work magic till you had a good vinegar. Or you could ferment the grape juice into must, boil it down for hours and let it mature for years in oak barrels to become a fine balsamic vinegar. Or you could simply squeeze a lemon—always delicious when combined with the freshness of herbs, salad and fish...OR with marinated capers, olives or anchovies...OR combined with sparkling water in "limonata." The zest is also a great culinary addition. If it hadn't already been done, we'd put the lemon on the cover of this book!
For more, see *Basic Cooking*.

# Amaretti

*[amarEtti], almondy*
Despite their name and their flavor, there's no Amaretto in amaretti—yet they're sweet and sinful all the same. Because people are rarely satisfied with just one of anything, amaretti come in many forms. If you just want a couple tiny ones, you can enjoy "amarettini." If you want to make amaretti, use Cornelia's recipe: Beat 3 egg whites until stiff and then beat in $2/3$ cup sugar until shiny. Fold in $2\frac{1}{3}$ cups finely ground almonds & several drops of almond extract. Dollop spoonfuls onto a lined baking sheet (covered with baking parchment). Bake for 30 minutes at 300°F. Or buy some at a specialty store or Italian bakery!

# Basil

*Ital. basilico [basEEleeco]*
We love this story: Columbus sailed for India but landed in the Americas and brought tomatoes back to Europe. Since they went so well with basil and America didn't have any, basil was sent to America. And where did the basil originate? From India! Basil not only goes perfectly with tomatoes but also with garlic, fresh mozzarella, olive oil, red wine and, most especially, pesto and pizza Margherita. Everybody loves basil, even though it quickly loses its best qualities with exposure to heat and time. To contain its magical spirits for as long as possible, combine basil leaves with salt and olive oil.

# Red Chiles

*Ital. peperoncino [peperonchEEno]*
These chiles are also called "diavolo"—this little brother in the famiglia peperone is devilishly hot. When fresh, it provides more than just heat, especially if you remove the seeds. Dried chiles are hotter, and lengthy cooking times intensify the heat. So be careful, particularly if you touch it after chopping (best to wear gloves). The heat sticks to your fingers like tar, and then if you rub your eyes or face, you'll be howling in pain. But you should never howl in pain while eating Italian peperoncino dishes—the rule is "aroma adagio" which more or less means "Hot? Only if it also tastes good!"

# Parmesan

*Ital. parmigiano [parmeejAno], grainy*
The nation that invented balsamic vinegar and sun-dried tomatoes wouldn't sprinkle just any old thing over its food. They take the best milk and concentrate it into large wheels, ripened for months or years in the pungent air till they harden for grating. Whether the cow's milk comes from the Parma or Reggio-Emilia region, it takes 18 to 24 months to become "Parmigiano-Reggiano." A grana padano from the Po Valley can mature in as little as 6 months, as can the pecorino from the south, one partially made from ewe's or goat's milk. The one thing they all have in common is that they taste best when freshly grated. Intense and perfecto!

# Anchovy

*Ital. acciuga [achOOga]*
What do crocodiles and anchovies have in common? The crocodile gives us a glimpse of what dinosaurs used to look like and anchovies teach us what ancient Roman cooking tasted like. The most important seasoning they used was "liquaman," fermented juice made from salted fish. Really good anchovies are still made by layering the fish with salt, creating a spicy-oily brine used to preserve. The result is an excellent flavoring for pasta and meat dishes—but as with Asian fish sauce, it should be used in moderation! For pizza and salads, rinse salted anchovies well or use the milder oil-packed type.

# Pine Nuts

*Ital. pinoli [peenOOlee]*
When God created Italy, he must have been in a playful mood. Not only did he conceal the best oil in olives, bury white truffles deep in the mountains and hide zucchini far away in the Americas, but he also sent the Italians on a culinary treasure hunt in their pine forests. When they soon managed to extract the finest kernels from the pine cones, God nodded benevolently. "Bravo, that's just what I had in mind!" But when the Italians used these nuts to make their first plate of spaghetti pesto, he was dumbfounded. "I never thought of that...bravissimo!" The Italians response? They nodded benevolently.

# 17 essentials for Authentic Italian cooking

# Salami

*Sing. salame [salAme], salted meat*
The good thing about salami is that you can see if it isn't good. Unlike pork sausages, they aren't chopped, mixed and boiled until all the ingredients are hidden in a homogeneous pink mass. The Italians would never do that! They chop bacon and meat into little pieces, throw in some salt, stuff it all into casings and hang it up to dry in the magic Italian air until it becomes air-dried salami. They slice the salami thinly and you can see the distinct red and white colors—there's no room for any secret ingredients. What's secret is that Italian air! Mmm...
For more, see p. 16.

# Olive Oil

*Ital. olio d'oliva [olyo dolEEva]*
The Spaniards make more, the Greeks have been making it longer, and it's even being made by Californians. But the best olive oil is made in Italy. And then they drizzle it, sauté with it, marinate stuff in it—delizioso! Italians like their oil to have a very distinct flavor of olives. That's not necessarily what you want on a green salad, so keep two kinds of oil in the house: One with a light olive flavor for tender salads, some pastas and delicate fish, veal and eggs; the other a very intense, extra virgin olive oil for hearty antipasti and robust pastas as well as for more substantial meats and fish. From Italy of course! For more, see p. 18.

# Bread

*Ital. pane [pAne]*
When you eat Italian, fresh white crusty bread is simply there—as surely as there are trees in a forest. If you really want to eat bread Italy-style, break it into pieces instead of cutting it; it's the difference between picking flowers yourself and cutting them down with a mower. Anyone who spreads butter on true Italian bread doesn't yet understand the dolce vita. And anyone who eats day-old Italian bread would rather view Italy in vacation photos than in person. Although—day-old bread does have its place—in soup, salads and baked goods. But while it's still today, grab a hunk of bread and enjoy!

# Sun-Dried Tomatoes

*Ital. pomodori secchi [pomodOree sEkee]*
Italians have almost always had dried tomatoes; the rest of the world only started clamoring after them in the last two decades. Is it true that those from southern Italy are dried only in the sun? Si, si and once again si! The plum tomato halves are salted to draw out moisture. Then they're marinated when either half-dried (mild) or fully dried (more intense flavor). Cornelia's recipe: Soak sun-dried tomatoes in 3 parts water and 1 part red wine vinegar for 2 hours, then pat thoroughly dry. Layer in jars with garlic, basil and capers. Fill jars with olive oil, seal and marinate for at least 1 week (refrigerated). Use within a couple weeks.

# Pasta secca & fresca

## Water and wheat? "Va bene," said the Italians, "We'll turn them into something wonderful."

The Germans invented the automobile, the English soccer and the Americans fitness. Well done! But the Italians thought, "We can do this better" so they reinvented everything and added a little more panache. Since then, the whole world wants to live like the Italians—not always possible, though, because Mediterranean contentment is ruled by the un-American motto, "Wait instead of crave." Which brings us to pasta…

For millennia, people have mixed together wheat and water. The Chinese and Arabs were the first to devise porridge-like iterations. At some point the Italians said "Va bene," and took the matter of wheat and water into their own hands. In the beginning, the south concentrated on making thin, durum-wheat pasta while the north made ribbon pasta with or without eggs. But then things started heating up all over Italy and generations of ambitious mammas, bakers and manufacturers continued to invent new pasta shapes. When the number reached about 300, they invited the rest of the planet to dinner, and the whole world was beside itself with joy.

Today "pasta" is an international culinary star. Children love spaghetti with anything; gourmets adore tagliatelle as a base for truffles; athletes draw their strength from rigatoni al burro; and researchers just can't get over the fact that pasta with tomatoes, olive oil and red wine—the "Mediterranean diet"—makes them so healthy and happy. And all this is based on nothing but wheat, water and sometimes a little egg? Well done, Italy! But is that all there is to it? At least a few basics for us non-Italians? Grazie.

## Hard Pasta

By this we mean all the dried pasta packed and stacked on the grocer's shelves. In Italy, this "pasta secca" is made from durum semolina and water. Durum wheat has a lot of protein gluten in its grains. When thoroughly kneaded with water, this wheat expands to form a fine, stable network, perfect for the wheat starch to establish itself. This makes pasta dough firm and elastic—easy to shape and dry. In durum semolina, the grains are ground to a size three times coarser than that of flour. If you were to make spaghetti (the traditional pasta secca) from soft wheat flour, it would swell too much during cooking and become spongy and sticky. Italy's first dry pasta specialists were the Sicilians who relied on their relationship with Arab durum wheat specialists. Then it was either Naples that perfected the product or those stubborn Ligurians—mountain dwellers but also seafarers, sturdy northern Italians but also olive oil chefs.

## Soft Pasta

It's the egg in the dough that makes this pasta exquisite. The northern Italians started kneading in egg—originally they had no durum wheat but only bread wheat, which didn't contain enough protein to stabilize the pasta. Calling the tender egg noodles in Italy "pasta fresca" is never wrong because in Italy it really is fresh, unlike much found in the rest of the world. Pasta fresca is not completely dry and therefore takes less time to cook. But fresh also means that it spoils faster due to the egg and increased amount of water (up to 30% as opposed to the 12.5% in dry pasta). You can really only enjoy true pasta fresca (untreated) purchased from the pasta maker on the day it's made. The pasta welded together in the refrigerated section of the supermarket is always pasteurized. If the pasta is directly treated with heat only once, it will keep for 3–5 weeks in an air-tight package. If the packaged pasta is again pasteurized, it will keep for up to three months refrigerated. True pasta fresca is rich and has a full flavor, which means it stands up well to heavy, rich pasta sauces from northern Italy. Typical pasta fresca shapes include lasagne and many ribbon-types from pappardelle to tagliatelle.

## Filled Pasta

Ravioli and tortellini essentially already contain their own sauce—often, they're served with little more than butter or a little tomato. Their wrapping is almost always pasta fresca because it's easy to work with and doesn't dry out as quickly. Originally, filled pasta was designed as a way to use leftovers. Anything extra was wrapped in dough and boiled in soup. Since then it has become a delicacy among pastas, provided the filling is right. Fillings can range from a

flavorful, light ricotta with spinach (see p. 72) to the more suspicious mixture like that found in dried, vacuum-packed tortellini.

## Cooking Pasta

Boil 1 quart water for every 4 oz. pasta, filling a pot no more than 3/4 full. This means that to cook 1 lb. pasta, your pot needs to hold at least 6 quarts. It doesn't have to be heavy nor expensive, but it's easiest to make spaghetti if it's a tall pot.

Let's use spaghetti as an example: hold the pasta vertically and lower into the pot full of boiling water (not salted yet) and let it go. If all goes well, the individual strands of pasta will feather out all around the edges of the pot; then you can gently push them down into the water as they begin to soften. Stir gently. Bring back to a boil. Then add the salt—you waited till this point because now the water will return to a boil faster—important, because you can't cook in lukewarm water! Once boiling, reduce to medium heat. Stir occasionally. The fresher and finer the dough, the shorter the cooking time. Fresh ravioli takes only a few minutes whereas rigatoni secchi can take more than 10. Each shape is different—it's best to remove a noodle after 3/4ths of the recommended cooking time (on the package directions) and test it. If it's still pretty hard and starchy, keep cooking and try again after 1 minute. If it's close to being done, shorten the test interval until the pasta is velvety but still puts up a little resistance to your teeth, meaning it's "al dente." Drain, using a little of the hot pasta water to warm plates or bowls (tip: place the colander in the serving bowl when draining). You can also add a little to the sauce as a cooking liquid and/or

thickener. And never forget that hot pasta continues cooking even when it's out of the water.

That said, it's not a good idea to hold the pasta under a stream of water after cooking. It's better to follow the Italian custom of quickly transferring the pasta to the serving bowl, mixing it with the sauce and perfecto! Then, if it's good pasta, it won't stick together. This also means you won't have to use the other trick of adding oil to the boiling water before cooking, which would keep the sauce from sticking to the pasta later on. And that really isn't the point, is it?

# Basic Speciale:

## Pasta Dough

Making hard pasta is as hard as it sounds, which is why homemade pasta dough typically contains egg (4 eggs per 4 cups flour). Combine these with 1 teaspoon salt and 1 teaspoon oil and knead together either in a food processor, electric mixer with dough attachment or by hand. In any case, the dough should become smooth, firm and elastic. Then shape it into a ball, wrap it in a towel and put it in a corner to rest for a little while. Knead it thoroughly once again and divide into four parts. Wrap up three of the parts and start with one: roll it out as thinly as possible and cut or shape it. A pasta machine makes it easier, but some connoisseurs prefer rolling it out on a floured surface with a rolling pin. In either case, it's a good idea to dry the pasta several hours on racks to let it age—but it's also delicious when cooked immediately.

# Basics: Pasta

### Long and Thin
*Spaghetti:* Thin pasta secca from 10–20" long. Spaghettini is thinner; spaghettoni is thicker.
*Capellini:* The thinnest pasta secca. Capelli d'angelo (angel hair) is the thinnest of thin.
*Fusilli bucati:* Long spiral spaghetti that's wound around a stick to dry.

### Long and Flat
*Pappardelle:* Ribbon pasta 1/2" wide, often pasta fresca, good with hearty sauces.
Tagliatelle ("cut up"): Northern ribbon pasta, fresca and secca; depending on size and region, can also be tagliatellini, tagliatini, taglierini, tagliolini, taglioni.
*Fettuccine:* Southern tagliatelle; sometimes narrower, often wound into nests.
*Linguine, bavette:* Ribbon pasta, narrower than fettuccine.
*Trenette:* The Ligurian compromise between spaghetti and ribbon pasta, narrow and flat, sometimes with wavy edges; typically served with pesto.

### Long or Short but Hollow
*Maccheroni, Maccaroni, Makkaroni:* Once the generic term for all pasta secca, now generally refers to long, hollow spaghetti.
*Ziti:* Thick macaroni, but usually a short pasta.
*Penne:* Hollow, diagonally cut, short pasta secca; penne lisce are smooth—rigate are ridged.
*Rigatoni:* Large, ridged, tube pasta.
*Cannelloni:* Largest tube pasta for filling.

### Miscellaneous
*Conchiglie:* Small and large shell pasta.
*Farfalle:* Butterfly/bow-tie pasta.
*Fusilli:* Ribbon pasta originally wound around knitting needles to form spirals.
*Orecchiette:* "Little ear" pasta.

# Risotto
## etcetera

## A quick introduction to risotto, polenta and gnocchi? How many hours do you have...

Those Italians! They play around with wheat, turn it into pasta and then they simply boil it. But give them something that's already done and they still play around with it. Mind you, We're not complaining! This is how they came to turn rice into risotto and corn meal into polenta. And they couldn't just boil a potato—it had to be gnocchi. Which is, of course, much better. Those Italians!

### Risotto

Is rice destined for anything tastier than risotto? "Nooooooo!" cry the Italians because Italy is such a wonderfully comfortable home for the finest things of this world...ingredients such as prosciutto, Parmesan, asparagus, saffron, truffles, etc. But what is a nice risotto? "Classico! All'onda!!! Nooooooo!!!" they all contend. We won't get anywhere like this, so let's start at the beginning.

The ancient Arabs were not only durum wheat experts but were also well versed in rice. Their grains traveled via Sicily and Spain to the peninsula where the Neapolitans, then fully occupied with their pasta and pizza, sent it on to the north. In northern Italy, the round-grain rice was planted in the Po Valley. Once the populace became accustomed to it, they started inventing risotto.

Since the rice grain couldn't be reshaped like pasta, the chefs focused their ambition and imagination on its preparation. That the result would be risotto was clear to everyone because the special characteristic of round-grain rice is that when cooked, it releases starch while itself remaining firm. The question was how to reach the perfect balance between a firm grain and creamy surroundings. So what is it? "Classico!, All'On..." Silenzio!! Let's take the techniques one at a time.

### Risotto classico

This is the method used by Italian risotto specialists from the Lombardy region and in this book (see page 82). Thoroughly sauté onions and then unrinsed rice (arborio or vialone, and maybe even carnaroli) in some butter and/or oil until translucent. A starch is released that forms a sort of roux. Then add a liquid (wine or stock), which sizzles and quickly boils away while you stir the risotto constantly.

Then add boiling stock (veal, chicken, vegetable), in gradual amounts, and allow to

evaporate down over medium heat. Continue to stir until almost done. Over medium heat, keep adding liquid and cooking it down. Constant stirring and simmering are essential because they cause the starch to swell and be released.

Keep going till you achieve the correct balance of a firm grain in creamy surroundings. Depending on your preference, the consistency can be porridge-like (beloved in mountainous areas) or soup-like (preferred along the coast). For the finish, stir in some butter (or cream or Mascarpone) and Parmesan (or pecorino). Then serve immediately before the grains surrender their firmness to the creaminess.

### Risotto "all'onda"

This is soupy risotto that forms gentle waves (onde) when you shake the pot, resembling the waves along Venezia where this method is revered. It's prepared the same as the Classico except that more stock is poured into the pot until it covers the rice, just as the Lido covers the streets of Venice.

### Risotto "tranquillo"

This technique takes the frenzy out of risotto preparation, making it pretty typical of Piedmont where it originated. Start out like the Classico. Then add all the liquid in a single shot, cover and simmer without stirring. When it's finally time to add the butter and Parmesan, you can simply toss it around a little with a fork to evenly distribute the starch that has quietly been swelling in the grains to all parts of the risotto. This works best with vialone or carnaroli. The result is very creamy, almost foamy risotto. It's Aunt Edna's favorite (see p. 80).

## Polenta

Corn became popular in northern Italy after its discovery in the Americas. But they were still missing something. Could it be that delizioso, filling porridge we now call "polenta"? Until then, they made their porridge out of buckwheat or semolina. It filled you up but... Well, anyway, after they had a chance to get used to corn, the northerners switched almost entirely over to yellow polenta made from dried kernels with an especially high starch content, ground into grits. Since it had less protein and firmer starch than wheat, polenta needed to cook longer than semolina. Medium-coarse corn meal makes this easy. Corn meal that is too fine tends to form lumps, and the coarser meal has to be stirred forever. Purchase corn meal labeled "polenta" and you're sure to get it right.

Polenta is best made in a deep pot (to prevent splattering) with a heavy base (to prevent burning). Two options: Traditional long-stirring method, best for the soft "polentina" (recipe below) or the basic method, good when making polenta for casseroles and for frying (and easy!). Purists can skip the next paragraph and continue reading from "Gnocchi."

Basic method: Bring liquid (e.g. stock) to a boil and add grainy polenta in a steady stream while stirring with a wooden spoon (see package directions for proportions). Don't wait for it to return to a boil but immediately reduce heat to low, cover and let polenta bubble away for 10 minutes. (On an electric stove, reduce heat before you start stirring in the corn meal.) Then reduce heat to the absolute lowest level (on an electric stove, turn off altogether) and let the polenta expand for 10 minutes (coarse texture) or 20 minutes (fine texture). And you're done—no lumps and hardly any sticking to the pan. Spread finished polenta out on a baking sheet and smooth it out, let cool and cut into rectangular pieces for pasticciata (see p. 89).

## Gnocchi

These "mini dumplings" from northern Italy have a lot in common with their flour-based cousins from nearby southern Germany and Austria. Like those dumplings, they're shaped from cooked potatoes, semolina, flour, bread and/or creamy cheese and are very filling. The difference is that in Italy, this would-be side dish is actually a main course Italians have spent much time perfecting. It can't get any better when the Italians are on the job.

In the course of research, the Italians quickly realized potato gnocchi that most resembled pasta were the best, so they devoted most of their attention and effort to this type. Ideal "gnocchi di patate" contain only potatoes and flour or semolina, and are very flavorful and firm. Egg just makes them softer and easier to work with. For the no-egg method, see p. 86.

All gnocchi are poached in barely-simmering water—the surface is moving but not yet bubbling. When done, the gnocchi are removed with a slotted spoon, drained, and often transferred directly to the serving bowl or plate, and garnished. Less often, they're tossed in a small amount of something, usually simple, such as a little melted butter enhanced by sage, Parmesan, or prosciutto OR a light tomato sauce OR a heartier sauce.

## Basic Speciale:

### Polentina

Soft polenta is made with less corn meal and served as a primo or side dish. To serve 4–6, bring to a boil 1 quart liquid (stock, can be mixed with milk) and add 1$\frac{1}{3}$ cups fine polenta corn meal in a steady stream while stirring constantly. Reduce heat and stir, stir, stir. Purists say you must stir in a clockwise direction—but this doesn't matter as much, as long as you stir in one direction. After 10 minutes, you can occasionally pause long enough to enjoy a couple sips of wine. Basic rule: The longer you stir, the softer the polenta—20 minutes is minimum and 30 is even better. Gourmets prefer 45 and purists insist on 1 hour if corn meal is coarse. Finally, stir in about 2 oz. ($\frac{1}{4}$ cup) softened butter and about 2 oz. grated Parmesan (separately or all together). Also good: Prepare polentina with buttermilk; or after transferring polenta to a plate, drizzle buttermilk on top; or top with browned butter and Parmesan.

## Basics: Risotto

*Arborio, avorio:* The most popular risotto rice; cooked a minimum of 15 minutes and a maximum of 25; releases a little less than 20% starch.
*Vialone nano:* Typical risotto rice; cooks in 15–20 minutes, releases over 23% starch.
*Carnaroli:* Gourmet risotto rice, a cross between vialone and Japanese round-grain rice; cooks in about 20 minutes, releases more than 24% starch while grains remain nicely firm.
*Riso comune, ordinario:* Ordinary rice grains slightly less than $\frac{1}{4}$" long for soups, etc.
*Riso semifino:* Rice with certain risotto-like properties around $\frac{1}{4}$" long.
*Riso fino:* Round-grain rice grains slightly larger than $\frac{1}{4}$" long or even longer—suitable for risotto.
*Riso superfino:* Like riso fino but with a more ideal starch content for risotto; the best.

## Basics: Polenta

*Polenta nera, polenta di grano saraceno:* "Black" polenta made from buckwheat semolina.
*Polenta bianca:* "White" polenta made from wheat semolina or flour, often used in desserts.
*Polenta concia:* Soft corn polenta containing milk, butter and Parmesan.

## Basics: Gnocchi

*Gnocchi di patate, gnocchi alla piemontese:* Potato dumplings (recipe p. 86).
*Gnocchi alla romana:* Semolina dumplings formed into balls, browned in the oven.
*Malfatti, strangolapreti, strozzapreti:* Spinach dumplings; depending on the region, thickened with flour or bread and/or softened with ricotta (recipe p. 88).

15

# Salami
## etcetera

What? We need a roof over our heads? First things first: Salame, prosciutto, formaggio. Then the vacation can begin.

Ah, we've finally made it. Several layovers and airplanes later, plus then we had to drive all over the place—we're very familiar with the autostrada by now. We're all worn out. But the cicadas are chirping at our campground, the air smells of pine and sunshine and we even have a view of the sea. All we need now is something tasty to eat. I saw an alimentari at the entrance. What? We need to put up the tent? Piano, piano! First things first: Salame, prosciutto, formaggio. Then the vacation can begin.

### Salami and More

A German, an Italian and an American have an argument. The German says, "We're the world's greatest sausage makers—we have over 1500 varieties!" So the Italian asks the American, "What do you think of beerwurst?" The American answers, "I don't know anything about that but I do know I love salami!" Why is this the case? Because the ancient Italians also applied their pasta trick to sausage-making: Use a modicum of ingredients and put them together simply. If everything's right, the result can't help but be good.

It started when the ancient northern Italians began wondering how best to use their pigs. They didn't see the point of fattening an animal for months and months and then having to gulp down all the meat in a single winter. So they took the whole animal, including the fat, and combined it with salt, packed it in casings and hung it up in the good mountain air. The salt drew the moisture out of the meat, thus robbing the bacteria of their element. Then the dry air worked its wonders. Then the fat worked to spread new flavors to all corners of the salami. As a result, the Italians not only had meat that would last but also had invented the world's most famous sausage.

However, the status of Italian salami today is similar to that of pasta a few decades ago. Only about five types are known outside Italy and all are called salami. Inside Italy, however, this name applies to 50 different varieties. And if you include their close relatives made from the same meat and salt, you'll find over 500 varieties of air-dried sausage that are prepared like salami from Aosta to Palermo. Their names are as varied as their shapes, but the contents have remained surprisingly alike: Lean pork, including wild boar, sometimes mixed with beef; a minimum of 10% white pork fat; about 2 to 3 tablespoons salt per 2¼ pounds raw meat; pepper, paprika or red chiles; frequently garlic with wine. The greatest difference between Italian salami is in the size of the pieces of meat, which are smaller in the north as in salame milano. In the south, the meat is often cut more coarsely. Another factor: the air in which the salami are dried—the whole mass can shrink up to ⅔rds its original size, depending on the air alone.

Originally the heat, humidity and wind velocity that contributed to the typical flavor of a particular region were left up to nature. Sausage makers had to pick out the best location and the best timing. Today, closer attention is paid to micro-climate, especially with the large salami that are exported worldwide. Initially they're dried a few hours or days at summer temperatures and then pre-cured around 68°F for a period ranging from days to two weeks, until the outside of the sausage dries and the mold that provides protection during curing starts to form. It is then dried at no more than 59°F for three to six months, during which the humidity levels and the airflow change several times. Finally, the world has another batch of the best salami to enjoy, which keeps almost forever—again, like dried pasta. This pasta principle is so ingenious!

## Prosciutto

If you ask for prosciutto in a store, you may be asked if you want it cotto (cooked) or crudo (raw). Crudo almost always refers to Parma or San Daniele ham. Both are made from the finest pork hindquarters to be found in Italy. These are first massaged with sea salt and then subjected to months of rest and care before aging in the air for 9–15 months. And since the air is especially dry, spicy and salt-free in the provinces of Parma and Emilia-Romagna as well as in the village of San Daniele, the resulting prosciutto is heavenly.

To be fully enjoyed, prosciutto must be sliced paper-thin at the time of purchase. It should be eaten neither at refrigerator temperature nor warm. It's best eaten with the marbled fat intact. If it's really good, it will be as soft as butter, only a little salty and almost a little sweet (dolce). It will have a heavenly forest-like scent. It tastes best with Italian bread or grissini (breadsticks). It's also delicious with delicately flavored, low-acid fruit such as melons, figs, grapes or pears.

## Formaggio

Okay, as far as the cheese platter goes, maybe the Italians could learn a little from the French. But if we look at the history of cheese from start to finish, we can only say, "Viva Italia!" What the Italians excel at are very fresh cheeses and very aged cheeses, evidenced by fresh mozzarella and Parmesan. Especially great cooking cheeses!

Each region varies their names for similar cheeses, and each considers a different stage of ripeness ideal. But perhaps some additional adjectives will be helpful: young cheese is called "giovane," "fresco" or "nuovo;" medium-aged to well-ripened are "stagionato" or "vecchio;" well ripened is "stravecchio;" the ripest is known as "stravecchione,"—cheese for the true connoisseur. In the recipes, we refer to types commonly known under a particular name and most widely available outside of Italy. But we only wish we could be in Italy learning about a thousand cheeses!

## Basics: Salumi

*Salumi:* Sausages (purchased in a salumeria)
*Salame:* Salami
*Salame genovese:* Mostly beef with a little pork and the rest fat; mildly spiced and dried for a short period of time.
*Salame fabriano:* Pork and beef, not much fat, heavily salted and peppered, without garlic.
*Salame felino:* Pork and fat, mildly salted with a slightly sweet, delicate flavor.
*Salame milano:* Milanese sausage; once prepared from pork and without garlic, now made of equal amounts of finely minced pork, beef and fat and a little garlic; smaller version: Milanino.
*Salame napoletano, napoli:* Spicy sausage from the south; 1/3 pork, 1/3 beef and 1/3 fat; coarsely cut with a generous amount of salt and garlic plus red chiles; slightly smoked just before the final drying stage, without mold; also used for pizza as is the smaller salamella napoli.
*Finocchiona, salame toscano:* Pork salami seasoned with fennel.
*Sopressata, sopressa:* Pressed sausage; often made of fancy cuts of meat or of leftovers, only from pork or pork and beef coarsely or finely chopped, smoked, dried or boiled.
*Salsiccia, luganega:* Italian pork sausage, 1–1 1/2" thick, can be short or long, raw or dried slightly (for sandwiches and cooking) or till hard.
*Cotechino:* Pork sausage including skin for (long) boiling; with beans and in bollito misto.
*Mortadella:* Italy's famous smoked, cooked sausage made of pork, veal and fat with pistachios; diameter can be up to that of the wheel on a Vespa.
*Prosciutto cotto:* Cooked ham
*Prosciutto di Parma:* Ham from Parma and Emilia-Romagna, air-dried 12–15 months (or more), whose aging process is strictly monitored.
*Prosciutto San Daniele:* Aged under controlled conditions similarly to Parma ham but first pressed into a mandolin shape; ready in as little as nine months.
*Coppa:* Salted, rolled and pressed pork neck or shoulder, also air-dried.
*Bresaola:* Salted, pressed and air-dried beef.
*Pancetta:* Narrow cut of pork belly, cured in salt and spices, air-dried.

## Basics: Formaggio

Parmesan, grana, pecorino and fresh mozzarella are discussed on pages 8–11. Unless otherwise indicated, cheeses below are from cow's milk.

*Ricotta:* A fresh cheese similar to sour cream and small curd cottage cheese (ricotta tipo dolce) derived from heated cow's whey; also available salted in block form (ricotta salata) and then often ripened; seldom made from ewe's whey (ricotta di pecora).
*Mascarpone:* Thick, sweet cream that becomes thickened after being drained in a sieve.
*Provolone:* The cheese mixture is simmered with hot water, kneaded, shaped and often dipped in wax; often ripened in the shape of a cone, sausage or sphere and some-times smoked.
*Robiola:* A small, round cheese shaped like Camembert; the most well-known type is ripened with red mold; also available as a fresh cheese.
*Taleggio:* A good high-fat soft cheese with a light mold, often square, sometimes made from raw milk.
*Asiago:* Asiago d'allevo is made from low-fat and regular milk; can mature from a compact semi-soft cheese to a hard cheese; asiago pressato and asiago grasso di monte have a higher fat content and mature in just a few weeks.
*Fontina:* Full-flavored, sweetish semi-soft cheese made from raw milk; melts well.
*Montasio:* Semi-soft cheese from raw milk that can mature in a few weeks or up to a year.
*Bel paese:* Buttery high-fat semi-soft cheese—very new to cheese history.
*Gorgonzola:* Famous blue-veined cheese; in its milder form, gorgonzola dolce and in the more powerful version, gorgonzola piccante.

# Aroma
## etcetera

All is fresh, all is pure, so all is good? Nothing is that simple when it comes to the miracle of Italian cuisine.

Even in southern Italy, they have their magic tricks for turning simple things into true works of art. No, not using a jar of ready-made spaghetti sauce but using an ingredient that takes well to rest and aging—the Italian formula for creating some of the best natural flavors in international cuisine. Take olive oil, for example. Just think what it can do to a simple piece of bread! And when combined with balsamic vinegar, you need nothing more to turn salad into a delicacy. But in order for these products to do their work, they must be carefully prepared. In the final analysis, all will be good only if all is fresh and pure.

## Olive Oil

Well, we've had a great time telling our little stories about pasta, risotto and whatever else has been produced in Italy's rural kitchens through the ages. But now we come to the diva of them all, olio d'oliva! The finest olive oil is like the finest wine, almost sacred and referred to in hushed tones. An overheard conversation between two Italian food purists might sound something like this: The ancient Egyptians..., ...trees that still, after 1000 years..., naturally, picked only by hand..., Giovanni from Lucca always saves the first bottle for me..., grassy with violets and a hint of green tomatoes with an aftertaste of avocado..., what do you mean you don't have any "olio extra vergine classico imbottigliato grand cru pizzica la gola?!"

You see, the best Italian olive oil must be as pure as the Mediterranean; it can bless you

or render you immortal; it is a Hallelujah Chorus dedicated to good taste! However, it's just not possible for every person in the world to fill their bottles with olio d'oliva before breakfast as it's virginally pressed, dripping from frantoio olives.

So what do you do when you can't get the best? How about using the second best, a very good Italian olive oil, because that's what mamma cooks with in Tuscany anyway. Plus, it's what you find right on the shelf at your corner market. Very good means that the oil is clearly olive, reasonably priced, fruity, bitter, full and a little unripe. It may taste more of hay or of flowers, or more like walnuts or almonds. Reasonably priced means olive oil is always more expensive than ordinary vegetable oil. Some are only a little more expensive and are good for frying (but so is corn oil, and it's also cheaper).

Olive oil is pricey because it's the only oil made from a fresh fruit rather than from grains alone. The olive fruit is also more sophisticated and complex than corn. Unripe, it's green and bitter; ripe, it's black with intense flavor. For good oil, however, olives are used at the intermediate green-blue stage. They are hard to remove from branches and must be hand-picked, knocked down with sticks or shaken out with machinery (the most common method). Because these little fruits are also highly sensitive (every scrape causes them to ferment, lowering the quality of the oil), the growers spread nets under the trees to cushion their fall. Think of how much easier it is to harvest corn and there's your price difference!

But even un-bruised olives start fermenting rapidly, so they're put through the olive oil mill as quickly as possible, preferably within 24 hours of picking but after no more than two to three days. The pits and fruit are crushed to a paste, which also ferments quickly, so immediate pressing of the paste is in order. According to the traditional method, the oily juice is squeezed out of the pulp and then separated into juice and oil. During this process, the heat in the press can rise to as high as body temperature. Using the modern method, pressing and separating occur in a single step, where a slight heating to 68°F helps out. Believe us, corn oil is much easier to make!

But now comes the reward for insisting on pure freshness and all the painstaking trouble: Rest and enjoyment because the oil is basically ready—no filtering, no washing, no chemicals as there are in corn oil, just tasting and testing until it's labeled. "Extra Vergine" or "Native Extra" is the highest quality, followed by "Vergine" or "Native." Since these European Union (EU) standards are based on the oil's acidity level, they only have an indirect relation to quality but, in any case, a level that's too high means that the fruit wasn't fresh or unblemished and therefore had started to ferment.

Like many oils made from grains, a lower quality, more acidic olive oil must be refined and, also like these oils, ends up being tasteless. But when "Vergine" or "Extra Vergine" oil is added to it, it can still appear in the store as "100% olive oil." Many also take advantage of another loophole permitted by the EU: They take olives from other countries and press them in Italy, calling it genuine Italian olive oil. This oil is not for purists (the olives spent far too much time traveling and were not pressed immediately!).

Purists go to specialized markets and read labels. If it not only says "Extra Vergine" but also specifies where the oil and olives came from, it can be trusted. "Each type yields a different oil," they say. "The soil, climate and location are all very important factors." Certainly, but there are still a few basics, including: Oil from the north, especially the oil from Liguria and Lake Garda, tends to be milder and more fragrant, excellent for fine cuisine. For a long time, no good oil came from the south, where they wait until the olives ripen in the heat and fall from the trees. It was fit only for the refinery. But now the south also produces delicious oils reminiscent of sun and herbs. Naturally they aren't as delicious as those from Tuscany, which embody all of Italy: Mild, fragrant, sunny, herby, elegant, rustic, straightforward, mysterious and with that little tingle in your throat, "pizzica la gola," which is how you know.

But there's one more thing—olive oil is also good for you. It provides large amounts of vitamins A and E and is beneficial for the blood and heart. But if your response to this is "Lay it on me, I want to be Italian and live forever!"—you haven't been listening. Italians live so long on olive oil not just because it's good for them but also because they love it! That's the secret of Mediterranean happiness.

## Aceto Balsamico

The dance around olio d'oliva is nothing compared to the balsamic vinegar cult. Its high priests and priestesses love to keep the cult alive in old attics where they mix mysterious substances back and forth, then come to the front door with a few ampoules of a black elixir while gourmets stand outside with their checkbooks ready and open. In fact, aceto balsamico prepared traditionally does have an alchemy-like aura about it. Everything it touches turns to culinary gold, whether salad, risotto, scaloppine, cheese, strawberries or liqueur. But for every drop of good balsamic vinegar in the world, there's a bottle of bad— black magic instead of black gold. This is all getting a little poetic so let's get down to facts.

## Tradizionale

You won't find "Aceto Balsamico Tradizionale" in a supermarket—not even in Italy. It's much too rare and at a much higher price than the "normale" type, it's used sparingly. It's mainly the location and time that make balsamic vinegar "tradizionale." First of all, it can only be produced in the Modena or Reggio Emilia regions from specific late-harvest grapes. Secondly, it must age for at least 12 years and thirdly, it is carefully controlled by a local consortium of producers.

For tradizionale, sweet "must" is slowly cooked down for hours or days and stored through the winter. It's then transferred to its first cask, open at the top. There the alcohol turns to vinegar, some of which evaporates—the rest absorbs the aroma of the wood. Then, it's moved on to the next smaller cask, where the same process occurs, and so on and so on. Only after at least 12 years of being transferred to a series of three to 12 casks made from different woods can a tradizionale be declared mature and ready for bottling. Just a couple drops from the typical 100 ml bottle are enough to ennoble any meal. And that is the result of about 5 pounds of grapes that bring forth about 1½ quarts of must!

## Normale

You should be able to find "Aceto Balsamico di Modena" in the supermarket—officially, to bear that name it should come from the Modena region of Italy. Whether it's also quality in flavor depends on the producer. Unlike the tradizionale, there are no testers monitoring production. This results in some producers coloring the wine vinegar with caramel or adding fruit juice. However, good, standard balsamic vinegar is similar to tradizionale but produced a little faster. It, too, is cooked down and matures over several years. A first-class "normale" can be quite expensive; some of them are very good. Balsamic vinegar sold at bargain-basement prices might be okay as vinegar but is probably not a properly produced version.

## Red Wine Vinegar

Authentic, good red wine vinegar gives your Italian salads power and jazzes up meat dishes. For quality red wine vinegar, pure acetic acid bacteria is added to red wine stored in a continuously aerated cask so the alcohol will become acidic. Water is then added, because pure vinegar is typically unusable without it. However, if another vinegar is added before fermentation, the result will no longer be authentic red wine vinegar (but it may still taste fine). The best red wine vinegars are then allowed to mature in a wooden cask after fermentation.

## Basics: Olive Oil

*Extra virgin olive oil, olio extra vergine:* Oil that has been cold-pressed directly (see below) from fresh olives and has less than 1% oleic acidity.

*Virgin olive oil, olio vergine:* Same as extra vergine but with up to 2% oleic acidity.

*Olive oil, olio miscelato:* Mixture of olive oil that was refined (because it wasn't good enough for virgin) and virgin or extra virgin olive oil.

*First pressing:* Oil is pressed directly from the fruit; always the case with virgin and extra virgin olive oil.

*Cold-pressed:* Oil does not reach 105°F when being pressed; always the case with virgin and extra virgin olive oil; 95–99°F is considered to be the range for high quality.

## Basics: Vinegar

*Aceto balsamico tradizionale:* Vinegar from Modena and Reggio Emilia that must age at least 12 years before it can receive the seal of approval from the Consortium of Producers.

*Aceto balsamico di Modena:* Unregulated term applied to vinegar from Modena that could be very good or very watered down.

*Authentic wine vinegar:* Vinegar made purely from wine.

*Inauthentic wine vinegar:* Vinegar made from wine + another vinegar.

# Haven't we all got a little dolce vita?

Oh, it's been such a wonderful day so far. I can't remember the last time I went to the market. It must have been with mamma when I was still living at home. Let's start doing this every Saturday, okay? And isn't that basil fantastic? I can smell it all the way over here. I can't wait to start cooking…Though it's cool to hang out here a little while and soak in the air…

Do you think they'll come tonight? Including the cute one with the beautiful eyes? At first I thought he was the waiter. He walked right up to the table when I tried to pay and said, "I have already paid thee beeell for you, signorina!" There was just something about him… Of course the other two weren't bad, either. Very Italian-looking. What, is it already that late? We'd better…

Well, one more little drink won't hurt.

But maybe we better get started cooking…

Just one more little sip…

# Vino
## etcetera

**Bordeaux-sniffer? Riesling-slurper? That's not very Italian! Vino is cool, but so are smiling and winking.**

*My friend, we've been sitting here eating for a long time and we didn't even raise a single toast. Since we're being so informal, maybe we should call each other by our first names. You're the type of guy I just can't see grating truffles over his pasta—but you sure do like your Parmesan. I've noticed that. I wonder what's in your cellar...probably some scary crates that don't even have wine in them. I'm going to guess you buy your vino with your pasta and Parmesan—and that for you, it must be fantastic...and that you drink it pronto! You're such an Italian hottie! I'll toss back a good glass of Barbera with you anytime...*

Italy has been producing wine for so long that it's a common staple. That's why it's so out of place to solemnly sniff Bordeaux or slurp Riesling at an Italian table. A smile and a wink are much more appropriate. Not that Italian wine goes only with women and song—there are also authentic Granati that are delicious with truffles and are best stored in wine cellars.

*What, you have a few interesting bottles lying around? Uh, what was your last name again?*

## Selecting Vino

People have finally come to realize that a gallon bottle of "Acme's Best Table Wine" for $2.50 isn't exactly what's needed for living the dolce vita. That's why, like snake oil, this type of wine is slowly becoming extinct. But then there are gorgeous bottles with avant garde labels, only $6, but once you open

them—ouch. Not even worth the trip to the store. These unpleasantries cause the old-time wine connoisseur to get a dreamy look and start to reminisce: "Remember when we took our first trip to Italy and ended up at that village wedding—there were all those bottles of vino rosso on the tables, I can still taste it, so pure, so..."

Scusi! Wake up! Right now you're standing in front of the Italian wine display and you need something to drink! Now! So which one should you buy?! Something good, of course. How can you know? By tasting is best, if they have a tasting counter. And if the store is a supermarket? First buy a cheaper one and try it out. You never know—it could be a disappointment, but the fun is in the trying. Sometimes you can find a decent wine to go with pizza on the balcony for $3 a bottle with a tacky name like "Ciao Bella." If not, you haven't lost much. If yes, you've found a "vino di vita," your everyday wine.

But to save you the trouble of drinking your way through the entire shelf, here are a few clues from the labels: "Secco," for example, means "dry," although this has milder connotations in the sunny south than in central Europe. Then there are abbreviations like the simple IGT or fancy DOCG that are awarded on the basis of origin and quality and constitute both an official act and a matter of taste. The better wines have additional adjectives like "Superiore." In any case, such wines then belong to the "vini della dolce vita" category, your wines for special occasions.

That's all very interesting but what are these words in big letters? "Montepulciano," for instance? Let's talk about Italy's wine regions. The best regions are in the north because that's where winemakers go to the most trouble, so their wines cater to true connoisseurs. Above all, Piedmont, where right under the noses of the French, Italy's vintners produce their very best effort with the nebbiolo grape. They then use it to produce a red Barolo or Barbaresco. Further to the northeast, the country has an experimental laboratory between the Po and the Brenner Pass. In this area where three countries come together, many wines are produced from grapes that come from outside Italy, including Chardonnay, Riesling, the Pinots, Merlot, Cabernet and Sauvignon, but also classics like white Soave and red Valpolicella and Bardolino.

The middle of the Italian wine country is at its heart. Perhaps the best winemaking ingredients anywhere in Italy grow in Tuscany in the Chianti region. But this region gained a stigma when chianti in the straw-covered bottle became a permanent symbol of cheap wine. Since then, the name "Chianti" appears on traditionally shaped bottles with more noble adjectives and Italy's most famous wine is again one of its best. The best also includes two other red Tuscans: Brunello di Montalcino and Vino Nobile di Montepulciano (which has nothing to do with the Montepulciano from the Abruzzo region further to the south). Next door is Lazio with Rome on its coast and the white Frascati as its principal wine.

Then there's the south and the Italian islands. Forty-percent of Italy's wines come from this area, but almost all the top-quality wines are from the central and northern regions. And even though the south and the islands are not known for high quality wine, winemakers are still drawn to these areas because of the seductiveness of the sun—especially Apulia and Sicily. Wines from these regions may not be as available outside Italy as wines from further north.

## Drinking Vino

Now you've brought the bottle home and it's simply waiting for you to drink it. If it will be a long wait, don't leave it standing on the kitchen counter—it's too warm there. It's better to keep it in a cool, dry place where it can lie flat, such as under your bed or in the cellar. The refrigerator should be used only as a temporary stopover for white wine and Prosecco because over the long run, it'll also cool the flavor. (We're too smart to advise you to use the freezer as an emergency wine cooler, but if you do, be sure to set a timer!)

And one more thing: Italian wines are made to be served a little cooler because in their hot homeland, they're designed to refresh. That's also the way they taste best outside Italy: Spumante and Prosecco at 40°F (the temperature in the door of a refrigerator that's not too cold); young, fresh white wine in a cold area of your house, in the "vini di vita" category at 45–50°F; white "vini della dolce vita" at 50°F; "vita" red wines at about 60°F; "dolce vita" reds at 60–65°F (open about an hour before serving).

## Vino and Dining

So what do I drink with my fish? "Drink whatever tastes good to you. Everything is allowed!" Hmmm. That's like asking the chef in a ristorante what he or she recommends and they snap back, "Everything I make is good, Dottore." Thanks a lot, maestro, but that doesn't answer the question. Or maybe it does: Many Italian wines, including many very good ones, are intended to be drunk with food and have been for centuries. So they've had plenty of time to be paired with dishes from their regions. Thus, it's seldom wrong to combine a typical northern dish like risotto with mushrooms with a typical northern wine such as a red Barbera, or fish sautéed in Tuscan olive oil with a Tuscan white such as a Vernaccia di San Gimignano.

## Basics: Vino

Designations
*VDT (Vino da Tavola):* Table wine without origin or year.
*IGT:* Wine from specific regions from a specific year; there are currently about 100.
*DOC:* Wine of controlled origin from a specific year that must meet defined conditions with regard to zone of origin, grape type, grape quality, cultivation, harvesting, alcohol content, acidity, bottling, storage and aging; there are currently about 300 DOCs.
*DOCG:* Top wines requiring additional controls that are made according to the highest DOC standards; there are currently 21 DOCG wines.

*Vino secco:* Dry wine
*Vino amabile:* Semi-sweet wine
*Vino dolce:* Very sweet wine
*Vino classico:* Wine from the best zone of a production area
*Vino scelto:* High-quality wine made from select grapes
*Vino in vecchiato, riversa, superiore:* Wine aged for lengthy periods depending on the type

## Basics: "Vini di Vita"
Our everyday wines

White
*Frascati:* Light, mild, from Lazio
*Vernaccia di San Gimignano:* Fresh, light, but elegant; Tuscany
*Orvieto:* Fragrant, round; Umbria
*Prosecco:* Lightly sparkling (prosecco frizzante) or sparkling (prosecco spumante) wine made from Prosecco grapes
*Soave:* Light, fruity, refreshing; Veneto

Red
*Barbera:* Hearty, fruity, medium-bodied; Piedmont
*Bardolino:* Light, slightly bitter; Veneto
*Chianti, young:* Fruity, tangy, earthy; Tuscany
*Montepulciano d'Abbruzo:* Dry, mild, light-bodied: Abruzzo
*Nebbiolo:* Fruity-tart to medium-bodied; Piedmont
*Valpolicella:* Medium-bodied; Veneto

## Basics: "Vini della Dolce Vita"

Our Italian wines for special occasions

White
*Arneis:* Full of character, light; Piedmont
*Gavi di Gavi:* Fresh, elegant, fruity; Piedmont
*Spumante:* Sparkling wines, including bottle-fermented (e.g. Talento); Asti Spumanti is a sweet version
*Soave classico:* Aged Soave

Red
*Barbaresco:* Robust but velvety and elegant; Piedmont
*Barolo:* Full-bodied, velvety; Piedmont
*Brunello di Montalcino:* Powerful, fragrant, smooth; Tuscany
*Chianti, aged:* Smooth, fine, elegant; Tuscany
*Vino Nobile di Montepulciano:* Rich, elegant, fragrant; Tuscany

# Caffè
## etcetera

My favorite Italian dish?
Espresso — scusi — caffè,
of course!

It's very strange. The most Italian substance people worldwide put into their mouths is espresso, and yet not a single bean comes from Italy. And the Italians don't even drink espresso! If they want a quick cup of the black stuff between or after meals, they simply call for a "caffè." Of course there's more to it than that, but every drop of milk, water or alcohol added to the cup usually means a new name. This, too, is very Italian when you consider all the pasta variations using one simple dough. Also, drinking coffee with a dessert is more typical outside of Italy. And, Italians would rather drink something alonside their coffee, sometimes water but more often something strong that can stand up to the "caffè" — often, the Italians enjoy their coffee in bars.

## About Caffè

Northern Italians irritate the Viennese with their coffee because Vienna considers itself to be Europe's first to have served it. The Italians claim they were already serving coffee in St. Mark's Square before the Turks left their famous sacks of beans outside Vienna, leading to the establishment of the "kaffeehaus" culture there. On the other hand, Austrians today drink more coffee than the Italians. Germans drink even more, the Dutch more than twice and the Finnish almost three times the amount. Bravo, Helsinki! But isn't it strange, then, that there are so few Finnish coffee houses in Munich, Los Angeles, Tokyo or Sydney? Could it be because the Italian Caffè Bars got there first?

It goes back to the pasta principle. Or rice. Or olives. When Italians get a hold of something good, they play around with it and turn it into something better. For their coffee, they go straight to the Arabica bean. This type grows at high altitudes along the coffee belt around the equator and is more sensitive than the second most-known type, Robusta. The Arabica makes better coffee — mild, aromatic, pleasantly acidic as well as less bitter and rustic than Robusta. And Arabica contains only 1–1.7% caffeine whereas Robusta has 2–4%.

Italy mainly imports its beans — raw — from Central and South America. Raw beans stay freshest and their subsequent flavor can be controlled. The first and most important step is the blending of different types of beans before actual roasting. Then the final flavor is determined in a later step. Good caffè is a combination of dry-processed Arabica beans, which have a full, balanced flavor, and "washed" beans, which are milder and more acidic. Naturally there are also espresso blends containing Robusta, sometimes added on purpose to help maintain the balance of the blend. True purists prefer Arabica.

The next step is the roasting, a 15-minute process at temperatures between 300 and 440°F. The beans are thus transformed into tiny reactors — aroma atoms are broken down into smaller units while releasing their energy. In order to prevent flavor from evaporating, the sensitive roasted beans are wrapped in a protective metal casing — typically foil packages or cans. With vacuum packing,

some of the aroma is unfortunately removed along with the air but it then stays fresh for three months. If the package is soft and mushy instead of hard and stiff, reconsider purchasing it; this means it has taken in air. In the case of pressurized cans, gas is pumped in when air is removed — the aroma is retained with this method. This keeps the coffee fresh for a year.

Naturally, purists buy only whole beans and grind them personally. The grinds for a well-made caffè can range from powder-fine to millimeter-sized. However, us Parmesan-instead-of-truffle-slicers and spur-of-the-moment wine buyers prefer to leave this to our favorite barista and take our coffee home already ground. After all, we need time to live the dolce vita!

## Making Caffè

Until now, it was okay for us to brew coffee grounds in a paper filter as usual (which is still fine for a café au lait). But now we're getting really Italian. We're going to make caffè with pressure and steam or pressurized air, a process invented by the Italians at the start of the 20th century. The principle is the same whether you're talking about your European countertop espresso maker or the gleaming caffè machine in Roma Centrale: Hot water that is not quite boiling is forced through the ground coffee at a high pressure and carries along everything it can get a hold of (more than brewed coffee does) while leaving behind most of the caffeine. In the

end, your cup contains a shot that stimulates you with its aroma instead of its punch—which is why Italians still drink it in the evening after dinner.

Do you want more details? Okay, let's talk about a good "macchina da caffè espresso" (the name espresso is, of course, what it's called outside Italy). Although not everybody has one at home, many of us never tire of watching our favorite barista perform the ritual. Here's what they do: Put about 50 beans in the form of ¼ oz. ground coffee into the filter and then tamp it down to increase the pressure. Then screw in the filter holder under the nozzle and turn on the intense steam or pressure (to about 9 "atmospheres"), which forces the 195°F water through the coffee in 30 to 35 seconds. Il caffè, va bene.

Too much detail? The essentials: This brief but powerful pressure has the effect of binding the ingredients already released by the hot water into the finer aroma. Since this aroma is mainly contained in essential oils, it takes on "body" and forms a "crema" that, like the cream on milk, is the best part of the whole deal. If the crema is nut-brown to reddish-brown, nice and thick, and is lasting, the caffè is well made. It indicates the caffè also contains all the other ingredients from the beans that, on the one hand, protect your taste buds from some of the bitterness and, on the other hand, allow your taste buds to blossom—which is why a caffè leaves such a long, heavenly aftertaste.

## Drinking Caffè

Besides the "how" of drinking caffè, we also need the where, when, with whom and with what. The "how" is simple: Hot, fast and sweet. As soon as it's placed on the counter, it should already be headed for your mouth because with every degree it cools, it loses taste. Which explains the "fast" part of it. You won't burn yourself, first of all because of the crema and secondly because you slurp it, which means you suck in air that simultaneously cools the caffè and gives it even more flavor. A bit of white sugar can also bring out the flavor (thus, the sweet), and it makes it more stimulating. Almost sounds like the dolce vita! You feel like a minor god, which is maybe too much of a jolt at breakfast time. That's why Italians prefer to approach the morning a little more cautiously with a cappuccino. "But only then!" insist the purists and point disapprovingly at non-Italians who sip a cappuccino just before knocking off work. Yeah, well, sometimes the afternoon in New York calls for some indulgence, meaning milk and cream, but perhaps we're missing out on the dolce vita! (If you haven't caught on yet, our shots of espresso are similar to the Italian caffè.)

The best time for your first Italian-style caffè is late morning when your biorhythm is slowly starting to pick up. And then another after lunch, of course, because this is another time when a cappuccino, etc., would be a little heavy. Then maybe another shot in the late afternoon, which Italians often drink in a bar on their way home. But what about that little glass next to the caffè? Ah, the aperitivo before dinner, naturalmente. Could you pass me the Gazzetta dello Sport? What do you mean, I have to get going, 'cuz my wife's not gonna hold dinner for me? Oh well, our dolce macho vita isn't what it used to be…But we'll see each other again later for a digestivo, eh? Va bene!

## Basics: Caffè

(For more on American espresso café lingo, see *Basic Baking* p. 84)

*Caffè:* One shot of thick, strongly flavored steam-brewed coffee (what the rest of the world calls espresso).
*Ristretto:* Caffè made with less water than usual for the amount of coffee grounds.
*Doppio:* A double shot of caffè.
*Lungo:* Caffè made with more water than usual for the same amount of coffee grounds.
*Americano:* Caffè diluted with hot water to approximate the strength of American coffee.

*Macchiato:* Caffè "stained" with a dollop of steamed milk.
*Caffè con panna:* Caffè topped with a dollop of whipped cream.
*Cappuccino:* ⅓ caffè, ⅓ hot milk, ⅓ foam.

*Caffè latte:* Caffè in a tall glass filled with a lot of hot milk, containing little or no foam.
*Latte macchiato:* Tall glass of steamed milk "stained" with a shot of caffè.

*Caffè corretto:* Caffè "corrected" with a shot of liquor.
*Caffè freddo:* Ice-cold caffè, usually with milk, sometimes with ice cubes; also called iced coffee.
*Granita di caffè:* See p. 156.
*Babychino:* Tiny cup of caffè with steamed milk topped with cocoa powder.

*Espresso:* Designates the method used to make the caffè.

# La dolce vita

## The full, sweet life. All day long. Yes, please!

You don't have to go to culinary school to cook Italian. And you don't have to cook for a family of 10 to eat like one. You can even have a name like Sally or François and still enjoy an Italian meal—the magic of Italian cuisine is that it transforms any place in the world into a piazza where François becomes Francesco and Sally becomes his signora and everyone becomes one big famiglia descended from the ancient Romans – don't we all have a little bella Italia in our blood? This phenomenon is called the "dolce vita miracle" that begins as soon as you slurp an espresso, and it can last all day long. Sound too good to be true? If you don't believe it, just keep reading. You're about to experience the most beautiful day of your life. It's called the:

## Sweet, Ordinary, Italian Day

If you've ever taken a day off just to do whatever you want, you know how sweet it can be. If you've never done that before, you must—a real pleasure. But if you just can't leave your boss for a day, then try a little Saturday dolce vita. It's a day when there's still some work to be done but with a vacation feel, without the Sunday pressure of having to recover. And even Saturdays have their unpleasant duties: Buying shoes, washing the car, looking for an apartment, being forced to take a trip. Forget all that for today but do get up early. Take your shower, dress in something both stylish and comfortable and step out your door. Did we forget something? Just what many people consider the epitome of pleasure, which is:

## Breakfast

You may not want to believe it, but breakfast has little to do with the dolce vita. For Italians it's just an unavoidable pit stop between getting up and having lunch. Nevertheless, it's when cappuccino-e-latte lovers can officially indulge their tastes, which isn't really permitted for the rest of the day. Unless it's your own sweet, ordinary, Italian day.

All that's very nice but you're still standing there in the street with an empty stomach. So what do you do? Do what the Italians do—go to a bar. The ideal would look something like this: Doors and windows are wide open because it's already warm and summery. Inside is a long counter with a brightly gleaming "macchina da caffè espresso" behind it with two baristi who have been running back and forth since 6:30 a.m. They're concentrating intently, making abrupt comments, pulling levers, banging coffee grounds out of metal filters amid hissing and steaming like train engineers at their stoker. Every once in a

while they spread out a handful of saucers on the counter like they're dealing out cards and let the clinking spoons slide over them. Then one-two-three, they give a call or simply nod and you can pick up your cappuccino, plus a sweet pastry or brioche, either fresh from the display case or wrapped in cellophane from a basket on top. That's an Italian breakfast.

There's no need to start any long conversations with your fellow drinkers—Italians like to keep to themselves at breakfast. Talkative types will do better at the:

## Coffee Break

This is the best excuse to go outside on an ordinary Italian day and get some air between 10 and 11 o'clock, but only long enough to go to the bar. This is when to have that first caffè, what we call espresso. Baristi often start the caffè for their regulars when they see them coming—a guy from the office across the street will immediately have something to slurp as he thumbs through the sports pages. He comes everyday. Then there are the readers of women's magazines who take this 15-minute break to chat a little or a lot. And if the conversation is good, they finish by throwing a few coins onto the counter and calling as they walk out the door, "Ci vediamo a pranzo!" meaning, see you at:

## Lunch

This is the center of the ordinary Italian day and most of the day's thoughts center around it. In the north, it usually starts between noon and 1 p.m. In the south, it starts at about 2 p.m. Traditionally, mamma has spent the morning at the market or in a shop and then at the stove while her husband sat in his office inventing a few new chaotic, bureaucratic rules. Then the wife phones just before starting the pasta water or heating the risotto pot and he drops whatever he's doing to go enjoy his "primo" at home "al dente." This initial filler is followed by a piece of meat or fish plus a side dish as a "secondo" and then a piece of fruit or cheese as a "dolce." Whether he then takes his caffè at home or in a bar depends on the balance of power between the spouses.

To avoid this dilemma entirely, you can simply move the whole "pranzo" to a restaurant, also very Italian. Whether you go to an osteria, trattoria or ristorante, the feast we would typically save till evening takes place at noon in Italy. This is the time to meet customers, colleagues, friends or family to have long discussions about what to order and even longer discussions about the rest of the world over a number of courses and beyond. This can take until 3 or 4 p.m., depending on when the businesses outside start raising their shutters again.

So how should you go about this on your sweet Saturday outside of Italy? Going out to eat is a good idea, but you can also do that in the middle of the week, and it won't feel like much of a siesta on a long Saturday. To get that siesta mood, you'd be better off slowly making your way home as the businesses fill up, to meet some of your favorite people who you've invited for lunch. One of them has brought along a few spicy anchovies and onions in balsamic vinegar from the market; another has cream puffs from the family bakery as a dolce, while a third brought some good cheese and wine. You yourself throw together spaghetti aglio e olio and sauté something elegant and fast such as saltimbocca or fish with olives and capers. When you're all sitting around fully satisfied with that last glass of wine, you can hardly believe you still have an entire weekend ahead of you and even time for an afternoon nap. Then you won't have long to wait till the:

## Aperitivo

In this context, aperitivo refers to what might otherwise be called "meeting for drinks after work" or "happy hour," the transition between the ordinary day and home life that is too precious to waste by going straight home. So Italians allow themselves a slight detour to the bar where, depending on the mood and their taste, they can find a glass of cold white wine, a decent red, a strong belt of clear alcohol or a little something that's nice and sweet. Traditionally, that's all they have because their spouse, children and dinner are waiting at home for papa (or mamma, theoretically, of course). But if you're still working on starting your own family, you might have a few spicy bites with your drink, as long as you leave one hand free for waving and for using the telefonino. Because this is the time spent organizing the rest of the evening, whether you're making a date for the movies or dancing or whatever else the night might bring. In this case, only minor importance is given to "la cena", which is to say the:

## Evening Snack

Although "la cena" is quite delizioso, "dinner" is too big a word for this meal. It often doesn't take place until late evening, for instance after a movie. In this case the distinctions between antipasti, primo and secondo are fuzzy. In Naples, for example, where there's no discussion of "la cena" any time before 10 p.m., pizza is the classic evening meal; according to ancient tradition, it's a pizza the size of the palm of your hand, eaten in the street in front of the bakery. Even outside Italy, good pizzerias won't refuse guests who walk in the door after 11 p.m. And even if you're too tired after your full evening program to do more than phone a pizza delivery service on this dolce Saturday, that's still more Italian than spending the entire evening in a ristorante over a ten-course meal. La dolce vita can be so simple!

## Italian Basics: Eating and Drinking

*Abbiamo fame:* We're hungry
*Antipasti:* "Before the dough"; cold (antipasti freddi) and warm (antipasti caldi) appetizers to stimulate your appetite
*Primo:* First course; fills you up more than an appetizer but is unique from the main dish; often pasta, risotto or a hearty soup
*Secondo:* Second and main course; often simply a fried or grilled piece of meat or fish with little or no sauce
*Contorni:* Side dishes, usually vegetables; simple
*Dolci:* Something sweet; can be fruit, pastry or ice cream; rarely fussy
*Formaggio:* Cheese; often just one good chunk and not an entire platter

*Abbiamo sete:* We're thirsty
*Bevande:* Beverages; alcoholic (bevande alcoliche), non-alcoholic (bevande analcoliche), hot (bevande calde) or cold (bevande fredde)
*Aperitivo:* Opening drink; for example, Prosecco, white wine or a liqueur
*Digestivo:* Closing drink; for example, brandy or bitters (amaro)
*Acquavite:* Schnapps
*Birra:* Beer
*Liquori:* Liqueurs, including other alcoholic beverages
*Succo:* Juice

ITALIAN SING-A

(WITH SPECIAL SING-ALONG LYRIC SHEETS)

VOLARE ■ CIAO, CIAO BAMBINA ■ ARR

TORERO ■ NON DIMENTICAR ■ TORNA

SANTA LUCIA ■ VIENI SUL MAR ■ MATTINA

# 16 Souvenirs
## for the
## dolce vita
### at home

## Aranciata — Orange Soda

"I've never had an orange soda like this before!" Did I have my first Aranciata in Marina di Grosseto or Polignano a Mare? I only remember I was badly sunburned and mamma was worried. She took me into a bar and cried, "Bambina sole mio, bibite subito e prego." About 10 men watched as I took that first sip. That's when I said the thing about the orange soda. First mamma started to laugh, then the whole bar laughed, for a long time. Then everybody got an Aranciata, including papa when he finally found us. Now I know Aranciata is so good because it contains real OJ. I always keep some handy 'cuz you never know when someone will cry out "sole mio!"

## Borsa — Bag

I got my beach bag in Naples, I do know that. Naturally, I haggled like crazy and, naturally, I paid way too much, but now I get to feel like I'm headed for the beach every time I go shopping. And it looks so nice with a giant bunch of basil from the market peeking out the top, or a head of romaine. Of course if I really want to look cool, I add a bottle of my favorite Chianti or even a Prosecco that's so cold it's covered with condensation. Of course, in colder months I'd still rather be carrying a towel and sunscreen and wearing a bikini. "Summer, here I come! Even if I don't know exactly where to find you."

## Giornale — Newspaper

When I really want to feel very, very Italian, I go to the airport and buy an Italian newspaper. I hardly understand a word of it but if I lay it out beside me while I drink a cup of coffee— even a hotdog stand starts to feel like the Bar Italia. Even better is to go to an outdoor café and hide behind the giornale. Molto italiano. But it does get a little embarrassing if an Italian walks up and starts talking to me. I also like to have a giornale when I give an Italian dinner party. Then we all read parts of it out loud, pronouncing lots of rrrr and ssss. Or I use it as the tablecloth. And if Bruno is there, he can even tell us what it says. But I never use the sports pages because he'll wind up spending the whole evening in the corner reading.

## Servizio di caffè — Coffee Service

Since everybody knows I collect souvenir espresso cups, each time I have my coffee I can have it in a different cup, every day for a week – and I drink at least four espressos a day! But sometimes I wonder if this is really the right thing to do. For example, the yellow one here that says "Hotel Capri" on it. I don't even like to remember that place: Because of souvenir hunters like me, there were hardly any of the mini espresso spoons left, only teaspoons. I had to use the handle of the teaspoon to stir my coffee to keep from destroying the delicate crema. Sometimes, I even toss back my espresso from a shot glass.

## Telefonino — Cell Phone

I love that word—it sounds so much better than "cell phone." Imagine you're in Rome on a Friday evening. You're out drinking Sambuca after work and feel like doing something fun. So you call Giovanna. She's drinking white wine somewhere, and she can hardly hear you because it's so loud. All you understand is, "Come stai? Why don't you meet me here?" So you say, "Va bene," pay, pick up your keys and take off. In the other bar, there's no Giovanna. Your telefonino rings. "Come stai. Where are you? I thought we were supposed to come to you!" You could spend a whole evening like this. If it weren't for the telefonino…

## Ospite — Guests

My aunt had a birthday party, as usual without sending out invitations. Whoever showed up, showed up. But who was that person at the door? "I've known a lot of people in my life," says my aunt from the window, "but I've never seen that man before." Well, didn't he look like the guy who always served her cappuccino at the campground kiosk on Sardinia? Or was he the taxi driver from Florence who took us to his sister's trattoria and came right in and ate with us? In the end, it turned out to be our family friend Xaver dressed as a gigolo (he thought it was a costume party) and it was all really funny. Which goes to show that surprise parties can be a lot of fun—but also pretty risky.

## Terrina — Bowl

Cooking Italian food for lots of people calls for a big serving bowl. I have to have a terrina for the pasta because I think serving pasta and sauce straight from the pot is despicable. So I put the colander in the bowl, pour in the spaghetti, and let the warm water filter through to heat up the bowl. Then I remove the water and fill the terrina with the spaghetti. (If it's earthenware, I first add a few ladles full of pasta water; if I poured it in all at once, the bowl could crack.) Then I pour sauce over the top, add a little Parmesan and perfecto! When I emerge from the kitchen, somebody is sure to exclaim, "Mamma mia!"—which always makes me feel good.

## Cantare — Singing

Winding along the roads in Liguria, we sang "Volare" at the top of our lungs at every blind curve because our horn was broken. Later on, looking for a lunch spot in a scorching-hot mountain village, we heard a distant and scratchy "Caruso" coming from some half-open shutters. Suddenly there was the osteria in front of our eyes. After our pranzo, we sat on the San Remo esplanade with glasses of Cinqueterre. Hey, isn't that Ramazotti sitting over there? "Azzurro!", we all cried. (It was him, all right, but the table next to us reminded us the song "Azzurro" is sung by Celentano.) We still laugh about it whenever we have pesto pasta out on our urban balcony—we belt out a rendition of "Volare" over our caffè, wishing the people in the street would join in.

## Tavola — Table

Even in the type of dives in America where you'd find incoherent graffiti carved into the bare wood tabletops, the Italians still prefer to use tablecloths. They can be wax-coated or checkered or flowered, which is either very authentic or very trendy, or both. A checkered cloth says "Benvenuto a casa" whereas red-and-white might say "Welcome to Little Italy." A large white cloth is always right for an Italian meal. Wine glasses without stems, pizza plates and a single, long-stemmed rose look as good on this type of cloth as Prosecco flutes, giant plates of arugula spaghetti and a designer peppermill. Cloth napkins are also right at home.

## Gelato — Ice Cream

I can still remember my first trip to a gelateria called Dolomiti. It's where as a teenager I had my first espresso (oops, I mean caffè) and that wonderful creamy ice cream that I now know is so typical in Italy. Gelato doesn't have as much air incorporated into it as American ice cream, so it is denser and creamier—and doesn't get as hard. Later in life I went back to the little village where I had found Dolomiti. Every little thing was as I had remembered. One taste and I felt so "choco-latta"!

## Oliera — Oil and Vinegar Cruets

Whenever I make spaghetti just for myself, I set the oil and vinegar cruets out on the table and I no longer feel so alone. They remind me of days in the trattoria in Modena where I went at lunch time to escape the frustration of the language school where I was enrolled. Maria, the owner, noticed right away I needed consolation. So she made me a salad with excellent balsamico from one cruet and dripped olive oil from the other onto my crusty bread. She did this every day. When I finally told her it was my last day in Italy, she brought her nephew over to have caffè with me. But I was too upset to be interested so she said, "At least take these with you." And that's how I came to have her oliera on my table.

## Magazzino — General Store

Now I must tell you about my summer in Abruzzo. We lived in a wonderful old farmhouse above the sea. There was nothing in the kitchen but an aluminum pot big enough to boil eggs and a tray depicting St. Peter's Square. But there was a shop down below in the village, selling everything from charcoal to laundry soap, the type I always get lost in when on vacation. When I finally emerged, I had a first-class espresso pot, a fusilli attachment for my pasta maker and a kitschy fly curtain. Now our vacation could begin! And because I brought the St. Peter's Square tray back home with me, the vacation lives on.

## Bella Italia

A Prosecco as an aperitivo—we're walking in the sun toward Veneto. But first a bruschetta with very young olive oil—it smells like the summer grass in Tuscany. An antipasti of marinated octopus—the waves gently lap onto the shores of Capri. A primo of risotto with scampi—we're watching the Romans do their shopping. A bollito misto as a secondo—at a large family-style table in the ristorante in Alba. Cinnamon doughnuts for our dolci—we're warming our hands in a wine bar in South Tyrol. Marsala as a digestivo—the Golfo di Palermo sparkles in the sunset. Need we eat or say more?

# 16 Souvenirs for the dolce vita at home

## Coperto — Cover Charge

I used to get so upset in Italy when I'd see something like "Coperto 3000 Lire" at the bottom of a menu. "What for?" I'd ask. Until one day a very nice waiter explained to me that it's for the water and bread, and that I was also paying less for drinks than I would at home (which was true in that particular restaurant, at least). This bread-and-water thing certainly is a nice idea. When people come to my house to eat, I always like to have a caraffa di acqua and a cestino di pane (bread basket) ready, because I find it makes it both a little "famiglia" and a little "ristorante." Another delizioso idea is to set out a small bowl of extra virgin olive oil for dipping the bread. That's all you need, really.

## Menù — Menu

Naturally, I'm not talking about the flashy, unreadable, hand-written menus on parchment that look like wedding invitations. It's much more authentic to stick my menù on the refrigerator door on a magnetic corkboard I got from the Bar Italia. Of course, I can also write it with chalk on a normal blackboard. On special occasions, I present it at the table with all the grandezza I can muster. And on very special occasions, I simply rattle it off in fake Italian trying to imitate Maria in her trattoria.

## Aperitivo

I'm no alcoholic but I like a little shot of something before a meal. Or sometimes a bit of wine while I cook. As guests arrive, I offer them a little something. Prosecco works great in stemmed glasses or flutes. I prefer using water glasses and stem-less Italian wine glasses for a good red wine with the pizza. If my guest is a regular, I know their aperitivo from the get-go. Andrew likes something bitter, preferably Averna. Anne prefers a sweet Strega. Maria loves my homemade limoncello, a lemon-flavored liqueur. And the handsome Sergio has to have his Campari, naturalmente. And me? Caffè. Somebody has to cook!

# the recipes

# Antip

Senza problema? Just turn the page...Bravo!

# asti

## [Before the dough]

Nothing against pasta—we love it as much as all the other delizioso Italian food. But man does not live by pasta alone. It makes a great, quick week-night meal—but it can seem lonely on the plate. How can you lead the dolce vita if you eat only a single course? Why not have a little something to go with it? Before it? In other words, "ante paste"?

So here we are again at the beginning. Whenever we visit our favorite Italian restaurant, we stop in front of the antipasti display case. Look at how colorful it all is! Marinated peppers, tomatoes au gratin, asparagus frittata, as well as marinated anchovies and even duck breast in balsamic vinegar. And with the salad bowl in between—pico bello! Plus a bottle of olive oil, extra virgin, with fresh-baked Italian bread. We wish we could have a little of everything. Senza problema? Just turn the page...Bravo!

Aunt Edna's Love Salad

# Italian greens with oil and vinegar

I once had a Japanese boyfriend who wanted me to cook him something special. I made a salad, and from that moment on I had him eating out of my hand. Why? Because it was an Italian salad! Watch out though—it's just like sushi—easy to make but even easier to make badly. Both dishes are based on years of tradition and require only a few ingredients, but the maneuvers have to be the right ones. So let's give it a try!

Start by deciding on the right combination: First something crispy: **lattuga** (head lettuce), **romana** (romaine), **lollo** or **lattughino** (leaf lettuce); then something wild and spicy is nice, like **arugula**, **mizuna** or **dandelion greens**. Plus add something bitter, like **radicchio**, **endive** or **frisée** (curly endive). Remove outer leaves, core and any tough stems, then tear leaves into manageable bite-sized pieces. Rinse greens well and pat dry (or use a salad spinner).

Italian chefs sometimes take greens straight to the table, pour vinegar into a salad spoon, stir salt and pepper into it and mix it into the salad. They then pour oil over the top, toss and they're done. Easier said than done! I prefer this method: In the salad bowl, mix your best vinegar (to serve 4, 2–3 tablespoons) with a little salt and pepper. Gradually whisk in olive oil—about twice the amount of the vinegar. That's it! Add the greens, toss and serve (leaves should be barely shiny—any more dressing is overkill). A genuine, romantic gesture...and Japanese aren't the only ones who love me for it.

# The Zucchini

### The zucchini is:
• Our favorite descendant of the squash family
• Not always green and long, sometimes yellow or lime green, pear-shaped or round
• Inexpensive and quick to prepare
• Often underestimated in the flavor department

### The zucchini has:
• An "o" on the end in Italian when singular (zucchino); called "zucchini" in Italian only when plural
• In the spring, huge luminous yellow blossoms that can be stuffed and baked or lightly battered and deep-fried. If a small zucchini is still attached, it's female. Blossoms without fruit are male.

### The zucchini needs:
• To be eaten when small, its most flavorful and tender stage. Longer than 8 inches, it's better used as feed for livestock.
• To be cooked at a high temperature, briefly, with little or no liquid—sautéing, grilling and deep-frying are ideal; braising it in its own juice also works.
• To be parboiled for a few minutes even when destined to be eaten cold. This brings out the full flavor.

### The zucchini loves:
• Basil, oregano, parsley, tarragon
• Garlic, capers, fennel seed, sugar
• Tomatoes, peppers, eggplant, green onions
• Olive oil, brown butter, lemon juice

# In the Paninoteca

Crostini, crostino, crostoni? Bruschetta or panunto? Or would you rather have focaccia? Italian bread can make you cry tears of joy then weep in despair because there are so many choices. Our bread glossary should save you some frustration and prepare you for a visit to the "paninoteca"— a small Italian sandwich bar with fine breads and wine.

## Five Time-Saving Tips:
# Antipasti

Oh no, any minute the hungry mob will start pounding on my door, and I haven't even gotten out the pasta. What do I do? Throw together a few quick, emergency antipasti to start, and the rest will fall into place.

### Salami carpaccio
Arrange thin slices of coarse, air-dried salami on a plate (coppa, prosciutto or serrano will also work). Drizzle fresh lemon juice and olive oil over the top with freshly ground pepper and some fresh basil. Serve with Italian bread such as pugliese, ciabatta or filone.

### Baked antipasti vegetables
For each serving, rinse ½ cup cherry tomatoes and chop a rinsed green onion. Mix with 1 table-spoon olive oil, ½ teaspoon rosemary needles, ½ garlic clove (thinly sliced) and salt and pepper. In a baking dish, bake in a 425°F oven for 10–15 minutes.

### Melon sticks
Cut any melon except watermelon into thick, julienned sticks. Just before serving, season with salt and cayenne pepper and serve alongside grissini (Italian breadsticks) and roasted-salted almonds. You'll be surprised how good the melon tastes, and it looks great if you use several types of melon.

### Prosciutto-egg brunch appetizer
For 4–6 as a starter: line a greased 9" square baking dish with 3–4 oz. prosciutto or salami. Whisk together 2 eggs, 2 tablespoons flour and 1 cup whole milk until smooth, then pour into the dish. Sprinkle a handful of grated Parmesan over the top. Bake in a 425°F oven for 15 minutes or until set. Cut into squares and serve.

### Mozzarella puffs
Cut thawed puff-pastry sheets into squares. Brush egg yolk along the edges and place a small piece of fresh mozzarella in the center of each. Top with one of these: an anchovy, capers, salami, pesto or garlic. Fold pastry over, press edges together with a fork and brush with egg yolk. Bake at 425°F for 15–20 minutes.

## Bruschetta
*Plural:* bruschette
*Pronounced:* brusketta
*Bruschetta is:* A slice of bread (from white to mixed-grain) toasted and rubbed with half a garlic clove while warm, then drizzled with olive oil and seasoned with salt and pepper. You can also add a simple topping such as crushed tomato pieces. See page 46.

## Crostino
*Plural:* crostini
*Pronounced:* just like it's written
*Crostino is:* A small slice of bread toasted like bruschetta and then immediately topped with a spread—often with strong pastes of marinated ingredients or even organ meats. If the slices are large, the whole thing is called crostone. Sometimes crostino refers to toasted tramezzino (sandwich). More on page 46.

## Focaccia
*Plural:* focacce
*Pronounced:* fokachia
*Focaccia is:* Flat bread containing olive oil and seasonings, sprinkled with salt and olive oil and baked in a very hot oven. Can also be topped like a pizza or used when cold to make a sandwich. See page 94.

## Panino
*Plural:* panini
*Pronounced:* just like it's written
*Panino is:* Actually just a plain roll. But if you ask for one in an Italian sandwich bar, it'll come filled with mortadella, ham or salami. More on page 49.

## Tramezzino
*Plural:* tramezzini
*Pronounced:* trametsini
*Tramezzino is:* An Italian sandwich—two slices of toast with something Italian in between. See page 48.

# Peperoni marinati
## Marinated bell peppers

### Numero uno on the antipasti plate

If you want bell peppers that live up to their best potential, you should roast and peel them first, before marinating (as described below). It's worth the effort. But if you are short on time, don't peel them—just sauté in 1–2 tablespoons olive oil for about 5 minutes; then marinate.

Feeds 4 as an appetizer:

2 red bell peppers

2 yellow bell peppers

2 cloves garlic

1 tablespoon fresh lemon juice

2 tablespoons cold-pressed extra virgin olive oil

Salt, freshly ground black pepper

$\frac{1}{4}$ cup parsley sprigs

**1** Set oven to 475°F. Rinse bell peppers and cut in half lengthwise through the stem. Then cut out stems and pull out interior, including seeds and ribs. Place pepper halves on a greased baking sheet with the cut sides down.

**2** Bake peppers for about 15 minutes or until the peels have blistered and are completely black in some places; remove. Wet a dish towel under cold water, squeeze it out and lay it over the peppers. Cool peppers to room temperature.

**3** Reserve liquid from the baking dish. Pierce blisters and slip peels off the peppers. Once removed (it's OK if a few traces remain), cut peppers into strips and place in a shallow bowl with the reserved pepper liquid.

**4** Peel garlic and slice cloves very thinly, and then cut into fine strips. Combine with lemon juice, oil, salt and pepper and pour over the peppers. Marinate at least 4 hours at room temperature, stirring occasionally and once again right before serving. Last minute: rinse parsley, shake dry, chop leaves very finely and sprinkle over peppers.

Prep time: 45 minutes
(not including marinating time)
Delicious with: Crusty Italian bread
Calories per serving: 60

# Acciughe piccante
## Spicy anchovies

Rapidissimo

Feeds 4:
3 $\frac{1}{2}$ oz. oil-packed anchovy fillets
$\frac{1}{4}$ cup parsley sprigs
1–2 cloves garlic
1 fresh red chile
$\frac{1}{3}$ cup cold-pressed extra virgin olive oil

**1** Drain anchovies.

**2** Rinse parsley, shake dry and chop leaves finely. Peel garlic and chop very finely. Rinse chile, remove stem and cut in half lengthwise (wear gloves). Now decide: if you like it hot, chop the pepper finely including ribs and seeds. If you'd rather be cautious, remove ribs and seeds. Mix all ingredients with oil and serve—or marinate several hours.

Prep time: 10 minutes
(not including marinating time)
Delicious with: Toasted Italian bread
Calories per serving: 345

# Funghi marinati
## Marinated mushrooms

Super-fast and super-easy

Tastes great not only as an appetizer but also as a small meal with a green salad — or as a side dish with meat.

Feeds 4 as an appetizer:
1 lb. oyster mushrooms
Salt, freshly ground black pepper
3 $\frac{1}{2}$ tablespoons extra virgin olive oil
$\frac{1}{4}$ cup basil sprigs
3 cloves garlic
3 tablespoons fresh lemon juice
2 tablespoons white wine
(if you have a bottle open)

**1** Preheat broiler. Break apart oyster mushrooms. Trim off stems. Combine mushrooms with salt, pepper and oil and place them in a baking dish pressed as closely together as possible.

**2** Broil the mushrooms about 4$\frac{1}{2}$" from the heating element for 10–12 minutes. Occasionally remove the pan and stir to turn the mushrooms over.

**3** While the mushrooms are broiling, rinse and pat basil leaves dry—cut into strips. Peel garlic and squeeze through a press. Stir basil and garlic into the mushrooms and broil another 2 minutes.

**4** Transfer mushrooms to a bowl. Pour lemon juice and wine into the baking dish and mix with the pan juices. Pour mixture over the mushrooms and serve hot; or, marinate for a few hours and serve at room temperature.

Prep time: 20 minutes
Goes with: Italian bread
Calories per serving: 140

# Cipolle al balsamico
Onions in balsamic vinegar

One more step towards the dolce vita

Makes enough for 4:

1 lb. young red onions (as small as

possible—try a farmers' market)

5–8 sage leaves

3 tablespoons olive oil

$\frac{1}{4}$ cup balsamic vinegar

$3\frac{1}{2}$ tablespoons dry red wine

2 teaspoons honey

1 dried red chile (optional)

Salt, freshly ground black pepper

1 Peel onions and halve lengthwise, then quarter. Rinse sage, pull off leaves and cut into thin strips.

2 Heat oil in a frying pan. Stir in onions and sage and sauté 1–2 minutes.

3 Combine balsamic vinegar, red wine and $\frac{1}{4}$ cup water, then add to onions along with honey and, if desired, the whole dried chile. Season with salt and pepper and cover. Simmer over medium heat for about

3 minutes and remove the chile; then simmer another 7 minutes.

4 Transfer onions to a bowl with any remaining liquid and let cool. Then refrigerate, covered to allow flavors to meld for at least 8 hours or longer. Serve at room temperature.

Prep time: 20 minutes
(not including marinating time)
Goes with: Toasted Italian bread and
a salad with arugula and diced tomato
Calories per serving: 110

# Melanzana grigliate
Grilled eggplant

Very easy to make

Feeds 4–6 as an appetizer:

$\frac{2}{3}$ cup olive oil

2 smallish eggplants (about 1 lb.)

Salt, freshly ground black pepper

2 stalks celery

$\frac{1}{2}$ lemon

$\frac{1}{2}$ cup parsley sprigs

4 oil-packed anchovy fillets

2 teaspoons capers

$3\frac{1}{2}$ tablespoons dry white wine

1 Heat broiler. Brush baking sheet with 2 tablespoons of the oil. Rinse eggplant and remove stems (peel if desired). Cut into slices about $\frac{1}{4}$" thick, either lengthwise or crosswise. Season with salt and pepper, place side by side on a greased baking sheet in a single layer; brush with olive oil, but reserve any remaining oil (do in two batches if necessary). Place in oven on the middle shelf and broil for about 10 minutes, turning halfway through.

2 While the eggplant is broiling, rinse celery, trim ends and any wilted parts and finely dice the rest. Rinse lemon and pat dry. Remove a thin layer of zest with a vegetable peeler, being careful to avoid the white part which imparts a bitter taste. Finely chop lemon zest. Squeeze out juice. Rinse parsley and chop finely. For dressing: mash anchovies with a fork and combine with lemon juice and any remaining oil; stir in celery, lemon zest, parsley and capers.

3 Remove eggplant from oven and place in a shallow bowl. Use wine to loosen any bits from the baking sheet and add to anchovy dressing. Pour over eggplant and marinate at least 4 hours. Serve at room temperature.

Prep time: 35 minutes
(not including marinating time)
Goes with: Italian bread
Calories per serving (6): 205

# Pomodori al forno
## Roasted-stuffed tomatoes

## Pack up for a picnic

Feeds 4 as an appetizer or side dish:

8 small, very ripe tomatoes

Salt, freshly ground black pepper

1/4 cup parsley sprigs

2 cloves garlic, 2/3 cup bread crumbs

2 oz. freshly grated Parmesan or pecorino

1/3 cup olive oil

1 Preheat oven to 375°F. Rinse tomatoes and halve through the equator. Cut out cores from top halves with the tip of a sharp paring knife. Sprinkle cut sides with salt and pepper and place face up, side by side in a greased baking dish.

2 Rinse parsley, shake dry, chop leaves finely and place in a small bowl. Peel garlic, squeeze through a press and add to parsley. Stir in breadcrumbs, Parmesan and oil.

3 Distribute bread crumb mixture over the tomatoes and gently press down. Bake tomatoes for about 30 minutes or until topping is nicely browned. Serve at room temperature.

Prep time: 45 minutes,
15 of which you're actually busy
Calories per serving: 250

# Verdura fritta con salsa verde
## Crispy fried vegetables with dipping sauce

## Fresh parsley makes the sauce green

Feeds 4 as a fancy appetizer:

**For the sauce:**

2 cloves garlic, 6 oil-packed anchovy fillets

1 cup parsley sprigs, 1 tablespoon capers

2 tablespoons white wine vinegar

2 tablespoons bread crumbs

About 1/3 cup olive oil

(or a little more as needed)

Salt, freshly ground black pepper

**For the vegetables:**

2 eggs

3/4 cup flour

1/3 lb. green asparagus

1 zucchini

1 large white onion

Vegetable or canola oil, for frying

1 For the sauce, peel garlic. Drain anchovies. Rinse parsley and discard any tough stems. Purée garlic, anchovies, and parsley together with capers, vinegar, bread crumbs and 1/4 cup water (using blender, hand blender or food processor). Add oil gradually, processing until desired consistency (add more oil if desired). Season sauce with salt and pepper.

2 For the coating ingredients, break eggs into a bowl and whisk. Spread out the flour onto a plate. Heat a quart or so of oil to 350–375 degrees over medium-high heat (test with an oil thermometer or by inserting a wooden spoon handle down into the oil—bubbles will rise when the oil is hot enough).

3 Rinse asparagus and zucchini. Trim tough ends off asparagus. Cut remaining spears diagonally into 1 1/2" long pieces (then in half lengthwise if large) . Cut zucchini lengthwise into slices 1/2" thick and then into julienne strips 1/4" x 1 1/2". Peel onion, cut in wedges and separate into layers.

4 Heat oil in a wide pot. Toss vegetables in batches in the egg and then dredge in the flour (try to coat lightly with flour on all sides, but shake of the excess). Transfer vegetables using a slotted metal spoon, a few at a time, into the hot oil. Deep-fry vegetable pieces for 3–4 minutes or until lightly golden. Remove and place on a thick layer of paper towels to drain, season with salt and pepper, then place in a 125°F oven to keep warm. When all the vegetables are done, serve with the sauce.

Prep time: 45 minutes
Delicious with: Lemon wedges
Calories per serving: 480

# Frittata agli asparagi
## Asparagus frittata

For adventurous types
who want more than
an omelet

Feeds 6–8 as an appetizer or snack:

3/4 lb. green asparagus

2 onions

2 cloves garlic

3/4 cup arugula leaves

1/3 cup olive oil

8 eggs

Salt, freshly ground black pepper

**1** Rinse asparagus under cold running water and drain. Trim off tough ends. Cut spears diagonally into 1 1/2" long pieces. Peel onions and garlic and chop both finely. Remove all wilted leaves and tough stems from arugula; rinse remaining leaves in cold water, shake dry and chop coarsely.

**2** In a large pan, heat 3 tablespoons of the oil. Add onions and sauté over medium heat until translucent while stirring. Add asparagus and garlic; sauté another 5 minutes, stirring often. Mix in arugula (reserve some fresh for garnish) and sauté only until it has wilted.

**3** Break eggs into a bowl and whisk briefly. Pour in asparagus-arugula mixture, stir and season with salt and pepper.

**4** Put pan back on the stove (no need to clean it!) and heat remaining oil. Pour in egg-asparagus mixture and cook over low heat for about 10 minutes until the egg mixture solidifies in the pan.

**5** Loosen the frittata from the edges of the pan with a flexible heat-safe spatula. Bring a plate to the edge of the pan and slide the frittata onto it. Place a greased second plate upside-down on top, turn the whole thing over and slide the frittata back into the pan with the uncooked side down. Cook for about another 3 minutes.

**6** Remove frittata from pan and let cool. Cut into pie-like wedges and garnish with fresh arugula to serve.

Prep time: 30 minutes
Goes with: Ciabatta and white wine
Calories per serving (8): 175

## Variations:

### With herbs
Buy a mixture of fresh herbs such as parsley, basil, borage, lemon balm and/or arugula. Rinse about 3/4 cup of herb sprigs and chop. Sauté herbs briefly with onions and garlic, stir into eggs and continue as described above.

### With artichokes
Remove a generous portion of the outer leaves and the stems from 6 small, tender artichokes, then cut lengthwise into eighths. If they contain fuzzy centers (which look like bristly hair), cut them out. Sauté artichokes like asparagus as described, then proceed. Or take artichoke hearts from a jar, drain, chop and stir into the egg mixture without sautéing.

### With tomatoes and olives
Drain 1/3 cup sun-dried tomatoes (oil-packed type) and cut into strips. Cut about 15 pitted black olives (preferably kalamata or Niçoise) into strips. Sauté onions, garlic and 1/2 cup chopped parsley sprigs; then stir into egg mixture along with sun-dried tomatoes and olives.

# Vitello tonnato
## Veal in tuna sauce

Tastes classy because
it is classy

Puts 6–8 in a good mood:

1 piece veal from the leg

(about 1¼ lbs. loin, rump or top round—

boneless. Ask your butcher)

1 onion

2 whole cloves

2 stalks celery

2 carrots

¾ cup fresh parsley sprigs

1 cup dry white wine

2 bay leaves

Salt

1 can water-packed tuna

4 oil-packed anchovy fillets

1 very fresh egg yolk

⅓ cup cold-pressed extra virgin olive oil

1 tablespoon fresh lemon juice

Freshly ground black pepper

2 tablespoons capers

**1** Rinse veal under cold water, pat dry and trim away any significant fat.

**2** Peel onion and cut in half. Pierce halves with whole cloves. Rinse celery, peel carrots and cut both into large chunks. Rinse parsley under cold water and shake dry. Place parsley, celery, carrots, onion, wine and 5½ cups water in a large pot. Add bay leaves, season generously with salt and bring to a boil.

**3** Place meat in boiling water mixture – this way, the pores are quickly sealed and the meat stays juicy. For this same reason, reduce the heat drastically, briefly removing the pot from the stove if necessary, at first. Simmer meat over low heat with the lid halfway off (block with a wooden spoon) for about 45 minutes. Let cool in the liquid.

**4** Drain tuna and purée with ½ cup of the veal cooking liquid; set aside. Drain anchovies, place in a bowl and mash finely with a fork. Whisk in egg yolk. Gradually drizzle very small amounts of oil into this mixture while whisking vigorously. When it starts to look like mayonnaise, you can add the oil a little more quickly.

**5** Stir in puréed tuna mixture. Season sauce with lemon juice, salt and pepper. Drain capers and add.

**6** Remove meat from liquid, pat dry and slice thinly with a very sharp knife. Pour a generous amount of sauce over the top and it's ready!

Prep time: At least 2 hours,
1½ of which you can relax
Goes with: Lemon wedges, fresh Italian bread and a sparkling white wine
Calories per serving (8): 205

# Carpaccio
## Raw appetizer

Feeds 4 lovers of tradition:

7 oz. beef tenderloin fillet (Inform the butcher you'll be eating it raw. Other options: sushi-grade swordfish, tuna or salmon fillets OR smoked fish sliced paper-thin.)

Several nice lettuce leaves or arugula

⅓ cup extra virgin olive oil

Salt, freshly ground black pepper

1 lemon

For beef version: 1 hefty chunk Parmesan cheese (5–6 oz.)

**1** If you're making it with meat or the fresh fish variation: Wrap in clear plastic wrap and place in the freezer for 1 hour. Then it will be so cold that you can easily cut it into thin slices. Or order meat from the butcher pre-sliced.

**2** Remove lettuce leaves from head, rinse in cold water and shake dry. Brush 4 plates with a thin coating of oil. Arrange lettuce around the edges of the plates. Remove meat or fresh fish from plastic wrap and cut into thin slices using a very sharp knife with a thin blade.

**3** Arrange meat, fish or smoked fish slices on the plates so they overlap slightly. Drizzle oil over the top. Season with salt and pepper.

**4** Cut lemon wedges and arrange on the edges of the plates. For the meat version, shave Parmesan cheese over the top. You can do this with a vegetable peeler but don't press down too hard, so shavings remain paper thin.

Prep time: 15 minutes
(not including freezing time)
Goes with: Italian bread
Calories per serving of beef fillet with
Parmesan: 340; per serving of salmon
fillet: 235

# Petto d'anatra al balsamico
## Cold duck breast with balsamic vinaigrette

## Extremely elegant

It's best to cook the duck breast one day ahead. If you want, make double the amount so you can enjoy half of it right after cooking, with a small salad and rosemary potatoes from page 110.

Feeds 4 in the mood to celebrate:

1 duck breast (about 10–11 oz.), skin-on

2 cloves garlic

1 dried red chile

or $\frac{1}{2}$ teaspoon crushed red pepper flakes

$\frac{1}{4}$ cup parsley sprigs

$\frac{1}{4}$ cup extra virgin olive oil

Salt, freshly ground black pepper

2 green onions

1 dash hot mustard

3 tablespoons balsamic vinegar

2 cups arugula leaves

**1** Rinse duck breast under cold water and pat dry. Peel garlic and squeeze through a press. Finely crush chile in a mortar or chop finely (omit seeds for less spice—wear gloves and don't touch your eyes)—or use flakes. Rinse parsley under cold water, chop finely and combine with garlic, chile and 1 tablespoon of the olive oil. Rub mixture into duck breast on all sides and let stand 1 hour.

**2** Heat a lightly-oiled pan (preferably a heavy one made of cast iron but other types are fine) over high heat. Place duck breast in the pan with the skin side down, reduce to medium heat and cook on that side for 8 minutes, then turn and cook another 10 minutes on the other side. Season with salt and pepper, wrap in aluminum foil and let cool.

**3** Remove roots and any wilted parts from green onions; rinse and chop rest finely. Combine mustard, balsamic vinegar, salt and pepper. Add remaining oil one table-spoon at a time, whisking vigorously until creamy. Stir in green onions.

**4** Remove wilted leaves and any tough stems from arugula. Rinse and dry arugula leaves and distribute evenly on 4 plates. Slice duck breast as thinly as possible. Arrange slices on arugula, drizzle with vinaigrette and serve.

Prep time: 50 minutes (not including marinating and cooling time)
Goes with: Italian bread
Calories per serving: 335

# Bruschetta

### Always good

Feeds 4 connoisseurs:

1/4 cup basil sprigs

3–4 tomatoes (must be ripe and fresh)

1/4 cup extra virgin olive oil

Salt, freshly ground black pepper

4 large round slices Italian white bread

4 cloves garlic

**1** Remove basil leaves from stems and cut into fine strips. Rinse tomatoes, pat dry and remove cores; dice. Mix tomatoes and basil with oil and season with salt and pepper.

**2** Cut bread slices in half and toast in a toaster or in a very hot oven (for about 4 minutes).

**3** In the meantime, peel garlic. Rub into hot, crispy bread (the bread works like a grater). Top with tomato-basil mixture and enjoy immediately.

Prep time: 20 minutes
Delicious with: Prosecco
Calories per serving: 140

# Bruschetta ai funghi
### Bruschetta with mushrooms

### For a change

Feeds 4 as an appetizer:

1 yellow bell pepper

1/2 lb. mushrooms

2 oz. pancetta or bacon

1/4 cup parsley sprigs

1/4 cup extra virgin olive oil

Salt, freshly ground black pepper

4 large slices Italian white bread

2–4 cloves garlic

**1** Rinse bell pepper, halve and remove the contents, then dice the rest. Trim ends of mushroom stems. Wipe off mushrooms and slice thinly. Chop pancetta. Rinse parsley and chop leaves finely.

**2** In a pan, heat half the olive oil. Sauté pancetta, mushrooms and bell pepper over medium high heat for 3–4 minutes, stirring occasionally. Add parsley and season with salt and pepper.

**3** Cut bread slices in half and toast in a toaster or in a very hot oven for about

4 minutes. Peel garlic and rub into crispy bread. Mix remaining oil with sautéed mushroom mixture and distribute on bread slices.

Prep time: 20 minutes
Delicious with: A hearty white wine or light red wine
Calories per serving: 210

# Crostini alla crema di olive
### Crostini with olive spread

This one's green. If you want black, see olive paste in *Basic Cooking*, page 62

Makes enough for 4:

1/2 cup basil leaves

3/4 cup pitted green olives

1 dried red chile

or crushed red pepper flakes to taste

1 tablespoon pine nuts + more for garnish

2 tablespoons olive oil

12 sliced bread rounds

**1** Rinse basil and remove leaves. Purée finely together with olives, red chile (seeds removed for less spice—or use flakes), pine

nuts and oil (using blender or hand blender). No need for salt—the olives are salty enough.

**2** Toast bread slices in a toaster or in a very hot oven for about 4 minutes. Spread with olive paste, garnish with pine nuts and enjoy immediately.

Prep time: 15 minutes
Delicious with: Toasted pine nuts sprinkled on top
Calories per serving: 155

# Crostini con fegatini
Crostini with liver paté

A classic for any occasion

Feeds 4 Tuscany lovers:

7 oz. chicken livers, 1 shallot or small onion

1 small carrot, 1 stalk celery

4–5 sage leaves

1 slice prosciutto or serrano ham

2 tablespoons olive oil, 1 tablespoon butter

1/2 cup dry white or red wine

1 fresh red chile (optional)

Salt, freshly ground black pepper

1 pinch lemon zest

12 sliced bread rounds

**1** Trim fat from livers, rinse under cold water and chop. Peel shallot and carrot. Rinse celery. Dice shallot, carrot, and celery finely. Cut sage into strips. Chop prosciutto.

**2** Heat oil and butter together. Briefly sauté shallot, carrot, celery, sage and prosciutto. Add and sauté liver while stirring constantly until liver changes color. Stir in wine and whole chile pepper, season with salt and pepper, cover and simmer over medium heat for about 3 minutes. Remove chile. Simmer for another 7 minutes. Let cool briefly, then purée (using blender, hand blender, or food processor). Season spread to taste with lemon zest and a little more salt and pepper, if desired.

**3** Toast bread slices in a toaster or in a very hot oven for about 4 minutes. Spread with liver paté mixture and serve.

Prep time: 40 minutes
Calories per serving: 240

## Variation:

### Bean caper paste

Purée 7 oz. cooked white beans from a can (about a half can), 1 tablespoon capers, 1/2 cup parsley leaves and 3 tablespoons olive oil. Season to taste with 1 tablespoon fresh lemon juice, salt and chili powder. Stir in more capers (chopped) to taste.

# Crostini alla crema di pollo
Crostini with a chicken-arugula spread

Simple and exquisite

Feeds 4 gourmets:

1 cup chicken stock, 7 oz. chicken breast fillets

2 tablespoons fresh lemon juice

1/4 cup olive oil

3/4 cup arugula leaves + more for garnish

Salt, freshly ground black pepper

12 sliced bread rounds

**1** Heat stock, add chicken, cover and bring to a low boil; reduce heat to low and simmer for about 10 minutes. Let cool slightly, remove chicken and dice (reserve stock).

**2** Finely purée diced chicken, lemon juice, oil and 3–5 tablespoons of the cooking stock (using blender, food processor or hand blender). Remove wilted leaves and any tough stems from arugula; then rinse leaves. Chop arugula leaves finely and add to paste. Add salt and pepper to taste.

**3** Toast bread slices in a toaster or very hot oven (for about 4 minutes). Top bread with chicken spread. Garnish with arugula and serve.

Prep time: 30 minutes
Calories per serving: 280

# Crostini al forno
## Crostini au gratin

### Off to a hot start!

Feeds 4 as an appetizer:

4 oil-packed anchovy fillets

1 heaping tablespoon butter

8 thin slices Italian bread

1 ball fresh mozzarella (about 5 oz.)

Salt, freshly ground black pepper

**1** Preheat oven to 475°F. Chop anchovy fillets finely or mash with a fork. Mix into butter and spread on bread.

**2** Drain fresh mozzarella, slice thinly and distribute on bread slices. Place on a baking sheet and bake on the middle shelf for about 5 minutes, until the cheese melts.

**3** Season with salt and pepper and serve while hot.

Prep time: 15 minutes
Calories per serving: 145

# Tramezzini agli scampi
## Tramezzini with shrimp

### Delicious anywhere— but especially under a clear blue sky

Makes 8 half sandwiches:

½ lb. cooked, peeled shrimp

2 small tomatoes, ½ cup basil sprigs

½ cup mascarpone cheese

¼ cup mayonnaise

Salt, freshly ground black pepper

4 nice lettuce leaves

8 slices sandwich bread

**1** Dice cooked shrimp finely. Rinse and halve tomatoes. Squeeze out juice and seeds; then dice the rest finely. Rinse basil and cut leaves into strips.

**2** Mix together mascarpone and mayonnaise. Add shrimp, tomatoes and basil and season with salt and pepper. Rinse lettuce and remove tough ribs from the leaves; pat dry.

**3** Cut 4 bread slices in half diagonally. Distribute the lettuce leaves among 4 of the slices; then top with shrimp mixture and

spread it out. Place other bread halves on top, press down gently. Cut half sandwiches in half again if desired (to make finger sandwiches).

Prep time: 25 minutes
Calories per half sandwich: 140

# Tramezzini al tonno
## Tramezzini with tuna spread

### Not just for beachcombers

Makes 8 half sandwiches:

2 cans water-packed tuna

½ cup parsley sprigs

2 heaping tablespoons mayonnaise

2 heaping tablespoons mascarpone or crème fraîche

1 tablespoon capers

1 teaspoon fresh lemon juice

Salt, freshly ground black pepper

4 nice lettuce leaves

8 slices sandwich bread

**1** Drain tuna and flake apart. Rinse parsley and chop leaves finely.

**2** Mix together mayonnaise and mascarpone. Add tuna, parsley and capers and season with lemon juice, salt and pepper.

**3** Rinse lettuce, pat dry and remove tough ribs from leaves. Cut 4 bread slices in half diagonally. Distribute lettuce leaves among 4 halves, then top with tuna and spread it out. Place remaining halves on top, press down gently and cut in half again if desired (for finger sandwiches).

Prep time: 20 minutes
Calories per half sandwich: 90

## Tip
Prepare half the amount of tuna spread and use as a topping for toasted crostini. Garnish with capers.

# Panini all'arrosto
## Roasted meat sandwiches

### Fast food alla Italiana

Makes 4 rolls:

¹/₄ cup parsley sprigs, ¹/₄ cup basil sprigs

3 green onions, ¹/₃ cup pitted black olives (preferably kalamata or Niçoise)

3 tablespoons mayonnaise

1 tablespoon cream

Salt, freshly ground black pepper

4 lettuce leaves, 2 firm tomatoes

4 sandwich rolls

5–7 oz. cooked, roasted meat, thinly sliced

**1** Rinse herbs and chop finely. Remove and discard wilted parts and roots from green onions, rinse rest and chop finely. Dice olives.

**2** Mix together mayonnaise and cream. Add herbs, green onions and olives and season with salt and pepper. Rinse and dry lettuce. Rinse tomatoes and slice thinly into rounds. Cut open rolls and place lettuce and tomato slices on bottom halves. Distribute roasted meat on each, top with herb-olive cream and cover with top halves of rolls.

Prep time: 20 minutes
Calories per roll: 200

# Panini alla Mozzarella
## Rolls with fresh mozzarella

### Makes a pond feel like the Mediterranean

Makes 4 rolls:

2 balls fresh mozzarella (about 8 oz.)

2 cloves garlic, ¹/₄ cup basil sprigs

1 tablespoon fresh lemon juice

1 tablespoon olive oil

Salt, freshly ground black pepper

3 small tomatoes, 8 radicchio leaves

4 sandwich rolls

4 slices prosciutto (or more if desired)

**1** Slice fresh mozzarella thinly into rounds. Peel garlic and squeeze through a press. Cut basil into strips. Combine garlic and basil with lemon juice, oil, salt and pepper and distribute over cheese slices.

**2** Rinse tomatoes and slice thinly into rounds. Rinse radicchio and pat dry. Cut open rolls and place radicchio and tomato slices on bottom halves. Top each with fresh mozzarella slices and 1 slice prosciutto (or more); cover with top halves of rolls. Serve or wrap for a picnic.

Prep time: 20 minutes
Calories per roll: 400

49

# Verdura grigliata
## Grilled vegetables

In summer on a charcoal grill...in winter under a hot broiler

Feeds 4 as a snack or small evening meal:

1 small zucchini

1 yellow bell pepper

1 red bell pepper

5 green onions

$1/2$ lb. mushrooms

$1/2$ cup olive oil

Salt, freshly ground black pepper

3 cups mixed salad greens

(e.g. arugula, radicchio and romaine)

3 tablespoons wine vinegar

1 tablespoon capers

$1/4$ cup parsley sprigs

**1** In the winter, start by preheating the oven broiler. Rinse vegetables and trim away ends and stems. Cut zucchini lengthwise into $1/2$" slices. Cut bell peppers into strips. Quarter or halve green onions lengthwise. Leave mushrooms whole or cut in half if large.

**2** Mix together all the vegetables with 3 tablespoons of the oil, salt and pepper and spread out in a single layer on a greased baking sheet. Broil on the middle shelf of the oven for about 15 minutes, occasionally removing the pan to stir the vegetables thoroughly. During the last 5 minutes, move the pan to the top shelf, closer to the broiler element.

**3** Rinse lettuce, pat dry and tear leaves into bite-sized pieces.

**4** In a small bowl, combine vinegar, salt and pepper. Gradually whisk in remaining oil until creamy. Drain capers. Rinse parsley, shake dry and chop. Mix parsley and capers into half the dressing and use as the dressing for the salad greens. Distribute dressed greens on plates. Drizzle remaining dressing on vegetables and serve alongside the salad greens.

**5** In the summer, prepare recipe as above, but cook the vegetables on an outdoor grill until crisp-tender. See tips below.

Prep time: 25 minutes
Goes with: Olive bread
Calories per serving: 175

## Basic Tip

### Summer Version for the Charcoal Grill

Scout's Rule No. 1: Alcohol, gasoline and oil are absolute no-nos for starting charcoal! They're just too dangerous. Buy charcoal lighter fluid instead (read directions on the package). Light the grill at least 30 minutes before you'll be using it so the coals will be glowing.

Scout's Rule No. 2: Wet your finger and test the wind. Whichever side feels cool is the direction the wind is coming from. Turn the back of the grill in that direction so the wind won't blow on the fire.

Scout's Rule No. 3: Arrange the charcoal in a pile, use lighter fluid, and light it in two different places with a match. When there's a white layer of ash on the coals, spread them out using a tool and place the rack over the top. And now comes the cooking. For grilling vegetables, cut the pieces large enough so they won't fall through the cracks once they shrink a bit. Place the vegetables (prepared as in the above recipe) on the rack and turn them occasionally. They're done when crisp-tender and when nicely browned in some spots.

# Pinzimonio
Raw veggies

Extra virgin olive oil
makes it extra good!

Feeds 4 as a snack while cooking

or as an appetizer:

1 fennel bulb

1 small head radicchio

2 carrots

1 red bell pepper

4 stalks celery

$\frac{1}{2}$–$\frac{3}{4}$ cup extra virgin olive oil

Salt, freshly ground black pepper

1 tablespoon fresh lemon juice (optional)

**1** Rinse vegetables. Remove root end and wilted outer leaves from fennel and radicchio. Peel carrots. Cut all vegetables into uniform strips for dipping.

**2** In a bowl, whisk together olive oil, salt, pepper, and fresh lemon juice vigorously until cloudy. Take out a small bowl for each person. Place 2–3 tablespoons of olive oil mixture in each one. Season with additional salt and pepper if desired. Italians prefer to eat the vegetables with oil alone (no lemon juice), especially if the oil is young and fresh.

**3** Dip vegetables and munch!

Prep time: 15 minutes
Goes with: Fresh, crusty white Italian bread
Calories per serving (with a hefty shot of olive oil): 300

# Insalata frutti di mare
## Seafood salad

**This one's without mussels**

Feeds 4 to 6:

$3/4$ lb. fresh, cleaned squid fillets

Salt

$3/4$ lb. cooked, peeled shrimp

1 stalk celery, 1 carrot

$1/2$ cup parsley sprigs

2 tablespoons fresh lemon juice

Freshly ground black pepper

$1/4$ cup extra virgin olive oil

1 lemon cut into wedges for

serving on the side

**1** Rinse squid well under cold running water; drain. Bring salted water to a boil. Add squid and boil for 1 minute, no longer or it'll become tough. (If frozen squid, prepare according to package directions).

**2** Place squid in a colander, rinse under cold water and drain. Cut into rings about $1/4$" thick. If you bought tentacles, leave those whole.

**3** Rinse cooked shrimp briefly and pat dry. Rinse celery and remove any wilted leaves, stalks and any loose "threads." Cut stalks in half lengthwise, then slice thinly on the diagonal. Peel carrots, slice lengthwise and then cut into short julienned strips. Rinse parsley, shake dry and chop leaves finely.

**4** Combine lemon juice, salt, pepper and olive oil in a bowl and whisk vigorously until creamy. Add squid, shrimp, vegetables and parsley and refrigerate for 2 hours. Before placing the salad on the table, stir again and taste. It may need a little more lemon juice or salt and pepper. Place lemon wedges on the edge of each person's bowl to serve.

Prep time: 30 minutes
(plus 2 hours marinating time)
Goes with: Fresh, crusty white Italian bread and a glass of white wine
Calories per serving (6): 145

## Basic Tip
### Mussels for the salad

If you like shellfish, buy 1 lb. mussels and 1 lb. clams. Rinse them well under running water and make sure they are all closed. Throw away any that aren't. Scrape any fuzz off the outside with a paring knife. Put them in a pot of water or stock (with a little white wine, lemon juice, salt and pepper) and bring to a boil, then cover and boil shellfish for about 3-5 minutes. Now they should all have opened. Make sure you throw away any that are still closed. Toss with other seafood salad ingredients as in recipe above.

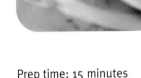

# Insalata di fagioli bianchi
## White bean salad

**Nothing could be quicker!**

Feeds 4 as an appetizer or 2 as a snack:

½ can cooked white beans (7–8 oz. drained)

1 medium red onion

1–2 tomatoes

½ cup basil sprigs

2 teaspoons capers

1 tablespoon wine vinegar

Salt, freshly ground black pepper

2–3 tablespoons extra virgin olive oil

**1** Pour beans into a colander and rinse well under cold water; drain.

**2** Peel onion, halve lengthwise and slice thinly crosswise into fine strips. Rinse tomatoes, cut out stem end and dice rest finely. Rinse basil, pat dry and cut into strips.

**3** Combine beans with onion, tomatoes, basil and capers. Thoroughly mix vinegar, salt, pepper and oil and stir into bean salad. Serve; or refrigerate briefly.

---

Prep time: 15 minutes
Calories per serving (4): 235

## Variation:

Instead of or in addition to tomatoes, drain 1 can water-packed tuna, flake apart and add. Instead of onion, thinly slice and add 1–2 stalks celery.

# Insalata di arance
## Orange fennel salad

**Sicily abounds in oranges and almost as many ways of preparing them**

Feeds 4 curious types:

2 small or 1 large fennel bulb

4 juicy oranges

16 pitted black olives

(preferably kalamata or Niçoise)

½ sprig rosemary or 3 sprigs parsley

1 tablespoon red wine vinegar

Salt, freshly ground black pepper

3 tablespoons extra virgin olive oil

---

**1** Remove tough outer layer from fennel and trim off root end. Remove fennel greens; rinse, chop coarsely and set aside. Rinse remaining bulb, halve lengthwise, then quarter. Slice fennel quarters crosswise, thinly into strips.

**2** Remove a slice from the top and bottom of each orange. Stand on end, then cut off the peel in strips from top to bottom, taking care to remove all the white membrane (use sharp knife). Then slice oranges thinly into rounds, reserving any juice that escapes.

**3** First arrange the oranges on four plates, then the fennel. Distribute olives over the top. Rinse rosemary; use only needles and chop them very finely. Sprinkle on top along with fennel greens. Add vinegar, salt, pepper and oil to reserved orange juice and whisk thoroughly. Pour over the salad. Enjoy salad immediately.

Prep time: 20 minutes
Calories per serving: 210

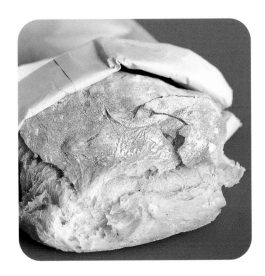

# Rucola e radicchio con parmigiano
## Salad with Parmesan

### Fresh and trendy

The dressing is also delicious with raw mushrooms cut into paper-thin slices.

Feeds 4 trendy types:

1 large bunch arugula

1 medium head radicchio

½ cup parsley sprigs

1 lemon

¼ cup extra virgin olive oil

Salt, freshly ground black pepper

1 large chunk Parmesan cheese (3–5 oz.)

**1** Remove wilted leaves and any tough stems from arugula. Separate radicchio leaves and cut off any tough ends; rinse together with arugula and shake dry. Tear radicchio and arugula into large bite-sized pieces.

**2** Rinse parsley, shake dry and remove leaves. Rinse and pat dry lemon; remove zest. Cut lemon in half and squeeze out juice.

**3** Purée parsley, 2 tablespoons lemon juice and olive oil in a blender and season with salt and pepper. Add zest.

**4** Toss arugula and radicchio lightly with enough of the dressing so that the leaves are shiny. Distribute on plates. Top the salad with paper-thin shavings of Parmesan made with a vegetable peeler or cheese plane. Enjoy immediately.

Prep time: 15 minutes
Calories per serving: 215

# Panzanella
## Tuscan bread salad

### Gives old bread a fresh look

Feeds 4 as a summer dish:

3 cups white bread cut into cubes

(can be up to 3 days old)

1 mild white onion

1 clove garlic

½ lb. firm, ripe tomatoes

½ cucumber (about ½ lb.)

1 yellow bell pepper

2 cups arugula leaves

½ cup parsley sprigs

2–3 tablespoons red wine vinegar

Salt, freshly ground black pepper

⅓ cup extra virgin olive oil

1 tablespoon capers

**1** Cut bread into small cubes. Toast bread cubes lightly in a pan without fat over medium heat until lightly golden.

**2** Peel onion, quarter and slice thinly crosswise. Peel garlic and chop finely. Rinse tomatoes, cucumber and bell pepper. Cut stem out of bell pepper and pull out ribs and seeds; cut stem end from tomato; and trim end off cucumber half. Finely dice all vegetables.

**3** Remove wilted leaves and thick stems from arugula. Rinse arugula and parsley, shake dry and chop finely. Thoroughly mix vinegar, salt, pepper and oil.

**4** Combine toasted bread cubes, tomatoes, cucumbers, bell peppers, herbs and dressing and let stand a little while before serving. Add salt and pepper to taste—stir up panzanella once more, sprinkle with capers and serve.

Prep time: 25 minutes
(plus 1 hour marinating time)
Calories per serving: 210

# Pasta

The dolce vita at home. Capisce? And now here's pasta. Basta! (Enough!)

[Dough]

*"Aren't we having anything but spaghetti today?"* But I thought you like it!
*"I do, but an Italian doesn't live by pasta alone."* Well, you're not Italian.
*"Maybe not, but what's good enough for Italians is good enough for me, and in Italy pasta's just an appetizer."* I don't believe you. *"It's true! It's because in the old days, meat was too expensive so the mamma filled up her family on pasta first and then served a smaller roast."* You don't really think the mamma always had a roast in the oven when she put on the pasta water...?
*"Well no, maybe not, but..."* ...or that she never just made the kids macaroni with a simple tomato sauce when they came home from school? *"I'm just saying that's the way Italians do it—even in restaurants!"* That's fine for them, but now you're in my house, the dolce vita at home. Capisce? And here there's pasta. Basta! *"You're right, I'll shut up now. Besides, it tastes fantastic. Could I have a little more?"*

# Eating Spaghetti in 10 Easy Steps

Real Italians eat spaghetti with a fork and save their spoon for the soup. Now you can be a real Italian, too!

**1.** As elegantly as possible, shift the spaghetti (that's already been mixed with sauce) from the serving bowl to a deep, pre-warmed plate. Try using tongs and/or pouring it from the pan.

**2.** Tuck the corner of a large, white napkin into your collar. It should be large enough to cover your front and lap, but don't get it mixed up with the tablecloth!

**3.** Sprinkle freshly grated Parmesan over the spaghetti and mix it all together. Make a little room on the left side of your plate (or right side if you're left-handed).

**4.** Hold your fork as though you're going to eat, grasping the handle flat between your thumb and middle finger. But now let the fork hang straight down and place your ring finger on the same side as your thumb. The index finger and middle finger are stabilizing the fork from the other side. Let your little finger take care of itself.

**5.** Stick the fork straight down into the small cleared space on your plate so that only a few loops of spaghetti encircle the tines.

**6.** Now comes the twirling. The thumb leads while the index finger lends support. Further down, the middle and ring fingers also work together and the twirling continues in this back-and-forth, up-and-down motion until the thumb is again in control. All this time, keep the fork perpendicular to the plate and tight against it.

**7.** Did it work? Good, but keep your eye on the tines, otherwise you'll end up with a gigantic ball of spaghetti. Two or three strands are enough to fill the fork. If you see more than that collecting around the fork, simply start over.

**8.** When the fork is well filled, bring it up with the tines held at an upward angle and insert it more or less elegantly into your mouth. If long strands are hanging down, either return the fork to the plate and twirl a little more (twirling in the air is only for pros) or just slurp it.

**9.** And what do you do with the other hand? Use it for caressing a cheek, patting a child, emphasizing your words, shaking other hands (when acquaintances come up to the table), waving (when a Cabrio or Vespa drives by), wiping your mouth and drinking wine.

**10.** But Italians are so tolerant, they'll even accept you twirling your spaghetti on a spoon. This is usually done using the fork to twirl pasta strands on the cupped part of the spoon. When all the strands are gathered, draw the fork away and bring it to your mouth. Hopefully in this case you'll refrain from caressing, gesticulating or waving with the other hand!

## We Want Pounds!

Cookbook authors have some pretty strange ways. And we're no exception, but we're changing our ways. Portions differ from cookbook to cookbook on how many ounces of pasta to use for 4 people—and often, the amount you use falls just short of using the whole package. Now we realize, that's irritating—what are you going to do with a couple of random dried noodles? Pasta usually comes in 1 lb. packages. Let's make this simple: from now on we want pounds—1 pound per 4 people. How did skimpier portions come about to begin with? We don't really know. Maybe during the course of a study of the digestion of astronauts, it was once determined that 3 oz. pasta per person is the ideal amount for weightless dining. Or perhaps years ago a manufacturer of pasta pots found that his latest product line was too small so he contacted a famous TV chef he'd met in school and asked him to always cook 12 oz. of pasta in front of the camera. Regardless of where it came from, those days are now over. Besides, what's the point in specifying ounces? We've never yet met anyone who actually weighs their spaghetti before cooking it. So go ahead and dump that whole bag or box into the boiling water. It will all get eaten.

So now it's official. Starting on the next page, this book will always measure pasta by the pound in recipes for pasta with sauce for four (except dishes that have to fit into a casserole or are especially filling, like pasta with beans).

## Our Favorite Pasta Ingredient

# The Canned Tomato

Canned tomatoes:
• Were once stored in canning jars so that housewives could bring a little summer into their kitchens in the middle of winter
• Are now a popular export all over the world, in 15 oz. and 28 oz. cans, that let us import a little Italian sunshine into our worlds, especially during non-tomato season
• Before canning, are usually of the plum tomato variety, perfect for preserving
• After canning, are often a better base for sauces than some fresh tomatoes

Canned tomatoes can:
• Be harvested when ripe in southern Italy, submerged in boiling water and peeled
• And then be canned whole, diced or puréed

Canned tomatoes need:
• To be chopped or puréed, preferably with any cores sorted out and removed
• To share their can or package only with tomato juice—purchase types without salt and other flavorings added. You'll add the flavor when you cook.

Canned tomatoes love:
• Basil, tarragon, mint, oregano, parsley, sage, thyme
• Chili powder, fennel seed, garlic, paprika, saffron, juniper berries, sugar
• Capers, olives
• Pasta, pizza, gnocchi, bread
• Seafood, canned tuna, anchovies
• Bacon, salami, ground meats, chicken
• Vegetables from artichokes to zucchini
• A shot of cream, a lot of Parmesan

## Five Tips for Using Leftovers:

# Pasta

If you really do have leftovers from your pound of cooked pasta, your next meal is practically made—leftover pasta is ideal for spontaneous concoctions.

### Pasta Toss
Cut up vegetables, such as leeks, bell peppers, mushrooms, green asparagus or zucchini into small pieces and sauté in olive oil. If you want to, add onions, garlic, salami or ham. Fill up the pan with hearty cooked pasta such as penne, fusilli or ziti plus fresh herbs. Salt and pepper to taste.

### Pasta Casserole
Similar to the recipe above: sauté about 4 cups vegetables. Mix with *cooked* pasta (originally a half pound of dry pasta) and some salt in a medium-sized baking dish. Then mix together 1 egg and 5 tablespoons whole milk and stir into pasta. Stir in about 2 oz. grated Parmesan and bake at 375°F for 20 minutes.

### Pasta Salad
For this, try penne, farfalle, orecchiete or even spaghetti. For a more intense flavor, toss the salad while the pasta is warm. Cut up eggplant, tender fennel bulb, bell peppers, green asparagus, celery or zucchini and sauté in olive oil until crisp-tender. Add red wine vinegar or lemon juice and toss with cooked pasta. As a finishing touch, add olives, capers, anchovies, pesto, canned tuna or herbs.

### Pasta Soup
You can make this with the same vegetables as the salad. Cook them in 1 quart vegetable or chicken stock—you can even include leftover tomato sauce—then add the cooked pasta to the stock mixture—speedy soup! Season with salt and pepper, sprinkle with Parmesan and serve with bread.

### Pasta Side
A specialty in parts of southern Italy: Sauté coarsely chopped, cooked ribbon pasta in butter. Sprinkle a handful of raisins (preferably marinated overnight in Grappa liqueur) and a little sugar over the top; sauté briefly and finish by topping with toasted bread crumbs.

## Aunt Edna's Memory Lane Pasta

# Spaghetti with Poor Man's Parmesan

Back when the owner of my favorite Italian restaurant was still a tyke in deepest Puglia, his favorite lunch was spaghetti with Parmesan made by his mamma. But Parmesan was often unavailable in those days, and they often lacked money to buy it. When that was the case, his mamma took three or four slices of the **airy white bread** of southern Italy (often day-old), removed the white part and tore it up coarsely, then smashed the pieces with the palms of her hands. She then heated **about ¼ cup olive oil** in a frying pan with **a peeled and coarsely sliced garlic clove**. When the garlic was brown, she removed it and threw in the bread with a little salt. When the bread was light-brown, she removed it, too.
At the same time, his mamma cooked and drained **one pound of** al dente **spaghetti** into which she stirred a little of the garlic oil she'd used for sautéing. She finally transferred the pasta to four wide-rimmed bowls (grandma and grandpa ate with them, too), ground pepper over the top and sprinkled it all with the mock Parmesan (chop or crumble any large pieces). And even today, it still tastes fantastic! I make it for myself when there's no cheese in the house, and finish by adding a handful of chopped parsley to the sizzling bread.

# Sugo al pomodoro
Tomato sauce

## The most basic of pasta sauces

Choose either the time-consuming version using fresh tomatoes or the quicker one using canned tomatoes—depending on the season, your appetite, your mood and your schedule.

Makes enough for 4:

**For a fresh tomato sauce:**

1¼ lbs. ripe, bright red tomatoes

1 small carrot

1 stalk celery

1 onion

2 cloves garlic

1 teaspoon fresh rosemary needles

3 tablespoons olive oil

Salt, freshly ground black pepper

½ cup fresh basil leaves

**For a canned tomato sauce:**

1 large can peeled tomatoes (28 oz.)

1 onion

2 cloves garlic

2 tablespoons olive oil

1 teaspoon dried Italian seasoning

Salt, freshly ground black pepper

**For both:**

1 lb. pasta

Salt

**1** For fresh sauce: Remove cores from tomatoes with the tip of a knife. Place tomatoes in a bowl, pour boiling water over the top and wait until the peels loosen, about a minute. Place tomatoes in a colander and rinse under cold water. Slip off peels; halve, then remove seeds with your fingers or squeeze them out. Dice tomatoes.

**2** Peel and rinse carrot, rinse celery and dice both very finely. Peel onion and garlic and chop both finely. Coarsely chop rosemary.

**3** Heat oil in a pot. Briefly sauté onion and garlic. Add carrot and celery and sauté briefly. Add tomatoes and rosemary, season with salt and pepper and simmer over medium-low heat for 20 minutes, or longer. Remember to stir occasionally! If the sauce becomes too thick, pour in a little water. Right before serving, check for salt and pepper and add fresh basil leaves (cut into strips) to the sauce.

**4** For the quick version: Take tomatoes out of the can, drain and chop (reserve juice from the can). Peel onion and garlic and chop both finely. As with the other recipe, heat oil. Briefly sauté onion, garlic and dried herbs (after crumbling them between your fingers). Add tomatoes and the juice, season with salt and pepper and simmer for at least 10 minutes. Before serving, add salt to taste.

**5** For both sauces, remember the motto: The sauce waits for the pasta but the pasta never waits for the sauce! So in the meantime bring 4–5 quarts water to a boil in a large pot. Add a large dose of table salt (a couple teaspoons). Add pasta and cook until al dente. Don't forget to stir occasionally and after 7 minutes, try a piece to see if it is tender yet "toothsome." Wait longer as needed.

**6** Pour al dente pasta into a colander to drain, then immediately mix with the sauce and transfer to wide-rimmed shallow bowls. Put 1 nice chunk of Parmesan in a cheese grater on the table.

Prep time: 45 minutes for fresh sauce, 20 minutes for quick sauce
Goes with the following pasta: Spaghetti, linguine, penne, fusilli (but really all types)
Calories per serving: 530

## Variations:

### Aurora Sauce
Prepare tomato sauce using only tomatoes, garlic and oil. At the very end, stir in $1/3$ cup + 1 tablespoon very fresh cream and about $1/2$ cup chopped fresh basil or arugula.

### Arrabiatta sauce
Prepare tomato sauce with onion and garlic plus 1–3 dried red chiles crushed in a mortar (wear gloves). At the very end, stir in chopped parsley.

### Sun-dried tomato sauce
Drain 12 oil-packed sun-dried tomatoes and cut into strips. Sauté 2 tablespoons pine nuts in 2 tablespoons olive oil until golden. Add sun-dried tomatoes, 1–2 teaspoons capers and $1/4$ cup finely chopped parsley; season with salt and pepper and mix with freshly cooked spaghetti or tagliatelle.

### Pesto Tip
If covered with a layer of oil and tightly sealed, pesto keeps well for several days in the refrigerator.

# Pesto

### Lay in a supply!

Some people say pesto tastes good only if you perform the tedious job of crushing all the ingredients in a mortar. We leave the tedium to a blender, hand blender or food processor and are just as happy with the results. Try it!

Feeds 8 once or 4 twice:

2 cups basil leaves (or one large bunch)

2 cloves garlic

$2/3$ cup pine nuts

$1/3$ cup + 1 tablespoon extra virgin olive oil

2 oz. freshly grated Parmesan

Salt, freshly ground black pepper

2 lbs. pasta once or 1 lb. twice

**1** Don't rinse the basil. Just pull the leaves off the stems. If the leaves aren't quite clean, wipe them off with a paper towel. Peel garlic.

**2** Combine basil, garlic and pine nuts and purée at medium speed (use blender or food processor) while gradually adding oil. Stir in Parmesan, salt and pepper—ready!

**3** In the meantime, boil the pasta till al dente. Stir together 1 tablespoon pesto and 1 tablespoon hot pasta water for each serving (add more pesto as desired); mix with drained pasta and serve.

Prep time: 15 minutes
(using blender or hand blender)
Goes with the following pasta:
Linguine, trenette and any other long, not-too-wide pasta
Calories per serving: 640

# Spaghetti alla carbonara
## Spaghetti with an egg-bacon sauce

### Stands up to those in most ristoranti

Feeds 4 as a complete meal:

Salt

1 lb.spaghetti

4 oz. pancetta or bacon

1 clove garlic

1 tablespoon olive oil

2 very fresh eggs

$^1/_3$ cup cream

2 oz. freshly grated Parmesan or Pecorino (or mixture)

Salt (as needed)

Freshly ground black pepper

**1** In a large pot, bring to a boil 4–5 quarts water and 1 tablespoon salt. Push spaghetti down into it with a mixing spoon until all the pasta is under water. Cook until al dente—it takes about 8 minutes but it's best to test it earlier. Place a large bowl and four spaghetti plates in warm oven (about 125°F).

**2** In the meantime, finely dice pancetta or bacon. Peel garlic and mince. Heat oil and cook diced pancetta until slightly crispy, then add garlic, stirring occasionally till garlic is lightly golden.

**3** Combine eggs, cream and Parmesan in the warmed bowl and whisk. Drain pasta and immediately add to the egg-cream mixture along with the hot bacon mixture. Season with salt if needed, and pepper; mix well and immediately transfer to plates.

Prep time: 15 minutes
Calories per serving: 750

# Pasta all'amatriciana
## Pasta with bacon sauce

### Something spicy from southern Italy

Feeds 4 lovers of fiery pasta:

1 small mild white onion

4 oz. pancetta or smoked bacon

1–3 dried red chiles or 1 teaspoon crushed red pepper flakes

3 medium tomatoes

2 tablespoons olive oil

$^1/_3$ cup dry white wine

Salt

1 lb. "long" pasta (e.g. bucatini, spaghetti, perciatelli, or any narrow ribbon pasta)

**1** Peel onion and chop finely. Cut bacon into small pieces. Crush red chile in a mortar or chop but be careful! Wear gloves and wash hands well; don't touch your eyes—or use flakes. Remove cores from the tomatoes and pour boiling water over rest; rinse under cold water and peel and dice finely.

**2** Heat water for the pasta. Heat oil in a large pan. Add bacon and brown over medium heat, stirring often. Add onion and chiles and briefly sauté. Pour in wine and stir in tomatoes; reduce heat to low. Cover and simmer sauce for about 5–10 minutes.

**3** Add salt to pasta water. Pour dried pasta into bubbling water, stir well and cook until al dente. Salt the sauce to taste. Drain pasta, mix well with the sauce in the pan and serve immediately.

Prep time: 30 minutes
Calories per serving: 660

# Pasta al prosciutto e panna
## Pasta with a prosciutto-cream sauce

**The sauce is done quicker than the pasta**

Feeds 4 in a hurry:

Salt

1 lb. pasta (e.g. tagliatelle, spaghetti, farfalle or fusilli)

5 oz. prosciutto or ham

1 large tomato (or 2 small)

²/₃ cup cream

³/₄ cup parsley sprigs

Chili powder

**1** In a large pot, bring to a boil 4–5 quarts water and 1 tablespoon salt. Cook pasta until al dente.

**2** In the meantime, dice ham. Rinse tomato, remove core and dice the rest. Purée diced ham, tomato and cream in a blender or food processor, coarsely.

**3** Rinse parsley, shake dry, remove leaves and chop very finely; stir into ham mixture.

Finish sauce by seasoning to taste with salt and chili powder.

**4** Pour pasta into a colander, drain and return to the pot. Stir in ham-cream sauce and mix with pasta until hot. Distribute on plates and serve.

Prep time: 10–15 minutes
Caloriés per serving: 650

# Pasta al sugo di salsicce
## Pasta with a sausage sauce

**Substantial, spicy and good!**

Feeds 4 with big appetites:

2–3 Italian pork sausage links (about 10–12 oz. total)

1 onion

2 cloves garlic

2 tablespoons olive oil

1 teaspoon fennel seed

1 (14 oz.) can peeled tomatoes

Salt

Black pepper or chili powder

1 lb. pasta (e.g. Italian macaroni [long and hollow], penne, rigatoni or orecchiette)

1 cup arugula leaves

**1** Peel onion and garlic; chop both finely. Squeeze sausage out of the skins and crumble into small bits.

**2** Heat oil and brown sausage well. Add onion, garlic and fennel seeds and sauté briefly.

**3** Chop the tomatoes and add along with their juice to sausage—salt to taste (carefully, because the sausage is also salty); spice it up with pepper or chili powder. Simmer uncovered on low for 20 minutes or more.

**4** In the meantime, fill a large pot with 4–5 quarts water, add 2 teaspoons salt and bring to a boil. Pour in the pasta, stir and cook until al dente.

**5** Rinse arugula, remove any tough stems and chop rest. Season sauce to taste with salt and pepper and/or chili powder. Stir in arugula. Drain pasta, distribute in wide pasta bowls and top with sauce. Serve with crusty Italian bread.

Prep time: 20 minutes
Calories per serving: 855

# Spaghetti al limone
## Spaghetti with lemon

Nice and refreshing!

Feeds 4 in the summer:

Salt

1 lb. spaghetti

2 cloves garlic

1 lemon

1 tablespoon butter

1⅓ cups tender, shelled peas

8 oz. very fresh cream

Freshly ground black pepper

**1** Bring to a boil 4 quarts water and 2 teaspoons salt. Add pasta, press under the water with a wooden spoon and cook until al dente.

**2** In the meantime, peel garlic and slice thinly. Rinse lemon and pat dry. Remove zest, carefully avoiding the bitter white part of the rind. Cut lemon in half and squeeze out juice.

**3** Melt butter in a pot. Briefly sauté garlic and peas. Add cream and lemon zest and simmer over medium heat until slightly reduced. Stir in 2 tablespoons of the fresh lemon juice. Salt and pepper to taste.

**4** Drain pasta in a colander; pour into the pot with the lemon cream and mix briefly, then transfer to wide pasta bowls and enjoy.

# Pasta al gorgonzola
## Pasta with a Gorgonzola sauce

Molto delizioso!

Makes enough for 4:

8 oz. gorgonzola

1 small onion

2 cloves garlic

1 tablespoon olive oil

1 tablespoon butter

1¾ cups cream

1 lb. pasta

(e.g. tagliatelle, spaghetti or penne)

Salt, freshly ground black pepper

**1** Cut gorgonzola cheese into small cubes. Peel onion and garlic and chop both finely.

**2** In a pot, heat oil and butter until butter melts. Stir in onion and garlic and sauté briefly. Turn heat to very low and add gorgonzola and cream. Heat sauce and

continue stirring until the cheese is melted and the sauce slightly thickened.

**3** At the same time, cook pasta in 4–5 quarts boiling water with 2 teaspoons salt until al dente. Drain in a colander.

**4** Season sauce to taste with pepper and, carefully, with salt (the gorgonzola is already salty); mix with the hot pasta and transfer to wide pasta bowls.

Prep time: 20 minutes
Calories per serving: 960

# Variation:

## Quattro formaggi (four-cheese sauce)
Cut 8 oz. total of four different types of cheese into small cubes (1 hard cheese such as pecorino, 1 medium-soft cheese such as Fontina or Taleggio, 1 blue cheese such as gorgonzola, 1 fresh cheese such as mozzarella—about 2 oz. of each but you don't have to be exact). Briefly sauté 1 minced onion in 1 tablespoon oil. Stir in 1 cup stock (vegetable or chicken) and the cheese; stir until melted. Add a little cream if desired. Mix with 1 cup rinsed and chopped arugula and 1 lb. cooked pasta.

# Pasta alla verdura
## Pasta with vegetables

### Senza carne

Feeds 4 veggie lovers:

1 small eggplant (about ⅓ lb.)

1 zucchini, 1 yellow bell pepper

1 onion

2 cloves garlic

3 tablespoons olive oil

1 (14 oz.) can peeled tomatoes

Salt, freshly ground black pepper

1 lb. penne or fusilli

½ cup basil leaves

1 ball fresh mozzarella (about 5 oz.)

**1** Rinse eggplant, zucchini and bell pepper. Trim ends of all, and remove stem, ribs and seeds from pepper. Cut each into ½" cubes. Peel onion and garlic; chop both finely.

**2** Heat oil. Briefly sauté onion, garlic and vegetables. Chop tomatoes and add along with juice to pan. Season with salt and pepper. Cover and simmer on medium-low for about 20 minutes, stirring occasionally.

**3** In the meantime, bring to a boil 4–5 quarts water and 2 teaspoons salt in a large pot. Pour in pasta, stir and cook until al dente.

**4** Cut basil leaves into strips, dice mozzarella and add both to the vegetable sauce. If desired, replace cover to let cheese melt slightly.

**5** Pour pasta into a colander, mix with sauce and serve immediately.

Prep time: 40 minutes,
25 of which you're actually busy
Calories per serving: 650

# Pasta agli asparagi
## Pasta with asparagus and shrimp

### Simple and elegant

Feeds 3 guests and 1 host:

1 lb. green asparagus

1 onion

2 cloves garlic

6 oz. peeled, cooked shrimp (tail-off)

Salt

1 lb. tagliatelle or linguine

1 tablespoon olive oil

7 tablespoons cream

Freshly ground black pepper

Nutmeg

**1** Rinse asparagus spears under cold water. Trim off tough ends up to the tender part of the stalk. Cut spears into ½–1" pieces on the diagonal. Peel onion and garlic; chop both finely. Rinse and drain shrimp; cut in half or into bite-sized pieces.

**2** In a large pot, bring 4–5 quarts water and 1 tablespoon salt to a boil. Add pasta, push under the water with a wooden spoon and cook until al dente.

**3** While the water is heating, continue making the sauce. Heat oil in another large pot. Briefly sauté asparagus, onion and garlic. Add 1 ladleful of pasta water, cover and simmer on low for 5–10 minutes or till asparagus is crisp-tender.

**4** Remove cover, stir in cream and turn up the heat so the cream boils down a little. Rinse shrimp (remove tails if necessary) and add to cream sauce; heat and season to taste with salt, pepper and a dash nutmeg.

**5** Drain pasta in a colander, then mix with the sauce and eat it while it's hot!

Prep time: 20 minutes
Calories per serving: 610

# Spaghetti vongole
## Spaghetti with clams

For a taste of the sea—best if ingredients are ordered in advance

Makes enough for 4:

$2\frac{1}{2}$ lbs. clams

Salt

1 lb. spaghetti

2 cloves garlic

1 large tomato (about $\frac{1}{2}$ lb.)

$\frac{1}{4}$ cup olive oil

1 cup parsley sprigs

Freshly ground black pepper

1 dried red chile or $\frac{1}{2}$ teaspoon crushed red pepper flakes (optional)

**1** Place clams in a colander and rinse off under running water. Clams close their shells if they're fresh. At this point, throw away any that don't close.

**2** Bring to a boil 4–5 quarts water and 2 teaspoons salt. Pour in pasta, push under water with a wooden spoon and cook until al dente.

**3** While the water is heating, continue making the sauce. Peel garlic, slice and then cut into thin strips. Rinse tomato and dice finely (discard core and stem).

**4** In a wide pot or pan, heat 2 tablespoons of the oil. Add wet clams and garlic, cover and cook over medium-high heat for 5 minutes. Now the shells should open. Make absolutely sure you throw away any clams that are still closed. Reserve pan liquid.

**5** Leave a few clams in the shells because it looks nice. Pull the others out of the shells with a fork or tweezers if desired. Pour the cooking liquid through a paper filter to remove any sand from the clam shells. Rinse parsley, shake dry and chop leaves finely.

**6** Heat remaining 2 tablespoons oil in a pot. Stir in tomatoes and heat. Add clams (if removed from shells), cooking liquid, parsley, salt, pepper and dried red chile (or use flakes) and simmer uncovered for about 3 minutes over low heat. Remove chile (unless flakes).

**7** Drain al dente pasta in a colander. Then mix well with sauce in the pot. Transfer to prewarmed plates. Place clams in shells on top. Ready to eat!

Prep time: 30 minutes
Calories per serving: 775

## Variation:
Cooking the clams with or without dried red chiles isn't the only variation possible with this pasta dish, which is known up and down the coast of Italy. You can also cook the clams without tomatoes, using just the cooking liquid from the clams. Or, add other herbs. Or, combine the clams with squid rings or mussels. It's also delicious with a hint of grated lemon zest.

# Pasta siciliana
## Pasta with a tomato almond sauce

Summer in Sicily!
Hot pasta, cold sauce

Feeds 4 curious types:

Salt

1 lb. spaghetti or hollow spaghetti

2 ripe but firm tomatoes (about 3/4 lb.)

1 cup basil sprigs

3 cloves garlic

1/3 cup skinless almonds

2 tablespoons extra virgin olive oil

Freshly ground black pepper

**1** Pour 5 quarts water and 2 teaspoons salt into a large pot. Cover and bring to a boil. When the water is bubbling, add the pasta and push it under the water with a wooden spoon. Cook until al dente.

**2** In the meantime, prepare the sauce. Rinse tomatoes, cut out cores, halve then remove seeds with your fingers. Then chop coarsely. Remove basil leaves from stems. Peel garlic.

**3** Purée garlic and almonds in a blender or food processor. Add tomatoes, basil and oil and blend until the sauce is nice and smooth. Season with salt and pepper.

**4** Pre-warm a serving bowl in a 150 degree oven for a few minutes. Drain pasta in a colander and mix with sauce in the warm serving bowl, and you're ready!

Prep time: 15 minutes
Calories per serving: 630

# Spaghetti alla puttanesca
## Spaghetti with a spicy tomato sauce

In Italy, this dish was once named after prostitutes

Makes enough for 4:

6–8 anchovy fillets in oil

2 cloves garlic

1 fresh red chile

Salt

1 lb. spaghetti

1/4 cup olive oil

1 (14 oz.) can peeled tomatoes

6 tablespoons dry red wine

2 tablespoons capers

2 tablespoons pitted black olives

(kalamata or Niçoise preferred)

**1** Drain anchovies well and chop finely. Peel garlic and mince. Rinse chile, trim off stem and then decide: If you like hot spicy food, finely chop the pepper with the seeds. If you're more cautious, remove the seeds first. Don't forget that the fiery heat sticks to your skin! (Wear gloves, and don't touch your face when working with hot peppers.)

**2** In a large pot, bring to a boil 4–5 quarts water and 2 teaspoons salt. Add pasta and press down with a wooden spoon until immersed. Cook pasta until al dente.

**3** While the water is heating, continue preparing the sauce. Heat oil in a pot. Stir in chopped anchovies, garlic and chile and sauté briefly. Chop tomatoes and add along with their juice and wine to the pot. Simmer uncovered over medium heat for 10 minutes.

**4** Drain capers. Cut pitted olives into halves or strips. Add to the sauce and season to taste with salt. Drain pasta in colander and quickly mix with sauce.

Prep time: 30 minutes
Delicious with: Fresh bread
and red wine, but no cheese
Calories per serving: 600

# Spaghetti aglio olio peperoncino
## Spaghetti with garlic, oil and chile pepper

Saves the day when your cupboard is almost bare

Feeds 4 suffering from

a sudden hunger attack:

Salt

1 lb. spaghetti

4 cloves garlic

1–4 dried red chiles or crushed

red pepper flakes to taste

Several sprigs parsley (optional)

$\frac{1}{3}$ cup extra virgin olive oil

**1** Bring to a boil 5 quarts water with 2 teaspoons salt. Pour in pasta and press down with a wooden spoon until immersed. Cook until al dente.

**2** Peel garlic, cut in half and slice. Crumble dried chiles (wear gloves and don't touch your face)—or use flakes. Chop parsley leaves. Heat oil briefly in a pot with garlic, chiles (or flakes), and parsley for about 30 seconds to 1 minute. Don't let it get

too hot or the garlic will burn and taste bitter. Remove from heat.

**3** Drain pasta, mix with the sauce and enjoy.

Prep time: 15 minutes
Delicious with: A hearty red wine
Calories per serving: 590

# Spaghetti al tonno
## Spaghetti with a tuna sauce

So simple and so good

Feeds 4 with small appetites:

1 yellow bell pepper

3 medium tomatoes

$\frac{3}{4}$ cup parsley sprigs

1 onion

2 cloves garlic

4 anchovy fillets in oil

Salt

1 lb. spaghetti

2 tablespoons olive oil

1 can water-packed tuna (5–6 oz.)

Freshly ground black pepper

**1** Rinse pepper, quarter and remove stem and contents, including seeds, then dice. Rinse tomatoes and chop very finely (discard cores/stems).

**2** Rinse parsley, shake dry, remove leaves and chop finely. Peel onion and garlic; chop both finely. Drain anchovy fillets and chop finely.

**3** Place a pot on the stove and fill it with 4–5 quarts water. Add 2 teaspoons salt, cover and heat. When the water boils, add the spaghetti. Press it down with a wooden spoon until immersed. Cook spaghetti until al dente. After no more than 7 minutes, test a strand for doneness. Should be a little tender but still have a chewy bite to it.

**4** As soon as you start heating the pasta water, continue preparing the sauce. Heat oil, stir in bell pepper, onion and garlic and sauté briefly. Add parsley, tomatoes and anchovies and cook over medium-low heat for a few minutes until the diced pepper is crisp-tender.

**5** Drain tuna, flake apart, mix into the sauce and heat. Season to taste with salt and pepper. Drain pasta in a colander, mix with sauce and serve immediately— without Parmesan, since it would not go well with tuna in this case.

Prep time: 20 minutes
Calories per serving: 560

# Orecchiette alla pugliese
## Pasta with broccoli

Spicy "earlets" from Puglia

Makes enough for 4:

Salt

1 lb. orecchiette

1 lb. broccoli

4–8 anchovy fillets in oil

2–4 cloves garlic

1–2 dried red chiles or crushed

red pepper flakes to taste

¼ cup extra virgin olive oil

**1** Bring to a boil at least 5 quarts water with 2 teaspoons salt. Add pasta, stir and cook until al dente. Orecchiette always take a little longer than other pasta—it will take about 10–12 minutes, but test one before that.

**2** While the pasta is boiling, prepare the vegetables: Rinse broccoli and cut off florets. Peel stems and slice (about ¼" thick). Cut large slices in half. After about 8 minutes, add broccoli florets and slices to pasta in the boiling water; cook together.

**3** With the rest of the time, drain anchovy fillets and chop finely. Peel garlic and slice, then cut into thin strips. Crush dried red chile in a mortar or crumble with hands (wear gloves and don't touch your face)— or use flakes.

**4** Drain broccoli and pasta in a colander. Heat oil, anchovies, garlic and crushed chile in the pot briefly. Stir in pasta and broccoli; mix well. Adjust salt to taste, then plate it up and dig in!

Prep time: 15 minutes
Calories per serving: 590

## Tip from Puglia
You don't have to use broccoli. In the land where this pasta originated, they use rapini (also called broccoli raab/rabe). Here, this is found in specialty markets or at farmers' markets. The dish is also good with chard, mature spinach, or tender strips of savoy cabbage.

# Pasta ai funghi
## Pasta with mushrooms

Puts you in a good mood

Makes enough for 4:

½ oz. dried porcini (can also be omitted,

but they give it that full mushroom flavor)

10–12 oz. mushrooms (⅔ lb.)

Salt

1 lb. tagliatelle or wider ribbon pasta

2 cloves garlic

½ cup parsley sprigs

2 tablespoons olive oil

½ cup cream

1 teaspoon fresh lemon juice

Freshly ground black pepper

**1** Place porcini in a shallow bowl, fill with lukewarm water and soak for about 30 minutes until they're soft. Remove from water and chop. Save porcini water for possible use in the sauce.

**2** Wipe off fresh mushrooms with paper towels. Discard tough stem ends (trim off) and then thinly slice mushrooms.

**3** Bring to a boil 5 quarts water and add 2 teaspoons salt. Add pasta and stir until immersed. Cook pasta until al dente.

**4** While pasta is boiling, continue with the sauce. Peel garlic and mince. Rinse parsley, remove leaves and chop finely. Reserve 1 tablespoon chopped parsley.

**5** Heat oil in a small pan. Add porcini and fresh mushrooms and sauté over medium-low heat for about 5 minutes, stirring.

**6** Add garlic and parsley (but not reserved parsley) to mushrooms along with cream, lemon juice and a hint of salt and pepper. If the sauce is too thick, add the porcini-soaking liquid a little bit at a time to taste. Drain pasta in a colander, then mix with sauce and reserved parsley. Enjoy, with Parmesan, if desired.

Prep time: 25 minutes
(+ 30 minutes soaking time for porcini)
Calories per serving: 580

# Pasta al ragu di coniglio
## Pasta with a rabbit ragu

Super-sophisticated

Makes enough for 4:

1 scant lb. of rabbit meat (purchase de-boned from specialty butcher)

2 oz. pancetta or bacon

1 onion

2 cloves garlic

2 stalks celery

3 medium tomatoes

4 small sprigs rosemary

3 tablespoons olive oil

½ cup dry white wine

Salt, freshly ground black pepper

1 lb. pappardelle, tagliatelle or hollow spaghetti

**1** Rinse rabbit meat under cold water, pat dry and cut into small pieces. Finely dice pancetta. Peel onion and garlic; chop both finely. Rinse celery and chop finely. Rinse tomatoes and dice very finely (discard cores and stems). Rinse rosemary; remove needles and chop.

**2** Heat oil. Add pancetta and rabbit meat, stirring until the meat is light-colored. Stir in onion, garlic, celery and rosemary and sauté briefly.

**3** Add tomatoes and wine, season with salt and pepper and simmer uncovered over low heat for at least 30 minutes. You can simmer it longer if on very low.

**4** Meanwhile, make the pasta. In a large pot, bring to a boil 5 quarts water with 2 teaspoons salt. When it boils, add the pasta, stir and cook until al dente. After 7 minutes, test a piece. Make sure you keep them from becoming too soft.

**5** Drain pasta in a colander and transfer to plates. Adjust salt and pepper in the rabbit sauce to taste. A courageous cook might also add a pinch of cinnamon. Pile sauce on the pasta and enjoy.

Prep time: 1¼ hours, 35 minutes of which you're actually busy
Goes with: Toasted pine nuts sprinkled on top, crusty white bread, white wine, water, arugula salad
Calories per serving: 750

# Ravioli

## A labor of love for very close friends

This dough isn't just for ravioli; you can also roll it out and cut it into pasta of any length or width and serve it with one of the sauces from the previous pages.

Pampers 6:

**For the dough:**

3 cups flour (or a little more as needed)

4 eggs

1 tablespoon olive oil

1 teaspoon salt

**For the filling:**

1 package frozen spinach

1 cup ricotta (about 8 oz.)

1 large egg

4 oz. freshly grated Parmesan or pecorino

1–2 cloves garlic

Salt, freshly ground black pepper

**Plus:**

Flour for the work surface

**For serving:**

4–5 sprigs fresh sage

3 tablespoons butter

3 tablespoons olive oil

1 decent-sized chunk of Parmesan

**1** Well ahead of time, remove spinach from package and let thaw in a colander (takes about 4 hours). If you omit this step, cook the spinach according to the directions on the package and then immerse in ice water or let cool.

**2** For the dough: Mix flour, eggs, oil and salt in a bowl until it becomes a mass. Then dump it all onto a lightly-floured work surface. Knead until the dough is smooth and a little shiny. It shouldn't stick to your fingers, so add a little flour if needed. Wrap the dough in a slightly damp non-terry dish towel and let stand at room temperature for at least 30 minutes.

**3** Meanwhile, start on the filling. Squeeze moisture out of spinach using your hands. Chop finely.

**4** In a bowl, combine ricotta, egg and grated Parmesan. Peel garlic, squeeze through a press and add. Then add the spinach; season with salt and pepper and stir together thoroughly.

**5** Now back to the dough: Take it out of the towel, knead it once more very thoroughly and divide into four pieces. Leave out only one-fourth. Wrap up the rest to keep from drying out.

**6** Sprinkle flour on a pastry board or the kitchen table and roll out the dough piece in all directions—the thinner the better. Cut into squares of about 2 1/4". Place about 1 teaspoon filling on half a square. Fold over the other half and press together around the filling, forming a fat triangle. Dip the tines of a fork in flour and use to press together the edges of the ravioli.

**7** Finish making all the ravioli and arrange side by side on non-terry dish towels. You can leave them like this for several hours till your guests arrive if desired.

**8** In a large pot, bring to a boil at least 5 quarts water with 2 teaspoons salt. Carefully lower ravioli into water so they don't break open. Boil gently 3–4 minutes. Fresh pasta doesn't need any more time than this. Meanwhile, pre-warm plates in a 150 degree oven.

**9** In the meantime, remove sage leaves from stems. Heat butter and oil and add sage; lightly brown the butter. Drain ravioli in a colander in batches so as to not overcrowd. Put ravioli on warm plates and spoon sage butter on top. Place on the table with Parmesan and a cheese grater. Then dig in!

Prep time: Just under 2 hours
(not including thawing time)
Calories per serving: 575

## Plus a lot more fillings:

### Meat:
Finely dice 14 oz. veal, chicken or rabbit and 2 oz. bacon, 1 carrot and 1 small onion. Sauté in 2–3 tablespoons olive oil for about 5 minutes or till meat is cooked through. Purée, mix with 1 tablespoon ricotta or mascarpone or 2 tablespoons cream, plus 2 eggs and 3 tablespoons grated Parmesan. Season with salt and pepper.

### Squash:
Mash 1 lb. cooked squash. Combine with 1/3 cup chopped pine nuts, 2 cloves garlic (pressed), 4 oz. grated Parmesan, 1/4 cup chopped basil and 1 egg. Season with salt, pepper and maybe some crushed red pepper flakes.

### Artichokes:
Finely purée 1/2 can (7 oz.) of marinated artichokes. Mix with 4 oz. mascarpone (1/2 cup), 2 oz. grated Parmesan and 1 egg. Stir in chopped parsley and a little lemon zest and season with salt and pepper.

## Basic Tip

### For Even More Enjoyment

Make a double recipe and freeze half (without cooking!)—lay ravioli out in a single layer on a cookie sheet and cover with saran wrap and freeze. When frozen, throw all the ravioli into a large freezer bag in the freezer. Throw frozen ravioli into boiling salted water until al dente. When starting frozen, they may take an extra minute or two.

# Lasagna

Hard work but a guaranteed success!

Try making the homemade pasta dough on p. 72 and cut into sheets (boil briefly before assembling); or purchase dried lasagne pasta sheets.

Feeds 6 with big appetites:

**For the ragu bolognese:**

1 carrot

1 stalk celery

2 oz. pancetta or smoked bacon

1 onion

2 cloves garlic

1 tablespoon butter

2 tablespoons olive oil

10–12 oz. ground meat

1 (14 oz.) can peeled tomatoes

1 1/4 cups beef broth/stock and red wine combined—or just stock

Salt, freshly ground black pepper

**For the béchamel sauce:**

2 oz. butter

Scant 1/2 cup flour

3 cups + 1 tablespoon milk

Salt, freshly ground black pepper

Freshly grated nutmeg

**Plus for the layers:**

About 1/2 lb. pasta sheets (see left)

Salt

2 balls fresh mozzarella (about 1/2 lb.)

4 oz. freshly grated Parmesan

1 tablespoon butter

**1** For the bolognese (which can also be used directly as a pasta sauce), peel carrot, rinse celery and dice both finely. Dice pancetta. Peel onion and garlic; chop both finely.

**2** Heat butter and oil in a pan or pot. Stir in pancetta, carrot, celery, onion and garlic and sauté briefly. Add ground meat and continue cooking and stirring until crumbly. Break up larger chunks of meat.

**3** Chop tomatoes and add along with their juice, plus the stock and wine to the pot; season with a little salt and pepper. Simmer covered over very low heat for 1 hour. Season with salt and pepper to taste.

**4** For the bechamel sauce: melt butter in a pot but don't let it turn brown. Stir vigorously with a mixing spoon while adding flour. Continue stirring until smooth. Gradually add milk, while whisking to keep it smooth. Simmer over very low heat for 5–10 minutes until thickened. Season with salt, pepper and a pinch nutmeg.

**5** If using dried lasagna sheets, bring to a boil 5 quarts water with salt. Cook lasagna pasta for 4–5 minutes until sheets are bendable and almost al dente; then rinse under cold water. If using fresh pasta, boil only briefly.

**6** Dice fresh mozzarella. Preheat oven to 375°F. Take out a large rectangular, baking dish (or oval if you're feeling artsy and experienced) and grease it. Pour in a little béchamel. Arrange pasta sheets on top, then ragu, béchamel, fresh mozzarella and more pasta. Continue layering until everything is in the dish. Top with remaining béchamel, sprinkle with Parmesan and bits of butter. Place in the oven—now you have 40 minutes to clean the kitchen, set the table and take a break.

Prep time: At least 2 hours,
40 minutes of which you can relax
Delicious with: Red wine and lots of salad
Calories per serving: 720

# Lasagne rapida
## Quick lasagna

New from bella Italia

Feeds 4 as a small meal:

2 cups frozen peas

Salt

16 dried lasagna pasta sheets

10–12 oz. salmon fillets or 8 oz. cooked ham

1 cup ricotta (about 8 oz.)

1/2 cup cream

From 1/2 lemon: 1 tablespoon juice and grated zest

Freshly ground black pepper

3/4 cup basil sprigs

2 tablespoons pine nuts

2 tablespoons freshly grated Parmesan or pecorino

2–3 tablespoons olive oil

**1** First remove peas from the package, break apart and thaw.

**2** To cook the pasta, bring 4–5 quarts water with 2 teaspoons salt to a boil. Add pasta sheets and boil until al dente. Pour into a colander, rinse under cold water and drain. Lay them out side by side on a damp non-terry dish towel so they don't stick together.

**3** Check salmon for bones. If you find any when you pass your fingers over it, pull them out with tweezers. Cut salmon into narrow strips. Or if using ham, trim any fat and cut into strips.

**4** In a bowl, stir together ricotta, cream, lemon juice and zest. Add a little salt and pepper. Rinse basil, shake dry and pull off the leaves but don't chop.

**5** Preheat oven to 425°F. Grease four small oven-proof dishes or one large shallow one.

**6** In each small dish, place 1 pasta sheet, a little salmon, peas and basil, spread with ricotta mixture, and then top with another pasta sheet. Repeat layers of salmon, peas, basil and ricotta until all the layers have been added (4 pasta sheets per dish). If using the large baking dish, layer 4 servings side by side.

**7** Finally, combine pine nuts and Parmesan and use to top the lasagna. Drizzle with oil. Then place lasagna in the hot oven and bake on the middle rack for about 10 minutes, until the surface is slightly brown and salmon is cooked through. Serve.

Prep time: 40 minutes, about 30 of which you're actually busy
Goes with: Fresh bread and white wine or Prosecco
Calories per serving: 725

## And for Vegetarian Lasagne:

Rinse 1 lb. vegetables (green asparagus, zucchini, yellow or red bell peppers, peas and green onions) and cut into small pieces. Briefly sauté in 2–3 tablespoons olive oil. Add 1/2 cup dry white wine; cover and simmer for 10 minutes. Season with salt and pepper. Layer in the pan as on page 74 with béchamel, pasta sheets and fresh mozzarella; bake in the same way.

75

# Crespelle
Filled crêpes

The Italian answer to
pancakes, crêpes, etc.

Feeds 4 as a full meal:

**For the batter:**

³/₄ cup flour

Salt

2 eggs

¹/₄ cup olive oil

²/₃ cup milk

**For the filling:**

1 package frozen spinach (1 lb.)

1 small zucchini (4 oz.)

Several sprigs fresh thyme

1 cup ricotta (about 8 oz.)

1 egg

2 oz. freshly grated Parmesan or pecorino

Salt, freshly ground black pepper

Grated nutmeg

**For the sauce:**

1 tablespoon butter

1 tablespoon flour

2 cups + 2 tablespoons milk

2 oz. freshly grated Parmesan or pecorino

1 tablespoon tomato paste

Salt, freshly ground black pepper

1 First of all, place the spinach in a colander to thaw at room temperature (takes 4 hrs.) or cook according to package directions and immerse in ice water or let cool.

2 For the batter, pour flour into a bowl and add a large pinch of salt. Mix together the eggs, 2 tablespoons of the oil and the milk and gradually whisk in. The batter should be liquid-like and, above all, smooth. Let batter rest for 30 minutes.

3 In the meantime, squeeze moisture out of the spinach and chop finely. Rinse zucchini and cut off ends; dice. Rinse thyme, shake dry, and strip off leaves (against the direction they're growing in).

4 Stir together spinach, diced zucchini, thyme, ricotta, egg and Parmesan. Season with salt, pepper and a little nutmeg.

5 For the sauce, melt butter in a pot. Stir in flour and cook until golden. Whisk in milk and make sure mixture is lump free. Simmer over low heat for about 5–10 minutes until thickened. Stir intermittently to keep from sticking to the bottom of the pan. Stir in Parmesan and tomato paste; season with salt and pepper.

6 Back to the batter. Brush a pan with a very thin layer of olive oil and heat. With a ladle, pour in a little batter and tilt and rotate the pan until the batter covers the base. Reduce heat to medium and cook crêpe until the batter is no longer liquid-like on top.

7 Shake the pan to loosen the crêpe. Turn it with a spatula and cook on the other side for about 1 minute. Remove it from the pan. If necessary, adjust flour and milk in the batter in order for the crepes to have the right consistency. Make the remaining batter into crêpes. There should be a total of 8.

8 Preheat oven to 425°F. Grease a large rectangular baking dish. Place 1 crêpe on a board, spread with spinach filling, roll it up and place it in the pan. Do the same with all the other crêpes and lay them side by side.

9 Finally, pour the sauce over the top and place in the oven. Bake for about 30 minutes or till the top is browned.

Prep time: 1 hour and 20 minutes, 30 minutes of which you can relax (not including thawing time)
Goes with: Mixed salad with tomatoes and cucumbers
Calories per serving: 615

# Cannelloni ai funghi
## Pasta tubes with a mushroom filling

### Definitely not for the lazy

Pampers 4:

2 small onions

2 cloves garlic

1⅓ lbs. white mushrooms

or oyster mushrooms

1 bunch basil

¼ cup olive oil

1 ball fresh mozzarella (about 4–5 oz.)

⅔ cup mascarpone or ricotta

1 egg

5 oz. freshly grated Parmesan or pecorino

Salt, freshly ground black pepper

About ½ lb. cannelloni tubes

(the type that do not need pre-cooking)

3 medium tomatoes

½ cup white wine

**1** Peel onions and garlic; chop both finely. Wipe off mushrooms with paper towels. For white mushrooms, trim off ends of stems. For oyster mushrooms, discard whole stems. Cut mushrooms into thin slices or strips. Remove basil leaves. If they're dirty, carefully wipe them with a paper towel and cut into strips.

**2** Place a large pan on the stove and heat. Add 2 tablespoons of the oil and briefly sauté onions. Then add mushrooms and sauté for about 5 minutes over high heat while stirring.

**3** Transfer the mushroom-onion mixture to a bowl and let cool slightly. Then add garlic and basil. Drain fresh mozzarella and cut into small cubes. Stir fresh mozzarella, mascarpone, egg and two-thirds of the Parmesan into the mushrooms (reserve rest of Parmesan). Season with salt and pepper, keeping in mind the cheese is already salty.

**4** If the cannelloni are the type that do not need to be precooked, you can fill the cannelloni with the mushroom mixture at this stage (if not, you need to boil the cannelloni in salted water for about 4–5 minutes to soften them a little bit, but they should still be a little starchy—then drain and proceed). Push in one heaping teaspoon of the mushroom mixture and follow it with another spoonful until the mixture is pushed all the way through. Grease a square baking dish and arrange the pasta tubes side by side.

**5** Preheat oven to 375°F.

**6** Rinse tomatoes and dice very finely (discard stems/cores). Combine with wine, remaining Parmesan and remaining oil, season generously with pepper and distribute over the cannelloni.

**7** Bake cannelloni in the oven on the middle shelf for about 35 minutes. Pierce them with a knife—they should be browned and tender. Before cutting them, it's better to wait 5 to 10 minutes so less juice will run out.

Prep time: 1¾ hours, at least 1 hour of which you're actually busy
Delicious with: Fresh Italian bread and arugula salad
Calories per serving: 760

### Tip
The crespelle filling (recipe on the far left) also goes well in the cannelloni.

# Risot

Where do those Italians get their inspiration?

# to
# etcetera

## [Rice Polenta Pizza and the like]

How about those Italians? They act as if the whole day were nothing but sunshine, children's laughter and espresso with a lot of sugar. In the meantime they're casually satisfying the appetites of half the world. And just so it doesn't get boring, they've come up with a few other magnificent hunger-stoppers to go with their 1001 pasta dishes. Take, for example, risotto, which is about the best dish rice can ever aspire to. Or polenta—who would have thought cornmeal porridge with cheese could taste so wonderful? Or gnocchi, that bite-sized potato dumpling. And then, of course, there's the giant-topped baked white bread from the oven known today from San Francisco to Tokyo (even if Italians might not recognize it) as pizza. Where do those Italians get their inspiration? From sunshine, children's laughter and espresso with a lot of sugar.

Aunt Edna's Racy Risotta

# Practically without Stirring

I always had a love-hate relationship with that seductive macho, Risotto. Whenever I wanted something from him, I first had to chain myself to the stove, stir him non-stop and feed him stock till he'd be nice to me for a few minutes. But if I let my attention wander even for a moment, he could get downright obnoxious. "He did the same to me," a good friend recently told me. But then she revealed her secret, about an Italian-Australian chef with a fantastic restaurant in Melbourne. He'd once made Risotto for an Italian president and won the silver medal in the Italian Rice Cooking World Championship. And he did so with a virtually no-stir recipe. Since I tried the recipe, my love for Risotto is rekindled. Here's how: Slowly sauté 1 diced onion in 3 tablespoons olive oil until translucent. Then add 1½ cups arborio rice and sauté another 2 minutes, stirring constantly. Meanwhile, bring 3⅓ cups stock to a boil and then add all but ⅓ cup of it to the rice at once. Season with salt and quickly bring to a boil. Reduce heat to low, cover and simmer for about 15 minutes. Without stirring! Because once stirred, it stays stirred. Meanwhile, grate 3½ oz. Parmesan. When the risotto is done, the grains should still remain a bit firm. Then add the finishing touches: Remove the pot from the heat, lift the lid, add Parmesan, 2 tablespoons butter and the remaining ⅓ cup hot stock and stir it up vigorously to make it nice and creamy. Then serve it immediately—don't give it time to get obnoxious!

## Five Tips for Using Leftovers:
# Risotto & Polenta

It's hard to reheat risotto and polenta. But Italian housewives have invented great ways to use their leftovers:

### Risotto al salto
Form leftover risotto on wax paper into small (3–4") pancakes, about ¼–½" thick. Heat 3–4 tablespoons olive oil in a frying pan and flip rice pancakes into it; sauté 2–3 minutes. When a light brown crust has formed, flip the risotto cakes and cook for 2–3 more minutes. Delicious with prosciutto or a mushroom-tomato sauce.

### Suppli di telefono
Mix 1¾ cups risotto with 1 egg yolk, 2 table-spoons bread crumbs and 2 oz. Parmesan (grated). Cut 1 fresh mozzarella ball into cubes. Flatten a heaping tablespoon of risotto mixture between your hands. Place a cube of fresh mozzarella on top, shape into a ball around the cheese; roll in more bread crumbs. Deep-fry balls in a large amount of hot canola oil (at 350–375°F, using an oil thermometer, until golden). During eating, the cheese stretches out like an old-fashioned phone cord.

### Pasticcio di risotto
Mix 1¾ cups risotto, 1 egg yolk and 2 tablespoons softened butter. Dice 1 fresh mozzarella ball and mix with 3 oz. grated Parmesan and 4 oz. salami strips. Beat 1 egg white until stiff and fold into mozzarella-salami mixture. Fill a greased baking dish with alternating layers of risotto mixture and mozzarella mixture, beginning and ending with risotto. Bake at 375°F for 45 minutes. Tasty with tomato sauce.

### Polenta al forno
Before it cools, spread leftover polenta on a greased baking sheet to a ½" thickness. When cooled, reverse it onto another surface. Use the top of a glass or cookie cutter to cut out circles; then halve the circles. Arrange in domino fashion on the bottom of a greased baking dish. Pour in just enough cream so polenta is still peaking out the top. Sprinkle with a generous amount of grated semi-soft cheese (e.g. mozzarella, fontina) and bake till browned at 350°F for 30 minutes.

### Bruschetta di polenta
Spread out the polenta as described above and let cool. Dice tomatoes and mix with chopped garlic, fresh basil, salt, pepper and a little olive oil. Cut polenta into slices and brown in olive oil in a pan (both sides). Top with tomato mixture.

# The Pizza Saga

The plot: A piece of dough sets out to see the world, has many experiences and suffers many setbacks. But in the end, love triumphs and Bella Pizza becomes a star.

## Pizza Originale

Its story begins in the southern Mediterranean region before the invention of the modern calendar. A dough pancake is baked on hot rocks over an open fire: first alone (now called flatbread), then spiced (like focaccia) and finally topped to become:

## Pizza Vera

In 18th century Naples, bakers make pizza the number one fast food in the city's narrow lanes – dough-cakes the size of one's palm, further enhanced by a topping of tomatoes imported from the Americas, and baked beside glowing logs in stone ovens. At the start of the 19th century, Naples' bakers serve pizza on the premises for the first time—the pizzeria is born. Just one step away from pizza delivered to your door, the:

## Pizza Mobile

When Queen Margherita visits Naples in 1889, she wants pizza. Since she doesn't feel like going out for it, she has it brought to her. "Something good," is her succinct order. The pizza baker she hires tops it with Italy's patriotic combination of red tomatoes, white fresh mozzarella and green basil—he names his creation after the queen. Today, Pizza Margherita is the most popular pizza in the world. But that slab of dough doesn't achieve international stardom until:

## Pizza Americano

When pizza emigrates to America in the 20th century, it declares that with any fewer than eight ingredients, it refuses to enter the oven. So it undergoes cosmetic surgery to thicken its crust. And in order to pile the ingredients even higher, the pan pizza is invented in Chicago in 1943. Today, US citizens eat 350 slices of pizza every second, a daily consumption equivalent to a pizza the size of a 250 square mile radius. Not the least of these being the:

## Pizza Industriale

Since 1957, ready-made pizza has been available frozen as Industriale Freddo or heated up as Industriale Caldo in all-night gas stations, company cafeterias and fast-food stands. We happen to think Pizza Niente ("no pizza") is preferable to this, and not just because this is a cookbook. The same goes double for Industriale Semi, which is thrown together in chain restaurants using a prefab crust and sauce. Anyone who would actually go out for this kind of pizza probably goes to the local pool to brush their teeth. If you are going out to eat pizza, get:

## Gourmet Pizza

With a thin and crispy crust like the Pizza Vera, it can be simple like Margherita or topped extravagantly as the Americano with fresh and marinated delicacies. If the ingredients can stand very high heat and go well with the rest of the pizza, the result can be a fantastic creation—for example a pizza with lamb fillet, rosemary and red onions. But more often, it's something even more bizarre like:

## Pizza Curiosa

If you think Hawaiian pizza with pineapple is exotic, you need to get out more. Pizza delivery services and restaurants on every continent offer the following debatable toppings: algae, avocado, cod roe, eel with soy sauce, grilled chicken, kimchi (spicy Korean marinated cabbage), mayonnaise, pickles, radishes, raisins, sauce bolognese, shark, squid ragu, strawberries, sushi ginger, tomato salad, and zickinic (an African spice mixture that increases potency). But by all means, make your own decision.

# The Green Asparagus

Green asparagus is:
• The tender shoot of a type of asparagus that, unlike white asparagus, is grown and harvested above ground
• Varying in length and has asparagus greens (for flower arrangements) and poison red berries if allowed to mature

Green asparagus has:
• More flavor and firmness than its white cousin
• A lot of vitamin C and B vitamins
• The magic ingredient asparagine that works as a diuretic and awakens your desire for more than just food

Green asparagus needs:
• To be purchased as fresh as possible. If the cut ends are smooth and moist, it's fresh.
• To be stored refrigerated, with stems in water OR whole spears in a damp cloth inside a bag.
• To be cooked immediately, if possible, because it quickly turns woody

Green asparagus can:
• Be boiled – in salted water without lemon because acid turns it gray
• Be cut up and sautéed in oil or butter, or braised in stock or cream
• Be sliced raw and mixed in a salad (but parboiled first is better)

Green asparagus loves:
• Garlic, nutmeg, saffron, mustard, sugar
• Basil, tarragon, chervil, mint, oregano
• Gorgonzola, mozzarella, goat cheese
• Pasta, potatoes, pizza, risotto
• Peas, carrots, mushrooms, tomatoes, onions
• Shrimp, salmon, swordfish, smoked fish
• Veal, poultry, ham
• Strawberries, raspberries, nectarines, oranges

81

# Risotto alla milanese
Saffron risotto

Old Italian rule:
Good stock makes
good risotto

Variety is the spice of life, especially in Italy. So it's no surprise Italians have more than one recipe for this classic. Here's our favorite!

Feeds 4 as a full meal or 6 lightly:

1 small onion

1 quart meat stock (preferably veal stock)

3 ½ tablespoons butter

A scant 2 cups Italian short-grain rice (arborio or vialone)

⅓ cup hearty dry white wine

A few threads saffron

2 oz. freshly grated Parmesan

Salt, freshly ground black pepper

**1** Peel onion and chop finely. Heat stock. Set aside half the butter. Melt the other half in a medium to large pot.

**2** Add onions and stir briefly. Then stir in rice (but absolutely do not rinse rice beforehand!). Using high heat, pour in the wine. When the wine has evaporated, change to medium heat.

**3** Now add a ladle of hot stock and cook, stirring, until the liquid has evaporated. Add the next ladle full, and keep stirring— this is the only way to make the risotto as creamy as Mamma makes it in Milano. Repeat the process.

4 When you're down to the last bit of stock, add the saffron into it (crumble threads with your fingers) and stir—then ladle that mixture into the risotto.

5 Keep stirring until you think your arm is going to fall off. If the risotto is creamy and smooth and the grains of rice are al dente, it's done—rice grains should still be a little firm in the middle. This should take at least 20 minutes.

6 Stir remaining butter and grated Parmesan into the rice and try a spoonful. Adjust salt and pepper to taste.

Prep time: 40 minutes
Delicious with: A light white wine
If you make risotto as a side dish,
it's best and most traditional with:
Ossobuco (page 139)
Calories per serving (4): 525

# Risotto ai funghi
Mushroom risotto

A meal in itself!

Feeds 4 as a full meal:

1½ oz. dried porcini mushrooms

1 small onion

1 small carrot

1 stalk celery

½ cup parsley sprigs

2 tablespoons olive oil

A scant 2 cups Italian risotto rice

(arborio or vialone)

2 canned, peeled tomatoes

(freeze the rest or use for a pasta sauce)

1 tablespoon butter

2 oz. freshly grated Parmesan

Salt, freshly ground black pepper

1 Put dried porcinis in a small bowl, cover with 1 quart lukewarm water and soak for about 30 minutes, until soft.

2 In the meantime, peel onion and carrot. Rinse celery and parsley. Finely chop all these ingredients and mix together—a combination Italians call "battuto."

3 Remove mushrooms from liquid and chop finely (reserve liquid). Pour porcini-soaking liquid through a paper coffee or tea filter. Almost exactly 3 cups should remain—heat to a gentle boil.

4 Now for the risotto. Heat oil in a pot and briefly sauté battuto mixture and porcini mushrooms. Stir in rice. Dice tomatoes and stir in.

5 From this point on, follow the technique in the previous recipe. Gradually add the hot porcini liquid to the rice while continuing to stir well—let someone else set the table. Add water or stock if extra liquid is needed. Finally, add butter and Parmesan to the rice, then adjust salt and pepper to taste.

Prep time: 1 hour
Calories per serving: 490

# Risotto agli asparagi
## Asparagus risotto

### Ready for its big debut

Feeds 4 with big appetites or 6 as a primo:

1 lb. green asparagus (about 4 cups)

1 small onion

2 cloves garlic

3 tablespoons butter

A scant 2 cups Italian risotto rice
(arborio or vialone)

3¼ cups stock

1 cup dry white wine

½ to 1 lemon

A few sprigs basil

3½ oz. fontina (makes risotto
creamy, but Parmesan also works)

Salt, freshly ground black pepper

**1** Act One for the risotto cook: Rinse
asparagus and trim off tough ends. Cut
off the tips as well (about 1"), because
you won't add them to the pot until later.
Cut the rest into ½" pieces. Peel onion
and garlic; chop both finely.

**2** Act Two: Melt half the butter but don't
brown. Briefly sauté onion, garlic and
asparagus in it while stirring constantly.
Add rice and stir until the grains are shiny.
Heat stock to a gentle boil.

**3** Add wine and let evaporate over high
heat while stirring. Then add 1 ladle stock
and switch risotto pot to medium heat.
Keep stirring diligently while gradually
adding the hot stock. After 10 minutes, add
the asparagus tips and after another 10
minutes, do a taste test. The grains should
be easy to chew but not entirely soft.

**4** Final Act: Rinse lemon, pat dry, and grate
off a thin layer from zest—without the white
part which would impart a bitter taste to the
risotto. Lemon zest should be in fine strips:
if not, chop. Remove basil leaves and cut
into narrow strips. Dice fontina cheese.

**5** Add cheese, lemon zest, basil and
remaining butter to the pot and stir only
until the cheese has melted in the hot rice
mixture. Season with salt and pepper and
enjoy the delicious Finale!

Prep time: 1 hour
Calories per serving (4): 580

# Risotto rucola e prosciutto
## Arugula risotto with Parma ham

### Unequaled in elegance

Feeds 4 gourmets:

1 thin leek

2 cloves garlic

2 cups arugula leaves

1 quart meat stock

3 tablespoons butter

A scant 2 cups Italian risotto rice
(arborio or vialone)

1 tomato

4 oz. raw smoked ham
(prosciutto di Parma or serrano)

2 oz. freshly grated pecorino cheese
(or Parmesan)

1 tablespoon mascarpone or crème fraîche
(optional)

Salt

Nutmeg

**1** Remove roots and dark-green, wilted parts from leek. Slit open lengthwise and bend apart individual leaves, rinsing very well under cold running water to remove any dirt. Then cut leek into fine strips crosswise. Peel garlic and mince. Remove wilted leaves from arugula and trim thick stems. Rinse and pat dry arugula leaves—reserve some for garnish and finely chop the rest. Heat the stock to a gentle boil.

**2** In a separate large pot, melt half the butter. Briefly sauté leek and garlic. Add rice and chopped arugula.

**3** Now it follows the same risotto technique: add a ladle of stock and stir diligently. Each time, when the stock has evaporated, add some more—and so on.

**4** When you notice the rice is almost al dente, rinse the tomato and dice very finely (discard stem/core). Trim fat from ham; cut ham into short strips. Finely chop remaining arugula.

**5** Stir in tomato, ham, pecorino, remaining butter and, if desired, mascarpone. Season risotto to taste with salt and nutmeg; top with arugula for garnish—enjoy.

Prep time: 1 hour
Calories per serving: 715

# Risotto al radicchio

## No translation necessary!

We admit, this risotto isn't exactly a feast for the eyes; unless you really like pinkish-red food. But it tastes so good that all eyes will be closed in ecstasy!

Feeds 4 curious types:

1 onion

1 head radicchio (about 10 oz.)

1 oz. beef marrow, optional (from beef

bones—ask a specialty butcher)

2 tablespoons butter

A scant 2 cups Italian risotto rice

(arborio or vialone)

4 cups hearty red wine (Barolo from

Piedmont would make it authentic,

but a less expensive wine will work fine)

2 oz. freshly grated Parmesan

Salt, freshly ground black pepper

**1** Peel onion and chop finely. Remove outer leaves from radicchio; then rinse the rest and cut into fine strips.

**2** If you were able to get beef marrow, remove it from the bone (if the butcher didn't already) and wipe it off with a paper towel to remove any bone splinters. Finely dice.

**3** In a large pot, heat 1 tablespoon butter and the marrow. Stir in onion and radicchio and sauté briefly. Add rice.

**4** Pour in 1 ladle wine and let it boil away. Reduce heat and gradually add more wine, one ladle at a time. And keep stirring! It will take at least 20 minutes.

**5** When the risotto is smooth and the rice grains are cooked but still firm, fold in remaining butter and the Parmesan. Adjust salt and pepper to taste; serve.

Prep time: 1 hour
Delicious with: Fresh Italian bread and the same red wine you used in the risotto
Calories per serving: 640

# Gnocchi di patate
## Mini potato dumplings

### A masterpiece from the "Nonna"

Italians have several types of gnocchi, including flour gnocchi. We don't have Italian flour but we talked to an Italian grandmother, the Nonna, and she let us in on a little secret: just mix flour and semolina.

Feeds 4 as a full meal with

the sauce of your choice:

2¼ lb. potatoes (russet or similar variety)

1 cup flour plus more for coating

½ cup durum semolina

Salt (kosher)

**1** Scrub potatoes, place in a pot and pour in cold water, covering the potatoes about halfway. Bring water to a boil, cover and cook over medium heat until tender (20 to 35 minutes). A tip from Nonna: You have to start with cold water when cooking potatoes for them to stay nice and starchy. If you don't believe it, try it yourself.

**2** Pour water off potatoes and let cool a little, but peel while still hot. Press through a potato ricer. A tip from Nonna: if you don't have a ricer, mash them with a fork or potato masher. But please don't purée the potatoes—otherwise you'll have paste instead of nicely mashed potatoes.

**3** Let mashed potatoes cool until you can hold them in your hand. Then add flour, semolina and 2 teaspoons kosher salt. Knead all this together with your hands and form sections of it into long rolls the thickness of an index finger. Cut the rolls into 1" pieces. Roll each piece in flour, then gently press down on one side of each with the tines of a fork so the gnocchi have ridges. Tip from Nonna: Spread the gnocchi out on non-terry dish towels and let stand 1 hour or even longer.

**4** In a large pot, heat a generous amount of salted water. When it starts boiling, drop in the gnocchi (in batches). When the gnocchi rise to the top, turn the heat to medium. Let cook for about 2–3 minutes. Take care not to let them become too soft nor soggy.

**5** Remove gnocchi with a slotted spoon and transfer to plates. Toss gently with sauce immediately: try melted butter and Parmesan; or serve with tomato sauce (page 60), ragu bolognese (page 74), pesto (page 61), or rabbit ragu (page 71). And now even Nonna is satisfied and quiet!

Prep time: 45 minutes
(not including standing time)
Calories per serving: 380

## Basic Tip
### For Consistent Success

Really starchy potatoes can't be found in the spring that's when the new potatoes that have very little starch content arrive on the market. As of the middle of the year you can buy really starchy potatoes and feel more secure about preparing gnocchi. If you still aren't sure, mix an egg into the dough with a little more flour. (The egg will give it a firmer texture.)

If you want to be adventurous use polenta instead of durum semolina. It looks nice and tastes great!

# Strangolapreti
*Literally "strangle the priests" in Italian*

**Ricotta dumplings with spinach**

In many regions, these little dumplings are also called gnocchi ignudi, because they lie naked on the plate with only a drizzle of sage butter and a smattering of pecorino. Elsewhere they're called malfatti, literally "badly made;" which means it's okay if you don't give them a perfect shape!

Feeds 4 gourmets:

1 package finely chopped

frozen spinach (1 lb.)

³⁄₄ cup parsley sprigs

8 oz. ricotta

2 eggs

4 oz. freshly grated pecorino

³⁄₄ cup flour

Salt, freshly ground black pepper

Grated nutmeg

2 tablespoons butter

1 tablespoon olive oil

A few sage leaves

**1** Remove spinach from the package and let thaw in a colander with a plate or bowl underneath (takes 4 hours, so plan ahead).

**2** Squeeze spinach to remove moisture, as much as possible, with your hands; then chop. Rinse parsley, shake dry and finely chop leaves.

**3** Mix together ricotta, eggs and pecorino. Stir in spinach, parsley and flour. The mixture should be soft but moldable. Season with a little salt, pepper and nutmeg.

**4** In a large pot, bring a generous amount of salted water to a boil. Meanwhile, form dumplings from the ricotta mixture using two teaspoons. The important thing is that the dumplings hold together—they don't need to win a beauty contest. Add small amounts of flour if necessary. Arrange the strangolapreti side by side on non-terry dish towels.

**5** When you've formed all the dumplings, roll the strangolapreti from the board into the boiling water. Turn down the heat a bit and cook for about 10 minutes. They'll float to the top when they're done.

**6** Heat butter and oil—the oil keeps the butter from burning so easily. Briefly sauté the sage leaves.

**7** Remove the strangolapreti from the pot with a slotted spoon, transfer to wide pasta bowls and sprinkle with sage butter. And even if it's hard to do, enjoy your strangolapreti slowly!

Prep time: 40 minutes
(not including thawing time)
Delicious with: A lot more grated
or sliced cheese
Calories per serving: 410

## Tip
If you want to use fresh spinach, remove thick stems from about 1¹⁄₂ lbs. Rinse leaves well in cold water and drain. In a large pot, bring 1" water to a boil, add a little salt, throw in spinach, cover and let wilt. Pour spinach into a colander, rinse under cold water and drain. Squeeze out moisture, and proceed with recipe.

These dumplings also taste fantastic without the sage, using only the oil, butter and cheese.

# Polenta pasticciata
## Oven-browned polenta slices

**Substantial, juicy and spicy**

Feeds 4 as a full meal:

Salt

1 2/3 cups dried polenta

1 onion

2 cloves garlic

2 carrots

2 stalks celery

4 oz. Italian salami

1/4 cup olive oil

1 lb. ground meat of your choice

1 (14 oz.) can peeled tomatoes

1/2 cup dry red wine

1–2 dried red chiles

or 1 teaspoon crushed red pepper flakes

1 teaspoon dried thyme

4 oz. freshly grated Parmesan

**1** In a large pot, bring to a boil 4 cups water with 1 teaspoon salt. Pour in polenta and stir well. Turn heat down to very low, otherwise the polenta will bubble and spurt—it also burns easily. Cover and cook for 10 minutes.

**2** Take out a large cutting board or baking sheet. Dump the polenta from the pot onto the board and using a rubber spatula, spread the polenta out to a thickness of about 3/4". Allow to cool and solidify.

**3** In the meantime, peel onion and garlic; chop both finely. Peel carrots. Rinse celery and trim ends. Pull off any loose "threads." Chop carrots, celery and salami very finely.

**4** In a pan, heat 2 tablespoons of the oil. Briefly sauté onion and garlic. Stir in vegetables and salami and sauté briefly. Add and brown ground meat until cooked through and crumbly. Chop tomatoes and pour into the pan along with their juice and the red wine. Crush dried chiles in a mortar or between your fingers but remember: your fingers will be almost as hot as the peppers so don't rub your eyes (best bet: wear gloves)—or use flakes.

**5** Season meat sauce with salt; stir in thyme and simmer slowly, uncovered, on medium-low heat for about 15 minutes.

**6** Preheat oven to 375°F. Brush a narrow, rectangular baking dish with a thin layer of the remaining oil.

**7** Hold a knife under cold water and then cut polenta into strips no more than 1" wide. Rinsing the knife periodically will make this job easier.

**8** Fill the dish with alternating layers of polenta slices and ground meat. Top with Parmesan and drizzle with oil.

**9** Bake polenta on the middle shelf for about 35 minutes until nicely browned. What more could you want?

Prep time: 45 minutes of activity,
35 minutes relaxing
Delicious with: Salad, such as tomatoes with balsamic vinegar and basil, and a hearty red wine to go with the spicy sauce
Calories per serving: 830

# Pizza—The Dough

## Jack of all trades

For 1 baking sheet or 2 pizza pans:

2 cups flour + flour for shaping

Salt, ¼ cup olive oil, 1 packet yeast

**1** Pour flour into a bowl with 1 large pinch of salt and the oil. Separately, stir yeast into ⅔ cup lukewarm water until smooth.

**2** Mix flour, oil, salt, and yeast-water together briefly—add a little flour if dough is too sticky. Then pour a little flour onto a work surface, put the dough on it and knead vigorously until pliable (takes some time and effort—or use the dough hooks on an electric mixer).

**3** Grease a bowl and put the ball of dough in it; cover with a cloth and wait. After 30–45 minutes the dough will have doubled in size and is ready to be punched down, formed, topped and baked.

Prep time: 15 minutes
(+ 30–45 minutes rising time)

## Variation from the South:

3 cups flour, 1 egg, 1¾ cup milk, salt, 1 packet yeast. This makes it a little thicker and fluffier.

# Pizza pane
### Pizza bread

## Truly basic

For 1 baking sheet or 2 pizza pans:

1 recipe pizza dough (see left)

4–5 canned peeled tomatoes

2 cloves garlic

2 sprigs fresh rosemary

3 tablespoons olive oil + oil for the pan

Salt, freshly ground black pepper

**1** Prepare dough, let rise and then roll out directly onto the greased baking sheet.

**2** Preheat oven to 475°F. Dice tomatoes. Peel garlic and mince. Remove rosemary needles; coarsely chop. Combine tomatoes, garlic, rosemary and oil; season with salt and pepper.

**3** Spread tomato mixture onto the dough. Bake pizza bread on the middle shelf until crispy, about 12 minutes. Remove, cut into pieces and eat it while it's hot.

Prep time: 1½ hours, 30 minutes
of which you're actually busy
Calories per serving (4): 450

# Pizza Margherita
### With tomato sauce and fresh mozzarella

## The queen mother of all pizzas

Feeds 4 purists:

1 recipe pizza dough (see far left column)

1 onion, 2 cloves garlic

2 tablespoons olive oil + oil for pan

1 large can peeled tomatoes (28 oz.)

Salt, freshly ground black pepper

3 balls fresh mozzarella (about 14 oz. total)

¾ cup basil sprigs

**1** Knead dough (from pizza dough recipe at far left) and let rise. In the meantime, peel onion and garlic and chop both finely. In a pan heat 1 tablespoon of the oil and stir in onion and garlic. Chop tomatoes and add to pan with the juice from the can. Season with salt and pepper and simmer for 20 minutes uncovered over medium-low heat, stirring occasionally.

**2** Brush baking sheet with a little oil and roll out the dough directly onto it so that it's a little thicker at the edges. Preheat oven to 425°F.

**3** Spread tomato sauce onto the dough. Slice fresh mozzarella. Pull off basil leaves (reserve some for garnish). Place mozzarella slices and basil leaves on top of tomato sauce; drizzle with remaining oil.

**4** Place baking sheet on middle rack and bake pizza for about 25 minutes. The cheese should be melted but not browned. Garnish with reserved basil, cut and serve.

Prep time: 1½ hours, 35 minutes of which you're actually busy
Calories per serving: 665

## Margherita's Splendid Sisters:
• Place anchovy fillets on the tomato sauce, use less cheese and it becomes a Pizza Napoletana.
• To make Pizza Rucola, top the baked Margherita with fresh arugula that you first dressed with a little lemon juice, olive oil, salt and pepper.
• Spread tomato sauce onto the dough and top one quarter with diced, cooked ham (about 5 oz.), one quarter with sliced mushrooms (preferably white mushrooms, about 1½ cups), one quarter with pitted black olives and one quarter with marinated artichoke hearts. Sprinkle cheese on top and call it a Pizza Quattro Stagioni (pizza with four stages).
• For a Capricciosa, cut ham into strips and arrange on the tomato sauce along with 8–10 anchovy fillets, ½ cup pitted black olives and ¾ cup chopped artichoke hearts. Top with cheese and bake.

# Pizza peperoni e carciofi
## Pizza with bell peppers and artichokes

La vegetariana

Feeds 4 veggie lovers:

1 recipe pizza dough (see recipe on p. 90)

1 (28 oz.) can peeled tomatoes

2 cloves garlic

Salt, freshly ground black pepper

2 yellow bell peppers

1 cup marinated artichoke hearts

2 balls fresh mozzarella (or about 8 oz.)

1 teaspoon dried oregano or thyme

2 tablespoons olive oil + oil for the pan

**1** Prepare dough, let rise and roll out onto a greased baking sheet.

**2** Drain tomatoes and squeeze juice out gently (juice not needed for pizza). Chop tomatoes very finely or purée briefly with a hand blender. Peel garlic, squeeze through a press and add to tomatoes. Season with salt and pepper and spread this sauce onto the dough.

**3** Preheat oven to 425°F.

**4** Rinse bell peppers and remove stem, ribs and seeds; quarter peppers and cut into strips. Quarter artichoke hearts. Dice fresh mozzarella.

**5** Distribute vegetables over tomato sauce and sprinkle with salt, pepper and oregano. Top with fresh mozzarella and drizzle with olive oil. Place baking sheet on middle rack and bake pizza for about 25 minutes until the cheese melts — but don't let it get too brown. Take pizza out of the oven, cut into pieces and enjoy.

Prep time: 1½ hours, 45 minutes of which you're actually busy
Delicious with: Green or arugula salad and a refreshing white or light red wine
Calories per serving: 635

91

# Pizza quattro formaggi
## Pizza with four cheeses

### Enlivened by a little fire

Feeds 4 as an appetizer or 2 as a full meal:

1 recipe pizza dough (page 90)

About 1 lb. cheese (mixture of mild and tangy types, e.g. fresh mozzarella, gorgonzola, ricotta salata and pecorino)

Several sprigs fresh thyme or sage

4–6 marinated pepperoncini

2 tablespoons olive oil + oil for baking sheet

**1** Prepare pizza dough as described on page 90, let rise and then roll out directly onto a lightly greased baking sheet. It can be a little thicker around the edges.

**2** Preheat oven to 475°F. Cut up cheese: dice mozzarella and gorgonzola, break up ricotta salata with a fork, grate pecorino. Mix all cheese and scatter on the dough.

**3** Rinse thyme or sage and shake dry. Strip thyme leaves from stems or cut sage into strips. Cut pepperoncini into rings.

**4** Sprinkle herbs over the cheeses. Season with salt only if you mainly used mild

cheeses. Place pepperoncini on top and drizzle with remaining oil. Bake pizza on the middle rack for about 15 minutes. Tastes best when medium brown.

Prep time: At least 1½ hours, 25 minutes of which you're actually busy.
Delicious with: Tomato salad and a hearty red wine
Calories per serving (2): 820

# Pizza al tonno
## Pizza with tuna

### Lots of taste— not a lot of Lire

Feeds 4 as a full meal:

1 recipe pizza dough (page 90)

1–2 tablespoons capers

2 cups + 2 tablespoons canned

chopped tomatoes

1 teaspoon dried Italian seasoning

Salt, freshly ground black pepper

1 small white onion

2 cans tuna packed in water (5–6 oz. each)

3 oz. freshly grated cheese

(e.g. fontina, younger pecorino, or Taleggio)

2 tablespoons olive oil + oil for baking sheet

**1** Prepare dough as described on page 90 and roll out onto a lightly greased baking sheet. Leave it thicker around the edges.

**2** Chop capers, combine with tomatoes and Italian herbs and season with salt and pepper. Spread three-quarters of the sauce onto the dough.

**3** Preheat oven to 425°F.

**4** Peel onion and slice thinly into rings. When the onion gets so small that you can't hold it in your hand anymore, lay it on the board and slice into strips. Drain tuna, flake apart and distribute on top of tomato sauce. Top with onion slices. Spoon on remaining sauce, sprinkle with the cheese and drizzle with oil.

**5** Bake pizza on middle rack for 25–30 minutes. The cheese should be melted but only slightly browned.

Prep time: 1¾ hours, 30 minutes of which you're actually busy
Delicious with: Tossed salad, acqua and vino rosso
Calories per serving: 590

# Pizza ai frutti di mare
## Pizza with seafood

### Without cheese, please!

Feeds 4 as a primo:

1 recipe pizza dough (page 90)

3/4 cup parsley sprigs

2 cloves garlic

1 dried red chile or 1/2 teaspoon crushed red pepper flakes

2 1/4 cups canned chopped tomatoes

Salt

3 tablespoons oil + oil for baking sheet

1 1/3 lbs. seafood (preferably purchased precooked from a fish market: shrimp, mussels, clams, squid rings, etc.)

Freshly ground black pepper

**1** Knead pizza dough, let rise and roll out onto greased baking sheet. Leave edges a bit thicker.

**2** Rinse parsley, shake dry and pull off leaves. Peel garlic. Chop parsley, garlic and dried red chile (wear gloves—or use flakes) very finely and mix with chopped tomatoes.

Add salt and 1 tablespoon of the oil. Spread sauce onto dough. Preheat oven to 450°F.

**3** Distribute seafood on pizza, sprinkle with remaining oil and grind black pepper over the top. Bake on middle shelf for about 20 minutes—just until the crust is brown. The rest just needs to be hot.

Prep time: At least 1 1/2 hours, 30 minutes of which you're actually busy
Delicious with: A fresh, light white wine
Calories per serving: 580

# Pizza al prosciutto di Parma
## Pizza with Parma ham

### Fantastico

Feeds 4 gourmets:

1 recipe pizza dough (page 90)

2 tablespoons olive oil + oil for baking sheet

1 lb. green asparagus

1 bunch green onions (5–6)

Salt

1 (14 oz.) can peeled tomatoes

Freshly ground black pepper

2 oz. freshly grated pecorino

4 oz. prosciutto di Parma, paper thin

**1** Prepare pizza dough and let rise, as described on page 90. Oil the baking sheet lightly and roll out dough onto it directly. Leave edges slightly thicker.

**2** Rinse asparagus and trim tough ends, up to the tender part. Cut spears into 2" pieces. Remove roots and dark-green parts from green onions; rinse rest and halve lengthwise.

**3** Preheat oven to 425°F.

**4** Bring a large amount of salted water to a boil. Boil asparagus and green onions for 2 minutes; rinse under cold water and drain.

**5** Chop tomatoes and mix with a little of their juice, salt and pepper. Spread onto the dough. Top with asparagus and green onions, sprinkle with pecorino and drizzle with the 2 tablespoons oil. Bake pizza on middle shelf for about 20 minutes. Trim any fatty edges from ham. Remove pizza from oven, top with ham, cut into slices and enjoy.

Prep time: 1 1/2 hours, 40 minutes of which you're actually busy
Delicious with: Arugula salad
Calories per serving: 580

## Focaccia al formaggio
Focaccia with a cheese filling

**For parties and picnics**

Feeds 4 as a snack:

2 cups flour

$\frac{1}{2}$ cup olive oil + oil for pan

Salt

$\frac{3}{4}$ cup basil sprigs

$\frac{3}{4}$ cup soft cheese

(e.g. goat cheese, fresh mozzarella, ricotta)

Course salt for sprinkling

**1** Pour flour into a bowl. Add 5 tablespoons of the oil, 1 large pinch of salt and about $\frac{1}{2}$ cup cold water. First mix well together, then continue on a work surface where it will be easier to knead the dough. Work it until it's elastic and smooth. You may need to add a little water or, if it sticks to your fingers, flour.

. Wrap dough in waxed paper and let relax
r about 30 minutes at room temperature
t won't rise because it is unleavened).

. In the meantime, pull the basil leaves
f the stems. Don't rinse, but rather wipe
ently with a paper towel if necessary.
ender plants don't tolerate rinsing very
ell, and basil is typically clean). Cut basil
to strips. Cut up cheese and mix with basil.

. Preheat oven to 475°F. Brush a little oil
nto a round pan (pizza pan, pie pan or
rge spring-form pan).

. Divide dough in half. Sprinkle a little
our on the work surface and roll out half
he dough in all directions so it's as round
s possible and the same size as the pan.
ace in the pan. Distribute cheese mixture
n top. Roll out the other half of the dough
nd pierce a number of times with a fork.
ace on top of cheese and press down
ently on edges. Brush with remaining oil
nd sprinkle with salt. Bake focaccia on the
iddle rack for about 15 minutes until nicely
rown—delicious warm or cold.

rep time: Just under 1 hour, 25 minutes
f which you're actually busy
alories per serving: 515

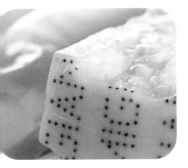

# Calzone
## Stuffed pizza

### The surprise is inside!

Feeds 2 with very big appetites:

**For the dough:**

1 2/3 cups flour

Salt

1/4 cup olive oil + oil for baking sheet

1 packet yeast

**For the filling:**

2 oz. cooked ham

1 small, firm tomato

1/2 cup parsley sprigs

1 ball fresh mozzarella (4–5 oz.)

2/3 cup ricotta

1 egg

2 oz. freshly grated Parmesan or pecorino

1 clove garlic

Salt, freshly ground black pepper

2 tablespoons olive oil for brushing on

**1** Combine flour, salt and olive oil in a bowl.
Separately, stir yeast into 2/3 cup lukewarm
water and then combine with flour mixture.
Transfer dough to a work surface and knead
vigorously. Grease the dough bowl and return
dough to it; cover and let rise for 1 hour. The
dough should approximately double in size.

**2** Meanwhile, prepare the filling. Dice ham.
Rinse tomato and dice finely (discard core
and stem). Rinse parsley, shake dry and
chop very finely.

**3** Dice fresh mozzarella and mix with ricotta
and egg. Stir in ham, tomato, parsley and
Parmesan. Peel garlic, squeeze through a
press and add. Season filling with salt
and pepper.

**4** Now back to the dough—first set the oven
to 425°F. Brush baking sheet lightly with oil.
Sprinkle a little flour on the work surface,
place the dough on top and roll it out thin
in all directions with a rolling pin, making
it as round as possible.

**5** Immediately lay out the dough on the
baking sheet so you won't have to move it
once you've added the filling. A good half of
it can hang over one edge. Distribute filling
on the other half but leave space near the
edge in order to press the ends of the dough
together. Fold the overhanging side over the
filling and carefully press the edges together
and pinch closed to seal. Brush calzone with
olive oil.

**6** Bake on the middle rack for about 25
minutes until nicely brown. Remove from
oven and wait another 5–10 minutes. Cut
in half and enjoy.

Prep time: 1 3/4 hours, 30 minutes
of which you're actually busy
Calories per serving: 1075

# Verdu

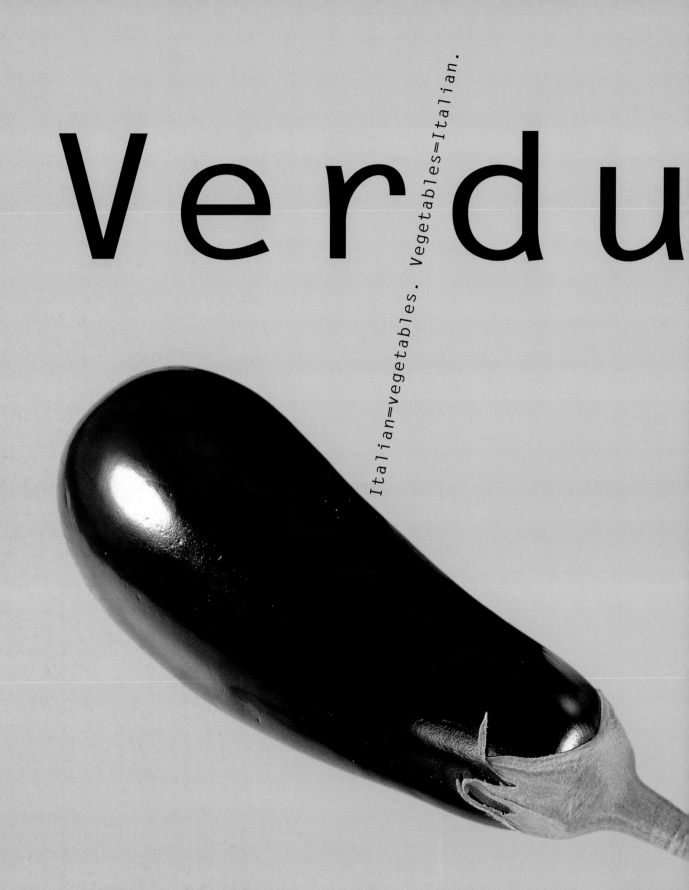

Italian=vegetables. Vegetables=Italian.

re

[Eat your greens...
          for living the dolce vita!]

Italian equals vegetables. Vegetables equal Italian. You can't have
one without the other. Asparagus green, fennel white, tomato red—
all seasoned to taste with olive oil, garlic and basil—that's as pure
as it gets! It's also why Italian chefs are so picky about their produce.
When buying vegetables, they inspect them just as closely—or
more closely—than they would fish, meat or cheese.

So what happens to a veggie once it has been so carefully obtained?
It doesn't just play second fiddle on a plate next to the saltimbocca,
I can tell you that much! Italians are generous lovers and their
treatment of food is no exception—the venerable vegetable gets
a plate of its own. The plate is deep if the vegetable is used for
soups such as minestrone or ribollita. The plate is flat if the veggie
is braised, stewed, sautéed or browned in the oven—leaving just
enough room for a tiny bit of saltimbocca. But only if absolutely
necessary.

## Aunt Edna's Vegetable Fling

# Recipe for whatever you have on hand

Sometimes people knock on my door and say, "My, Edna, what a coincidence that we should find you here! How are you? By the way, could you cook us something Italian?" Well, on the spur of the moment...ur...um...I guess I can do it because I have some basics on hand and I bet we can find some other characteristically Italian ingredients in the refrigerator and cupboard, too! **The beginning is always the same: A shot of olive oil in a hot pan, 2–3 chopped garlic cloves and 1 onion sliced into rings.** I let it sauté slowly on medium-low while I look through my other vegetables. Depending on what I have, I might throw in a bunch of diced eggplant, bell pepper strips or sliced zucchini—maybe even green asparagus spears or frozen peas. In any case, I use 1 teaspoon dried oregano. I sauté the vegetables for 1–5 minutes, time enough to look for leftover antipasti because artichoke hearts, capers, olives and sun-dried tomatoes will taste great alongside the vegetables. Then to the pan, I always add 1 can of diced tomatoes (14 oz.). When that comes to a boil, I add a bit of salt and pepper. Now I clear a space in the vegetables and drop in one egg. I cover it, turn the heat way down or off and wait 5 minutes. Then I remove the cover, sprinkle on some freshly-grated Parmesan and serve with ciabatta bread. "My, Edna, this is so good!" they say, and "From now on we'll never call ahead!" Bravo!

# Good Italian cooking comes from good stock

You don't have to be a vegetarian to cook Italian food with vegetable stock. But to cook well with stock, it's best to use homemade. Here's how:

Peel 4 onions and 4 cloves garlic. Dice onions coarsely. Peel two carrots and cut into thick slices. Rinse 4 outer stalks of celery, clean and dice. Rinse 4 tomatoes. Rinse a lemon and remove zest from half.

In a very large pot, heat olive oil and slowly sauté onions, carrots and celery. Pour in a good 5 quarts of cold water.

Add tomatoes, lemon zest and garlic plus 3 bay leaves, 1 whole dried red chile (optional), $1/2$ teaspoon fennel seeds, and a few sprigs of fresh thyme and oregano. And if you want, 1 tablespoon dried porcini mushrooms. Use cheesecloth, cinched up with kitchen string, to contain these items if desired.

Slowly bring to a boil and simmer for 2 hours (you can remove the chile even after a few minutes of boiling if desired). Pour the stock through a colander, season lightly with salt and return to a boil. Take what you need, let the rest cool; then store it in the freezer. Good for soups, stews and cooking liquid in general.

## Tourists and natives

Not all vegetables associated with Italian cooking originated in Italy. Only three of the seven vegetables listed below were born somewhere between Bolzano and Palermo—the rest are immigrants. Who can tell the difference?

**Eggplant**
Originated in: a) India b) Southern France c) Italy

**Broccoli**
Originated in: a) America b) Central Asia c) Italy

**Fennel**
Originated in: a) North Africa b) Southern France c) Italy

**Garlic**
Originated in: a) Central Asia b) Greece c) Italy

**Tomato**
Originated in: a) America b) North Africa c) Italy

**Savoy cabbage**
Originated in: a) Germany b) Ireland c) Italy

**Zucchini**
Originated in: a) America b) Greece c) Italy

Answer: Only broccoli, fennel and savoy cabbage are answer C and therefore Italian. For all the rest, the answer is A.

# Our Favorite Green Ingredient

# The Celery Stalk

**Celery is:**
• An absolute must in many vegetable soups and vegetable dishes from southern Italy
• Descended from wild celery, whose flavor has been tamed by Italian growers
• The half-brother of celery root—except its power lies in the stem, not the root
  Also related to carrots, fennel and parsley

**Celery has:**
• A lot of vitamin C (good for the immune system), especially when eaten raw
• A good amount of calcium (strengthens bones, teeth, blood, nerves), potassium (makes you relaxed and strong) and manganese (good for the brain and immune system)

**Celery needs:**
• To have its threads removed sometimes: Cut partway through the top of the stalk, hold ends of threads between the knife blade and your thumb and pull downward
• To be boiled when in a soup
• To be braised or stewed when a side vegetable
• To be deep-fried or sautéed for some excitement—but not the pale, inner stalks
• To be mixed in a salad—raw and sliced
• To be enjoyed along with its heart (pale inner stalks), which can be quartered and braised

**Celery loves:**
• Basil, savory, oregano, parsley, bay leaf, mint, thyme and its own greens
• Fennel seed, capers, garlic, dried red chiles, pesto, anchovies, mustard
• Eggplant, peas, fennel, carrots, potatoes, bell peppers, mushrooms, tomatoes
• Fish, shrimp, anchovies, canned tuna
• Poultry, pork, prosciutto, pancetta
• Eggs, mayonnaise, creamy sauces
• Blue cheese (e.g. gorgonzola), fresh mozzarella, goat cheese

## Five Time-Saving Tips:
# Stock with Eggs

Italian housewives are experts in using almost identical ingredients to whip up a variety of different dishes—such as these five quick ideas using stock and eggs:

## Stracciatella
From 1 quart of quality stock, set aside one ladle full, and bring the rest to a boil. Whisk together 3 eggs, 3 tablespoons Parmesan, the ladle of stock and 1 pinch salt. If you want, also add 2 tablespoons semolina. Season the stock you just boiled with salt and nutmeg and remove from heat. Gradually whisk egg mixture into soup. Return to a simmer, for 3–4 minutes, while stirring constantly until nothing but "egg drops" are swimming in the stracciatella. Ready!

## Semolina e prosciutto
For semolina soup, sauté 3 tablespoons semolina in 3 tablespoons butter. While stirring, add 1 quart of quality stock and simmer 5 minutes. Cut 4 slices prosciutto into strips. Mix together 2 egg yolks, 1/4 cup mascarpone cheese, a little bit of whole milk or cream to thin it a bit and 2 tablespoons chopped basil. Remove soup from heat. Whisk 1 ladle full of soup into the egg-mascarpone mixture and then whisk that whole mixture back into the soup. Add prosciutto, season and serve!

## Zuppa Spatzli
Bring to a boil 1 quart of quality stock and season with salt and nutmeg. In a bowl, stir together 1 egg, 2/3 cup flour and 2 tablespoons pesto (prepared, from a jar) to create a batter. Add to lightly simmering soup teaspoonful by teaspoonful—miniature dumplings will form. Simmer for 1 minute—or test the dumplings till they're done to your liking!

## Zuppa Pavese
For this soup from Pavia, toast 4 slices white bread in butter (day-old works fine) and put one each in 4 wide soup bowls. Bring to a boil 1 quart of quality stock and season to taste with salt and nutmeg. Top each bread slice with 1 tablespoon freshly grated Parmesan and 1 fresh raw egg. Pour boiling hot stock slowly over the top (which cooks the egg).

## Acqua aglio e salvia
Although its original Provençal version is tedious to make, the Nonna from Genoa values this "garlic-sage water" because it doesn't require use of stock. Peel 6 cloves garlic, chop, sprinkle with salt and then crush coarsely with the side of a heavy knife blade. Simmer in 1 quart water for 15 minutes along with 2 bay leaves; add 2 sage sprigs and simmer for 5 more minutes. Distribute 4 slices of toast in 4 wide soup bowls, drizzle with olive oil and top each with 1 egg yolk, 1 tablespoon grated Parmesan and some salt and pepper. Pour hot liquid mixture on top slowly and enjoy!

# Minestrone

Nothing's more popular—nothing tastes better!

Feeds 4 as a full meal:

1 lb. mixed vegetables (preferably celery, zucchini, carrots, young savoy cabbage, spinach)

4 tomatoes

1 onion

2 cloves garlic

3 tablespoons olive oil

6 cups vegetable or meat stock

2 cups dried pasta (short type)

1 (14 oz.) can cooked white beans (e.g. cannellini, navy, great northern)

Salt, freshly ground black pepper

4 tablespoons freshly grated Parmesan or pecorino

1 Rinse all the vegetables. Peel carrots. Dice these types of vegetables: celery, zucchini, carrots, including the tomatoes for this recipe. Cut these types into strips: savoy cabbage, spinach. Peel onion and garlic; chop both finely.

2 In a large pot, heat 1 tablespoon oil. Stir in onion and garlic and sauté for a minute or so. Add vegetable stock, mix in vegetables and heat to a low boil.

3 Then, simmer the vegetables for about 15 minutes over medium-low heat with the lid halfway off (block with a wooden spoon if necessary).

4 Rinse beans in a colander under cold water, discarding liquid from the can. Add pasta and beans to soup; simmer for about 10 more minutes until the pasta is al dente.

5 Adjust salt and pepper. Ladle soup into wide bowls, drizzle with remaining oil and sprinkle with Parmesan. A great Italian zuppa!

Prep time: 45 minutes, 30 of which you're actually busy
Delicious with: Fresh Italian bread (toasted if desired)
Also good with: 1 teaspoon pesto per bowl (prepared, from a jar)
Calories per serving: 400

# Pasta e fagioli
## Soup with pasta and beans

Buon appetito!

Feeds 4, also as a full meal:

2½ cups dried white beans (for the ambitious—see steps 1 & 2—otherwise buy 28 oz. of canned white beans)

4 oz. pancetta or streaky smoked bacon

1 onion

2 tablespoons olive oil

1 to 1½ quarts vegetable or meat stock

1 (14 oz.) can peeled tomatoes (or 2 tomatoes)

2 cups short pasta (e.g. penne, orecchiette, fusilli)

¾ cup parsley sprigs

Salt, black pepper

1 If you always wanted to learn how to cook dried beans: pour them into a bowl, cover with water and let stand overnight. If this does not appeal to you, just buy 2 (14 oz.) cans of cooked beans.

2 But back to the ambitious student: After the beans have soaked overnight, pour off and discard the water.

3 For everyone: Chop pancetta. Peel onion and chop finely. In a large pot, heat pancetta and onion in 1 tablespoon of the oil. Keep stirring and sautéing until the fat on the bacon is translucent; add the softened beans and 1½ quarts stock. Simmer slowly for about 2 hours until the beans are tender. (For using canned beans, add beans and only 1 quart stock—then bring to a low boil. No need to simmer.)

4 Drain tomatoes and chop (omit juice). Or rinse fresh tomatoes and chop very finely. Stir into the soup. Purée two ladles of soup

with a blender or hand blender. Return purée to the pot – this provides a smooth texture. Add pasta and continue simmering until it is al dente.

5 Meanwhile, rinse parsley and shake dry. Chop leaves very finely. Season soup to taste with salt and pepper. Sprinkle with parsley and drizzle with remaining oil. Serve at the table from the pot.

Prep time: 2½ hours, 30 minutes of which you're actually busy
Delicious with: Toasted bread slices and a stream of fresh olive oil (put a small bottle on the table)
Calories per serving: 645

# Zuppa di lenticchie
## Lentil soup

You won't even be able to tell it's good for you!

Makes enough for 4:

2 stalks celery

2–3 sprigs fresh sage

2–3 cloves garlic

4–6 anchovy fillets in oil

¼ cup olive oil

1 cup dry brown lentils

3 cups vegetable or meat stock

1 (14 oz.) can peeled tomatoes

Freshly ground black pepper, salt

8 small sliced bread rounds

2 tablespoons freshly grated Parmesan

**1** Rinse celery and cut off ends. Pull off any visible "threads." Save celery greens if fresh. Slice stalks thinly crosswise. Rinse sage and cut leaves into strips. Peel garlic and chop finely along with the drained anchovy fillets.

**2** In a large pot with a lid, heat 1 tablespoon of the oil. Stir in garlic and anchovies, plus sage and celery; sauté briefly. Pour in lentils and stir well.

**3** Pour in stock and bring to a low boil. Chop tomatoes and add to pot along with their juice.

**4** Season soup with pepper (salt comes later). Cover and simmer over medium heat for about 40 minutes until the lentils are done, stirring occasionally. Keep it at a low simmer, or you may need to add more liquid (if too much evaporates). Adjust salt and pepper to taste.

**5** In a pan, heat 2 tablespoons of the oil and toast bread slices on both sides until crispy. Pull apart celery greens. Distribute bread slices in wide soup bowls and ladle lentil soup over the top. Drizzle with remaining oil, sprinkle with a little freshly grated Parmesan and the celery greens—enjoy.

Prep time: 1 hour, only 20 minutes of which you're actually busy
Calories per serving: 375

# Ribollita
## Reheated vegetable bean soup

But it also tastes great freshly ladled!

Feeds 4 but only 2 as a full meal:

½ lb. greens (preferably a mixture of savoy cabbage, spinach and arugula)

1 carrot

1 stalk celery

2–3 cloves garlic

1–2 slices white bread (day-old works fine)

1 sprig fresh rosemary

¼ cup olive oil

4 cups vegetable or meat stock

1 (14 oz.) can cooked white beans (e.g. cannellini, navy, great northern)

Salt, freshly ground black pepper

1 small red onion

**1** Rinse greens and chop coarsely. Peel carrot, rinse celery and cut both into lengthwise strips, then into tiny cubes. Peel garlic and mince. Cut bread into cubes. Rinse rosemary; remove and chop needles.

**2** In a large pot, heat 1 tablespoon of the oil. Briefly stir carrots, celery and garlic into the oil, then stir in greens with rosemary.

**3** Add bread and stock and heat. Reduce heat to medium-low; cover and cook vegetables for about 15 minutes until tender.

**4** Drain and rinse canned beans well in a colander. Pour beans into the pot and cook everything for about 25 more minutes, remembering occasionally to stir well—the soup should turn into a thick type of porridge (which will happen only if the bread dissolves thoroughly). Taste and season with salt and pepper as needed.

**5** Here's how to serve: peel red onion, cut in half and slice thinly into strips. Place onions, remaining olive oil, and soup pot separately on the table; give each person a wide soup bowl. Let each guest take some ribollita, which they can top with onion strips and drizzle with olive oil.

Prep time: 1 hour, 45 minutes of which you're actually busy
Calories per serving (4): 295

# Zuppa di pesce
Fish soup

### Soup that's a meal in itself

The more types of fish in the pot, the better.

Feeds 4 as an entire meal:
1¼ lbs. mixed fish (Salt water fish are best—have them filleted by your fishmonger, or purchase fillets)
4 oz. raw peeled and cleaned shrimp
½ lb. clams (or 4 oz. calamari rings)
3 cloves garlic
¾ cup fresh parsley sprigs
1 dried red chile
1 (14 oz.) can peeled tomatoes
1 tablespoon olive oil
½ cup dry white wine
1½ cup fish or vegetable stock (homemade or prepared)
4 large slices of white bread
Salt, freshly ground black pepper

**1** Cut fish fillets into pieces of about 1½". Leave shrimp whole. Rinse clams—throw away any that don't close during rinsing.

**2** Peel two of the garlic cloves. Rinse parsley, shake dry and pull off the leaves. Chop garlic, parsley and red chile very finely and mix together (always wear gloves when working with hot peppers). Chop tomatoes (reserve their juice from the can).

**3** In a large pot, heat olive oil and stir in garlic-parsley mixture. Add tomatoes, along with their juice, wine and fish stock and simmer uncovered for 15 minutes.

**4** Add clams to pot and bring to a rolling boil. Cover and cook for 5 minutes. Remove any clams that don't open. Now add fish and shrimp and turn the heat down low; cover and simmer 6–8 minutes.

**5** In the meantime, toast bread in the toaster or oven at 475°F. Peel remaining garlic clove and rub into bread slices. Cut bread slices in half and place in wide soup bowls. Season fish soup to taste with salt and pepper and ladle over the bread slices.

Prep time: 45 minutes, 30 of which you're actually busy
Delicious with: The wine used for cooking it
Calories per serving: 350

103

# Parmigiana di melanzane
## Eggplant au gratin

Also tastes great served at room temperature

Feeds 4 as a main dish or 8 as a side:

3–4 medium eggplant (about 2 lbs.)

Salt

3 balls fresh mozzarella (14 oz. total)

3/4 cup fresh basil sprigs

1 large (28 oz.) can peeled whole tomatoes

Freshly ground black pepper

2–3 tablespoons flour

2/3 cup olive oil

2 oz. freshly grated Parmesan

1 Rinse eggplant and trim off a little at both ends. Now slice lengthwise into slices about 1/2" thick. Sprinkle slices with salt and let stand 15 minutes.

2 In the meantime, drain the fresh mozzarella balls and slice thinly; set aside. Pull off basil leaves and chop finely. Chop tomatoes and put in a bowl with a little of the juice from the can.

3 Mix basil, salt and pepper with the tomatoes. In the meantime, the eggplant should have formed tiny water droplets. Pat them dry with paper towels. Spread flour on a plate. Season eggplant with pepper and dredge in the flour on both sides. Gently knock off extra flour so eggplant is only lightly coated.

4 Preheat the oven to 350°F. In a pan, heat 2 tablespoons of the olive oil, then turn it down to medium heat. Sauté one-fourth of the eggplant slices until brown on both sides. Remove. Put more oil in the pan and sauté the next batch of eggplant, continuing in this way. If desired, drain sautéed slices on paper towels.

5 Line a large baking dish (greased) with a layer of eggplant, spread with tomatoes and top with fresh mozzarella slices. Add another layer of sautéed eggplant and continue layering until all the ingredients are in the dish. Sprinkle with Parmesan and drizzle with remaining oil. Bake parmigiana on the middle rack for about 30 minutes until temptingly brown. Let rest 10 minutes, then cut and serve.

Prep time: At least 1 1/4 hours, 35 minutes of which you're actually busy
Delicious with: Bread and a light red wine; delicious as a dish to accompany roasted or grilled meats and fish
Calories per serving (4): 590

## Basic Tip

### Variations for experimenting

•Peeling the eggplant first with a vegetable peeler or sharp paring knife makes an even finer parmigiana.
•If desired, prepare a "genuine" tomato sauce (recipe on page 60), which makes the dish taste even better.
•Italians sometimes like to prepare this with 2 hard-boiled eggs, sliced thinly, and layered in with the other ingredients.

# Asparagi al forno
## Asparagus au gratin

It has to be green

Feeds 4 as a side dish or 2 as a small meal:

1 lb. green asparagus

Salt

1 tablespoon butter

1 tablespoon flour

2 cups milk (warmed)

3 oz. freshly grated Parmesan or pecorino

Freshly ground black pepper

Freshly grated nutmeg

**1** Rinse asparagus spears under cold water. Trim off the tough stem end up to the tender portion.

**2** In a pot wide enough to fit the length of the asparagus spears, bring salted water to a boil. Add asparagus and boil for 2 minutes; remove from water and transfer to a greased baking dish.

**3** For the sauce, melt butter in a pot over low heat but don't let it brown. Sprinkle in flour and stir thoroughly into the butter with a wooden spoon. Continue stirring until the flour changes to a more golden color. Then take a wire whisk and stir constantly while gradually adding the milk. Bring to a simmer and cook for about 5–10 minutes, stirring occasionally, till thickened.

**4** Preheat oven to 425°F.

**5** Stir half the Parmesan into the milk sauce and season with a little salt, pepper and nutmeg. Pour over the asparagus and then sprinkle remaining Parmesan on top. Bake on the middle rack for about 20 minutes until lightly browned.

Prep time: 20 minutes of activity,
20 minutes relaxing
Delicious with: Grilled or roasted meat or fish; as an appetizer with fresh bread or as a main dish served with potatoes
Calories per serving (2): 210

# Finocchi al forno
## Fennel au gratin

Costs almost nothing!

Feeds 4 as a side dish or 2 as a small meal:

2 fennel bulbs (about 1½ lbs.)

Salt

2 tomatoes

¼ cup bread crumbs

¼ cup freshly grated Parmesan

Freshly ground black pepper

2 tablespoons butter

**1** Remove wilted stalks/leaves from fennel and cut off thick green stems. Save the nice green fronds and set aside. Cut both bulbs in half lengthwise and then cut in half lengthwise once more. Cut out core and remove outer portion of bulb if tough. In a pot, bring to a boil about 2" of salted water. Add fennel quarters, cover and boil for 5 minutes.

**2** Meanwhile, rinse the tomatoes and dice them very finely (discard core/stem). Chop fennel fronds very finely. Drain cooked fennel in a colander and rinse under cold water.

**3** Preheat oven to 375°F. In a greased baking dish, lay the fennel quarters side by side. Top with tomatoes and season with salt. Combine bread crumbs with Parmesan, pepper and fennel fronds and sprinkle over the top. Cut butter into bits and lay on top.

**4** Bake fennel on the middle rack for about 20 minutes until the bread crumb mixture is nicely browned.

Prep time: 50 minutes, the first 30 of which you're actually busy
Delicious with: Grilled fish or meat; as a main dish served with potatoes or as a warm or room-temperature appetizer
Calories per serving (2): 250

## Variation: Cipolle al forno

### Roasted Onions
Peel 1 lb. onions, boil in salted water for about 10 minutes, rinse under cold water and drain. Cut onions into round slices 3/4" thick and lay out side by side in a large greased baking dish. Finely chop 1/2 cup fresh parsley sprigs and 8 sage leaves. Sprinkle the herbs, salt and pepper over the onions and drizzle with 1/4 cup olive oil. Bake onions on the middle rack at 375°F for about 40 minutes until nicely browned.

# Pomodori ripieni
## Stuffed tomatoes

### Filled with pleasure!

Feeds 4 as a side dish:

4 large or 8 medium tomatoes

1 can oil-packed sardines (don't confuse with anchovies; about 3 1/2 oz.)

2 tablespoons pitted black olives (preferably kalamata or Niçoise)

1/2 cup fresh parsley sprigs

1 onion

2 cloves garlic

1/4 cup olive oil

1/4 cup bread crumbs

1/4 cup freshly grated Parmesan

1 tablespoon fresh lemon juice

1 teaspoon lemon zest

Salt, freshly ground black pepper

**1** Rinse tomatoes and cut top off of each one—scoop out contents (reserve). Discard seeds and chop the rest of the contents finely. Drain outer shell of tomatoes upside down on paper towels (to be stuffed later).

**2** Drain sardines and chop. Dice pitted olives finely. Rinse parsley, pull off leaves and chop finely. Peel onion and garlic; chop both finely.

**3** Preheat oven to 350°F. In a pan, heat 1 tablespoon of the oil. Add and sauté onion and garlic. Stir in chopped tomato and parsley and cook uncovered over medium heat for about 5 minutes.

**4** Stir in olives and sardines. Remove pan from heat and let cool slightly, then add bread crumbs, Parmesan, lemon juice and lemon zest. Season with salt and pepper. Stuff the whole tomato shells by filling generously with the tomato-Parmesan-bread crumb mixture (overflowing is desirable). Arrange tomatoes side by side in a greased baking dish and sprinkle with remaining oil.

**5** Bake tomatoes on the middle rack for about 30 minutes until the tops are nicely browned.

Prep time: 50 minutes,
20 of which you're actually busy
Delicious with: Grilled fish or meat; or as a main dish with bread or risotto
Calories per serving: 220

# Fagioli all'uccelletto
## White beans with tomatoes and sage

Truly inexpensive

Feeds 4 as a side dish:

1 cup dried white beans

2 cloves garlic

6 leaves fresh sage

2 tablespoons olive oil

1 (14 oz.) can peeled tomatoes

Salt, freshly ground black pepper

**1** Pour water over beans in a bowl and soak overnight. For this recipe, canned beans don't work very well—they get too soft when stewed with the tomatoes.

**2** The next day, drain beans and transfer to a pot with fresh water. Cover, heat and simmer over medium heat for 1–1½ hours until almost tender.

**3** Peel garlic and mince. Rinse sage, shake dry and cut into strips.

**4** Chop tomatoes (reserve juice from can). Drain beans. Heat oil in a pot. Stir in garlic

and sage and sauté briefly. Pour tomatoes (along with juice) and beans into the pot, season with salt and pepper and simmer uncovered over medium heat for 20 minutes. Test a few beans for doneness. Adjust salt and pepper to taste.

Prep time: 2 hours, 20 minutes
of which you're actually busy
(not including overnight soaking)
Beans are also delicious with: Arista
(page 137) and fried salsicce (sausage)
as well as grilled meat and fish
Calories per serving: 200

# Peperonato
## Sautéed bell peppers

Tastes like southern Italy—served warm or cold

Feeds 6–8 as a side dish or appetizer:

2 yellow and 2 red bell peppers

(about 1¼ lbs.)

2 white onions (about ½ lb.)

2 cloves garlic

3 tablespoons olive oil

1 (14 oz.) can peeled tomatoes

Salt, freshly ground black pepper

1 pinch chili powder

2 tablespoons white wine vinegar

**1** Rinse bell peppers and cut off tops. Remove stem, seeds and ribs; cut rest into strips. Peel onions and garlic. Cut onions into rings and finely chop garlic.

**2** In a large pan, heat oil. Add bell peppers, onions and garlic and stir well.

**3** Chop tomatoes and pour along with their juice into the pan and season with salt, pepper and chili powder. Reduce to medium heat, cover and simmer peppers for 15–20 minutes until crisp-tender.

**4** Remove peppers from heat and let stand for about 5 minutes, then season to taste with vinegar and maybe a little more salt and chili powder. Serve immediately or let cool.

Prep time: 45 minutes,
20 of which you're actually busy
Bell peppers are also delicious with:
Grilled fish and meat, with pasta, or
as an appetizer (great for buffets)
Calories per serving (8): 70

# Spinaci al limone
### Spinach with lemon

### Simply good!

Feeds 4 as a side dish:

1½ lbs. spinach

Salt

½ lemon

2 cloves garlic

2 tablespoons olive oil

Freshly ground black pepper

**1** Rinse spinach several times and drain (make sure it is free of grit). Bring a pot of salted water to a boil. Throw in spinach, boil for 1 minute, drain and rinse under cold water.

**2** Rinse lemon and zest half. Squeeze out juice from half. Peel garlic.

**3** Heat oil in a pan. Add spinach, lemon zest and salt. Squeeze garlic through a press and add. Season spinach with salt and pepper, stir and heat quickly till very hot. Done!

Prep time: 20 minutes
Spinach is also delicious with: Meat and fish
Calories per serving: 75

# Caponata
### Sicilian eggplant

### Best with sunny summer eggplant

Feeds 4 as a side dish or appetizer:

2 stalks celery

1 onion

2 cloves garlic

1 eggplant (about ¾ lb.)

2 medium tomatoes
(or 1 large, about ½ lb. total)

6 tablespoons olive oil

Salt, freshly ground black pepper

1 tablespoon pitted green olives

½ cup fresh basil sprigs

2 tablespoons red wine vinegar

½ tablespoon sugar

1–2 tablespoons capers

1 tablespoon pine nuts

**1** Rinse celery, trim off ends of stalks and slice thinly. Peel onion and garlic. Cut onion in half and then into thin strips. Mince garlic. Rinse eggplant, cut crosswise into thin slices, then cut slices into fourths or eighths depending on how large the rounds are (bite-sized pieces). Rinse tomatoes and dice very finely.

**2** In a large pan, heat half the oil. Stir in at least half the eggplant and brown well over medium heat. Then remove, add another 2 tablespoons of the oil to the pan and brown the rest of the eggplant. Remove from the pan.

**3** In the pan, combine remaining oil, onion and garlic. Stir in eggplant, celery and tomatoes and season with salt and pepper. Cover and simmer vegetables over medium heat for about 5 minutes.

**4** In the meantime, chop olives; pull off basil leaves (brush off leaves if necessary) and leave whole.

**5** Add basil, olives, vinegar, sugar and capers to eggplant and cook uncovered for about 15 more minutes until the vegetables are almost creamy, stirring occasionally.

**6** Heat a small pan and toast pine nuts while stirring constantly until they're golden. Let caponata cool and sprinkle with pine nuts.

Prep time: 45 minutes,
25 of which you're actually busy
Caponata is also delicious with: Grilled fish and meat, with lamb dishes, with gnocchi (page 86) or even as an appetizer
Calories per serving: 180

# Patate con rosmarino
Rosemary potatoes

They rival
fried potatoes

Feeds 4 as a side dish:

1¼ lbs. potatoes (firm type: red, fingerling, or Yukon gold)

2 sprigs rosemary

3–4 tablespoons olive oil

Salt

**1** Scrub potatoes under running water. Then boil, for 20–30 minutes depending on size, until tender but not mushy. Drain and let cool.

**2** Peel cooled potatoes and quarter lengthwise. Rinse rosemary, shake dry and strip off needles. Chop needles if desired.

**3** In a large frying pan, heat oil. Add potatoes, preferably side by side. Brown over medium heat and turn. Add rosemary, season with salt and pepper and cook for another 5 minutes or less.

Prep time: 50 minutes (not including cooling time), 20 of which you're actually busy
Calories per serving: 210

# Carote al Marsala
Carrots in a Marsala sauce

Just like mamma in Sicily used to make

Feeds 4 as a side dish:

1¼ lb. carrots

2 tablespoons butter

½ cup dry Marsala

Salt, freshly ground black pepper

½ cup fresh parsley sprigs

1 teaspoon fresh lemon juice

**1** Peel carrots and trim ends. Quarter lengthwise, then cut into strips about 1½" long.

**2** Melt butter in a pot but don't let it brown. Add carrots and sauté over medium-low heat for 5 minutes. Stir diligently.

**3** Pour in Marsala. Season carrots with salt and pepper. Cover and cook for 10–15 minutes or until carrots are crisp-tender.

**4** In the meantime, rinse parsley, shake dry, pull off leaves and chop finely. Add to carrots along with fresh lemon juice. Adjust salt and pepper and serve.

Prep time: 30 minutes,
15 of which you're actually busy
Carrots are also delicious with: Roasts, poultry, scaloppine (page 132) and costolette alla milanese (page 134)
Calories per serving: 100

# Funghi trifolati
Herbed mushrooms

So good, there's never any left over

If you do have leftovers, enjoy mushrooms cold, since they don't reheat well.

Feeds 4 as a side dish:

1 lb. fresh mushrooms (very fancy: mixed, with fresh porcini)

2 cloves garlic

3 tablespoons olive oil

½ cup fresh parsley sprigs

Salt, freshly ground black pepper

Freshly grated nutmeg

1 teaspoon grated lemon zest

**1** Wipe mushrooms with paper towels (moisten paper towel if necessary). Cut off and discard ends of stems and slice mushrooms thinly. Peel garlic and mince.

**2** Heat a large pan (cast iron is especially good). Pour in oil, add mushrooms and sauté well over high heat while stirring constantly.

**3** Add garlic. Turn heat down to low, cover and cook for another 10 minutes.

**4** In the meantime, rinse parsley, shake dry, pull off leaves and chop finely. Stir into mushrooms and season generously with salt, pepper, a pinch of nutmeg and the lemon zest. These mushrooms taste best when hot.

Prep time: 30 minutes
Mushrooms are also delicious with:
scaloppine (page 132), lamb and game, pasta and gnocchi (page 86)
Calories per serving: 90

# Carciofi arrostiti
## Sautéed artichokes

### Don't use the big fat French artichokes!

Feeds 4 as a side dish:

6 small artichokes (the Italian ones, about 1¼ lbs.)

1 tablespoon fresh lemon juice

½ cup fresh parsley sprigs

2 cloves garlic

2 tablespoons olive oil

Salt, freshly ground black pepper

**1** Tear off outer leaves from artichokes until you get to the lighter, more tender leaves. A tip from Mamma: Test a leaf by biting it near the root. It should be fresh and tender! Then cut off the dark leaf tips. Pare the stems down to a point. Cut artichokes into eighths lengthwise (i.e. through the stems). Mix with fresh lemon juice.

**2** Rinse parsley, shake dry and pull off leaves. Peel garlic; chop parsley and garlic finely.

**3** In a large pan (preferably cast iron), heat oil. Stir in artichokes and sauté on medium heat for about 5 minutes, stirring occasionally.

**4** Stir in parsley and garlic. Season artichokes with salt and pepper and cook for about another 2 minutes until crisp-tender. Serve warm.

Prep time: 30 minutes
Artichokes are also delicious with:
arista (page 137) and roast lamb
Calories per serving: 80

### Tip

How about using marinated artichoke hearts? No, that won't work. They'll heat up fine but they'll never achieve that delicate flavor. This dish can really succeed only if you use the small, fine, fresh artichokes that are even eaten raw in Italy. They're easiest to find in the winter and early spring—at farmer's markets or specialty grocery stores.

# Pesce

Mackerel, sardines, sole, scorpion fish, trout, tuna, swordfish...

# etcetera

## [Fish and so on]

Even though many Italians have moved to the big cities instead of dwelling in the fishing villages on Capri AND even though Italian fishermen haul fewer catches out of the Mediterranean...pesce is still a big part of Italian cuisine.

If you went to see an Italian fishmonger and they were out of your favorite fish, you'd hardly notice. There would still be mackerel, red mullet, sardines, sole, all types of bream, scorpion fish, trout, tuna and swordfish, as well as various crustaceans, squid and Mediterranean mussels—no lack for sea creatures to choose from!

With a selection like that, you don't need much more to put a good meal on the table. Italian fish cuisine is quick and uncomplicated—grilled, pan-fried or deep-fried whole—with olive oil, garlic and herbs.

In America, it takes some effort to find fresh fish. Seek out your local fishmonger, try reputable farmer's markets, or even Asian markets or specialty markets. If you live by the coast—you can go to the dock and see who's selling!

# Help, how do I fillet a fish?

If necessary, scale the fish: Because this makes a big mess, do it in the sink with a towel wrapped around the tail. With the back of a knife blade, scrape off the scales from the tail side to the head side. Cut off the fins (top and bottom) with scissors (from tail to head).

To gut the fish, carefully slit open the belly (under-side) with the tip of a sharp knife from the tail to the head. Starting at the tail, loosen the entrails with your finger but don't rupture the dark bladder. (It's OK to wear gloves!) The dark spot (kidneys) can be flushed out under cold water.

In the case of small fish (e.g. fresh sardines), make a slit behind the gills and up to the spine on both sides. Holding the knife even with the spine, cut through from the head to the tail with a single cut—releasing tiny fillets on both sides. For larger fish, cut off the head and make a cut down the back, close to the spine. The underside is already cut. Then cut the fillet away from the skeleton by sliding your very sharp knife between the fillet and the bones. Cut off the tail.

To skin the fillet, lay it on a cutting board, skin side down. In one hand, hold one side of the fillet. Slide a very sharp knife between the skin and the fillet and slide it away from you to remove the skin.

### Aunt Edna's Lonely Baked Fish
## Filetto delizioso

Whenever I'm down, I make fish. But just for myself. I've always done this, even back when I couldn't cook and shoved frozen fish sticks into the oven. Now, I bake "Filetto delizioso": I salt 1 fresh fish fillet—fresh cod, sole, or halibut—and massage it with olive oil. Then I mix 1 tablespoon bread crumbs, 1 tablespoon Parmesan, 1 teaspoon ground almonds and 1 teaspoon chopped parsley and spread a thick layer of this mixture on the fillet. Then I finely chop some fresh and marinated ingredients to add: either 1) green onions and sun-dried tomatoes (oil-packed type, drained), 2) cherry tomatoes and artichoke hearts or 3) radicchio, mushrooms and bacon. If I'm not planning on socializing, I mix in some minced garlic, too. The amount depends on how long I want to be left alone. In any case, I add 1 tablespoon olive oil and a squirt of fresh lemon juice. I put all this in a baking dish, lay the fillet on top, sprinkle with a little more olive oil and bake at 375°F for at least 10 minutes. What a mood-lifter!

Our Favorite Seafood

# The Whole Fish

Whole fish are:
• Beloved when mackerel (sgombro), gray mullet (cefalo), red mullet (triglie), sardine (sarde), dentex/sea bream (dentice), porgy (pagro) and trout (trota)
• Sophisticated when gilt-head sea bream (orata), sole (sogliola), turbot (rombo) or sea bass/loup de mer (branzino)
• A rarity when scorpion fish (scorfano) and young hake (nasello)
• Often available frozen—ask your fishmonger about the availability of the above

Whole fish should be:
• Very fresh, recognizable by bulging clear eyes, moist red gills, shiny skin and firm meat that springs back to the touch
• Scaled if necessary and already cleaned if possible
• Refrigerated on ice, tightly covered, and kept no longer than 1–2 days
• Thawed slowly in the refrigerator (if previously frozen)

Whole fish need:
• To be prepared simply with few but distinctive flavors—such as herbs, olive oil, lemon, garlic, salt and pepper—in a pan or on the grill
• Or to be baked in the oven, with vegetables or a simple stuffing in their cavity
• Or to be deep-fried when very young
• To be cut open before cooking if large

Whole fish love:
• Butter, olive oil, pesto, white wine, lemon
• Fennel greens, oregano, bay leaf, rosemary, sage and thyme when grilled and sautéed
• Basil and parsley in stuffings and side dishes
• Fennel seed, capers, garlic, almonds, olives, Parmesan, pine nuts, anchovies
• Peas, fennel, bell peppers, mushrooms, green asparagus, spinach, tomatoes, zucchini
• Potatoes, pasta, rice
• Sometimes even: bacon, red wine

Five Tips for the Pesce-Challenged:
# Even More Fish
## (and Seafood)

There were days when Italian fisherman netted nothing but sardines and sole out of the Mediterranean. But now look what can you find on an Italian seafood platter:

### Tuna & Swordfish
Tonno and spada are warm-blooded and muscular, which is why their meat is more like beef or veal than fish. They're available as steaks that taste best sautéed.

### Dried & Salt Cod
Although it comes out of the Atlantic, "baccalà" is genuine Italian. On the coasts of Portugal, Spain and Norway, cod, pollock and shellfish are dried in the sun and wind to produce dried or salt-preserved fish. Italian salt traders of old are believed to have introduced "baccalà" to Italy in the course of their business. They get soaked in water for 1 to 7 days and stewed for hours in milk and olive oil or with tomatoes, or even deep-fried.

### Scampi & Gamberi
As can be seen by their claws, scampi are related to crabs and lobsters. Gamberi are prawns with feelers instead of claws and a sharply curving tail. Both taste especially delicious grilled in the shell.

### Squid & Octopus
This is complicated because Italians don't agree among themselves. Let's just say that in Italy, calamaro and seppia are squid whose body (never longer than 3 inches) is grilled, stuffed or deep-fried. Polpo is small octopus, cooked whole (never larger than 6 inches), either briefly or for a minimum of 1 hour.

### Mussels & Clams
Mussels (cozze) are usually cooked with wine, vegetables and herbs (page 118). Clams (vongole) are used in the popular Italian dish spaghetti vongole (page 66). The same rule applies to both: Throw away any that stay open before cooking. Throw away any that stay closed after cooking.

# Pesce misto ai ferri
Grilled fish

### BBQ Italian-style

Italian mayonnaise (maionese) is made with extra virgin olive oil.

Feeds 4 garlic lovers:

$1^3/_4$ lbs. fish fillets (preferably mixed: monkfish, swordfish, rockfish, tuna); whole sardines or whole trout; raw shrimp with peel-on

Salt, freshly ground black pepper

$1/_4$ cup olive oil

**For the maionese:**

2 very fresh egg yolks

(from pasteurized eggs if possible)

$1/_2$ cup extra virgin olive oil

2–4 cloves garlic

$1/_4$ cup fresh parsley sprigs

2 teaspoons capers

$1^1/_2$ tablespoons lemon juice or to taste

Salt

A little chili powder

**1** Place rinsed fillets, whole fish and shrimp in a glass bowl. Stir salt and pepper into oil and drizzle over the top; briefly toss. Set aside while making the maionese. Also, make sure grill is heating up (takes 30 minutes) — or you can use the broiler.

**2** For the maionese sauce, place room temperature egg yolks in a small bowl and whisk until smooth. Place a towel under the bowl to stabilize, then add the oil (also room temperature) drop by drop, whisking vigorously. When it takes on a fine sheen, you can be a little braver and add the oil by the teaspoonful. Most importantly, keep whisking. You should end up with a bowl of thick sauce.

**3** And now you'll pep it up: Peel garlic, squeeze through a press and add to the sauce. Finely chop parsley and capers and stir in. Season the maionese with fresh lemon juice, salt and chili powder. Keep maionese refrigerated until serving time. Always remember not to serve raw egg products to young children or the elderly.)

**4** Hopefully the grill is hot, or you can heat up the oven broiler (takes 3 minutes). Place fish pieces on the rack or under the broiler and grill/broil for 5–7 minutes, then turn and grill/broil another 5–7 minutes. Serve with maionese!

Prep time: 30 minutes
(not including heating grill)
Delicious with: Crusty white bread, a tossed salad and a light, dry white wine
Calories per serving: 555

# Pesce aglio olio
## Fish in garlic olive oil

Presto!

Feeds 4 in a hurry:

3–4 cloves garlic

6 tablespoons olive oil

1³/₄ lbs. fish fillets (cod, salmon, swordfish, sole, halibut) or raw, peeled shrimp

Salt, freshly ground black pepper

2 tablespoons flour or more as needed

Lemon wedges

**1** Peel garlic; quarter and slice half into thin strips and chop the rest.

**2** Rinse fish fillets and pat dry. Sprinkle salt and pepper on both sides of each and dredge with flour: spread flour on a large plate and simply lay the fish on it (do both sides). A little flour will stick, and that's enough.

**3** Heat oil in a large pan. Add garlic strips and sauté over medium heat for about a minute or until lightly golden.

**4** Remove garlic strips from oil; set aside. Place fish fillets in the oil, sprinkle with the chopped garlic and sauté for 1–2 minutes on each side (longer for thick fillets—until opaque throughout). Done! Cut lemon into wedges and serve alongside.

Prep time: 15 minutes
Delicious with: Spinach or caponata (page 109), fresh white bread and a hearty white or light red wine
Calories per serving: 330

# Involtini di pesce
## Fish spirals

**Important: The fillets must be nice and thin**

Feeds 4 as a secundo:

8 thin slices of fish fillets (halibut, sole or get a fishmonger's recommendation, about 3 oz. per slice)

4 anchovy fillets in oil

1 onion

2 cloves garlic

1/3 cup olive oil + oil for the baking dish

2 tablespoons Grappa liqueur (optional)

2 tablespoons bread crumbs

4 bay leaves

Salt, freshly ground black pepper

4 1/2 oz. fresh mozzarella

1/2 cup fresh parsley sprigs

3–4 sprigs fresh oregano

1/4 cup fresh lemon juice

1 Rinse all fish fillet slices and pat dry. Finely dice 2 fish slices. Drain and finely chop anchovies. Peel onion and garlic; chop both finely.

2 In a pan, heat 2 tablespoons of the olive oil. Add and sauté onion and garlic briefly. Add diced fish, chopped anchovies and whole bay leaves; sauté a couple minutes, stirring. Add Grappa and bread crumbs; season with salt and a little pepper and transfer to a mixing bowl. Remove and discard bay leaves.

3 Preheat oven to 375°F. Now back to the fish slices: Cut them in half lengthwise so you'll have 12 pieces on the table. Top each piece with a little of the sautéed fish mixture. Drain fresh mozzarella, cut into paper-thin slices and lay on top of each strip. Grind pepper over the top.

4 Roll up fish slices. Place side by side in a large, greased baking dish.

5 Rinse parsley and oregano and shake dry; remove from stems and chop very finely. Combine fresh lemon juice and remaining oil in a small bowl and whisk vigorously until cloudy. Stir in herbs. Season oil mixture with salt and pepper and drizzle over the fish rolls.

6 Bake rolls on the middle rack for 20 minutes until fish is opaque throughout.

Prep time: 50 minutes, 20 of which you can relax
Delicious with: Rosemary potatoes (p. 110), spinach with lemon (p. 109) and a dry white wine
Calories per serving: 350

# Cozze al vino bianco
## Mussels in white wine

**Finger food from bella Italia**

Loved by many and abhorred by as many, mussels are a matter of taste. We love them! Basic tip: the cooking liquid must be boiling when you add the mussels.

Feeds 4 as a small meal:

6 1/2 lbs. live mussels

1 carrot

1 onion

4 cloves garlic

2 stalks celery

3/4 cup fresh basil or parsley sprigs

1–2 sprigs fresh thyme

(or 1/4 teaspoon dried thyme)

2 tablespoons olive oil

2 whole canned peeled tomatoes

2 1/4 cups dry white wine

1 bay leaf

Salt, freshly ground black pepper

1 Rinse live mussels under cold water. If the shells are dirty, scrub with a brush—but the fishmonger can do this for you. Throw away

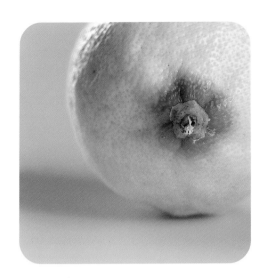

any mussels that remain open when you rinse them.

**2** Peel carrots, onion and garlic and rinse celery. Finely chop all four ingredients. Pull off basil leaves (or parsley) and chop. Rinse thyme and strip off leaves.

**3** In your largest pot, heat oil. Stir in chopped vegetables and sauté briefly; stir constantly. Add herbs. Finely chop tomato and add along with wine. Add bay leaf, season with salt and pepper and bring to a boil.

**4** When the liquid is boiling, throw in the mussels, cover and keep the heat turned up high. Wait 8–10 minutes. Don't remove the lid but from time to time shake the pot back and forth to shift the mussels.

**5** Remove the lid and look at the mussels. Most of them should be open. If a large number are closed, boil for another 2–3 minutes. Throw away any that are still closed. Remove and discard bay leaf. Serve open mussels in the cooking liquid. Add more chopped herbs, salt and pepper to taste.

Prep time: 45 minutes, 35 of which you're actually busy
Delicious with: A lot of fresh, crusty white bread and vino
Calories per serving: 265

# Cozze gratinate
## Mussel gratin

### Also can be an appetizer for a large number

Feeds 4 as a full meal:

4$^1$/$_2$ lbs. mussels

2$^1$/$_4$ cups dry white wine

1 bay leaf

Salt, freshly ground black pepper

1$^1$/$_2$ cups day-old bread chunks

or $^3$/$_4$ cup breadcrumbs

3 cloves garlic

1 dried red chile or $^1$/$_2$ teaspoon crushed

red pepper flakes (optional)

$^3$/$_4$ cup fresh parsley sprigs

4 tomatoes

2 small eggs

2 oz. freshly grated Parmesan

2 tablespoons olive oil

**1** Rinse mussels under cold water (scrub if necessary). Throw away any that remain open.

**2** In a large pot, bring to a boil wine, bay leaf, salt and pepper. Add mussels, cover and leave heat turned up high. Boil vigorously for

8–10 minutes, then look to see whether the mussels have opened. If most are still closed, try another 2–3 minutes. Then, throw away any that are still closed.

**3** Preheat oven to 425°F. Get the broiler pan ready (the deep baking pan part).

**4** Crumble bread/break into bits. Peel garlic, squeeze through a press and add to bread. Finely crush dried red chile in a mortar or chop (wear gloves and don't touch your eyes)—or use flakes. Rinse parsley, shake dry and chop leaves very finely. Rinse tomatoes and dice very finely. Add chopped garlic, chile, parsley, tomatoes, eggs and Parmesan to bread; mix well and season with salt.

**5** Drain mussels and break off empty shell halves and discard. Place all shell halves containing mussels in the broiler pan. Sprinkle bread mixture on to the top of each mussel. Drizzle with oil. Bake mussels on the middle rack for about 10 minutes until the topping is slightly browned. These taste best warm!

Prep time: At least 1 hour, 15 minutes of which you can relax
Calories per serving: 330

# Pesce al forno
## Roasted fish with tomatoes

Fresh and refreshing!

Makes enough for 4:

1½ lbs. fresh fish fillets

(e.g. salmon, sole, halibut)

Salt, freshly ground black pepper

2–3 fresh tomatoes or 1 (14 oz.) can

whole peeled tomatoes

2–3 cloves garlic

½ red onion

½ cup fresh basil sprigs

½ cup fresh parsley sprigs

1 sprig fresh rosemary

½ dried red chile or ½ teaspoon

crushed red pepper flakes (optional)

3 tablespoons olive oil

1 Preheat oven to 375°F.

2 Rinse fillets and pat dry, then cut each into serving portions. Season on both sides with salt and pepper and arrange side by side in a greased baking dish.

3 Rinse tomatoes (unless canned type), cut in half and slice thinly into wedges. Peel garlic and halve red onion; finely chop both.

4 Rinse herbs and shake dry; remove leaves from stems and chop finely. Finely crush dried red chile in a mortar or chop (wear gloves and don't touch your face)—or use flakes.

5 Combine chopped onion, garlic, herbs and crushed chile and sprinkle over fish fillets. Top with tomato wedges and season with salt and pepper. Drizzle oil over everything, then bake fish in the oven on the middle shelf for 15–20 minutes or until opaque throughout.

Prep time: 35 minutes, 15 of which
you're actually busy
Delicious with: Lemon wedges, rosemary
potatoes (page 110) or fresh Italian bread
and a light white wine
Calories per serving: 220

## Variations:

### With Whole Small Fish

For special occasions, try baking whole small fish such as cleaned sardines or red mullets (ask your fishmonger). The cooking time and temperature is about the same. Prepare the same mixtures as above and sprinkle on or stuff a bunch of the small fish before drizzling oil on top. Bake until fish are opaque throughout—test one for doneness.

### With Whole Large fish

To make orata alla pugliese, buy 1 cleaned, gilt-head sea bream weighing about 2¼ lbs. (ask your fishmonger). Or use another type of whole fish, such as trout (cook 2 to 3 of them if 10–12 oz. each). Have fish cleaned by the fishmonger. Rinse, season with salt and pepper outside and inside and likewise drizzle with 2 tablespoons fresh lemon juice. Peel about 1 lb. potatoes (any type) and slice paper thin or as thinly as possible. Put in salted water until ready to use. Finely chop 1 fresh red chile or jalapeño (optional—omit seeds and ribs for less heat), ¾ cup fresh parsley sprigs and 2 peeled garlic cloves. Brush olive oil onto a baking dish large enough to hold the sea bream or several whole trout (or other fish). Drain and pat dry potatoes—line baking dish with a layer of potatoes arranged in an overlapped fashion. Season with salt and pepper and lay the fish on top. Cover with remaining potatoes. Sprinkle with parsley-garlic mixture and drizzle with about ⅓ cup olive oil. Bake at 350°F for about 50 minutes or until fish is/are opaque throughout. Cut into one to check for doneness. Serve, but remind guests to check for bones.

# Trote al vino bianco
## Trout in white wine

### Simple, fast and impressive

Feeds 4 who don't mind picking out bones:

4 whole trout (about 10 oz. each)

½ lemon

Salt, freshly ground black pepper

1 carrot

1 stalk celery

2–3 cloves garlic

½ cup fresh parsley sprigs

1 sprig each of fresh rosemary, thyme and marjoram

¼ cup olive oil or more as needed

2¼ cups dry white wine or more as needed

**1** Rinse trout well inside and out. The slightly slippery coating should rinse off. Pat fish dry with paper towels, especially on the outside.

**2** Rinse lemon, dry and remove zest from half. Halve and then squeeze out juice from one half. Combine lemon zest and juice with salt and pepper—use to season fish, especially the inside.

**3** Peel carrot. Rinse celery and trim ends. Pull off any loose threads. Cut both carrot and celery into long strips; then dice finely.

**4** Peel garlic and mince. Rinse herbs, shake dry, remove leaves from stems and chop very finely.

**5** And now the big question: Do you have a pan large enough to hold all the fish side by side? If yes, great! If not, you'll have to use two pans plus a little more oil and wine.

**6** Heat oil in one pan, or in two simultaneously. Combine garlic, carrot, celery and herbs and sauté (if necessary, divide equally between the pans). Add fish and brown lightly on each side.

**7** Now pour in the wine. If you're using two pans, you'll probably need a whole bottle (about 2 cups in each pan). To reduce the sauce, cook the fish uncovered at medium-high for about 15 minutes, turning once halfway through. To keep the fish from falling apart, lift each fish individually with a spatula underneath and a spoon on top and turn very carefully. If it does fall apart, it will still taste delicious with the tangy sauce. Season the pan juices with salt and pepper right at the end, otherwise it may become too salty. Then bring it to the table where each person can fight with their own fish bones!

Prep time: 40 minutes, 25 of which you're actually busy
Delicious with: Fresh Italian bread, possibly spinach, and the same white wine you used for cooking, but make sure it's chilled!
Tip: buy 2–3 bottles of the same wine to begin with
Calories per serving: 420

# Pesce con olive e capperi
## Fish in olive caper oil

### Ready to eat in a flash

Feeds 4 in a hurry:

1 tablespoon fresh lemon juice

4 fish fillets (halibut, sole, turbot, cod, pollock, or swordfish—in any case, saltwater/ocean variety, with each portion weighing around 6 oz.)

Salt, freshly ground black pepper

10 sun-dried tomatoes in oil

10 pitted black olives, preferably

kalamata or Niçoise

1 tablespoon capers

2 cloves garlic

½ cup fresh parsley sprigs

3 tablespoons olive oil

**1** Rinse fish fillets and drizzle lemon juice on them. Season both sides with salt and pepper.

**2** Drain sun-dried tomatoes and chop. Chop pitted olives finely. Coarsely chop capers and peel and chop garlic. Rinse parsley and shake dry; remove leaves and chop finely. Combine all these chopped ingredients on a plate (spread out) and dip the fish fillets into them on both sides.

**3** Pour oil into a large pan and heat. Sauté fish for 1-2 minutes on each side or more, until opaque throughout. Stir remaining herb mixture into the pan and sauté briefly to use as a condiment for the fish—dinner is served!

Prep time: 15 minutes
Delicious with: Tossed salad or spinach with lemon (page 109) and crusty white bread
Calories per serving: 230

# Seppie in umido
## Squid stew

The tiny pinch of cinnamon makes it buonissimo!

Feeds 4 who don't mind waiting:

1¾ lbs. squid tubes/fillets (cleaned by your fishmonger)

2 fresh red chiles or jalapeños (optional)

4 cloves garlic

1 onion

1 cup fresh basil sprigs

¼ cup olive oil

1 (14 oz.) can peeled tomatoes

½ cup dry red wine and/or fish stock

Salt, 1 pinch cinnamon

**1** Rinse squid under cold water and pat dry. Leave small ones whole. Cut the larger squid fillets into pieces or rings, depending on the type. (Just make sure all are bite-sized.)

**2** Rinse chiles, remove stems and cut open peppers. And again the question: Very hot or mildly hot? If you don't want it too hot, scrape out the seeds and membranes and chop rest very finely. For the super-hot

version, finely chop whole chiles. (In either case, wear gloves or wash your hands well, and don't touch your eyes.) Peel garlic and onion and finely chop. Rinse basil, shake dry and remove leaves; set a few aside for later and chop the rest finely.

**3** Heat oil and sauté chiles, garlic, onion and basil. Add squid and sauté briefly.

**4** Chop tomatoes and add with their juice to squid along with wine (and/or stock). Season all with salt and 1 tiny pinch of cinnamon. Turn heat down to low, cover and simmer stew for about 1 hour until the squid is very tender (test a piece). See if the sauce needs a little more salt or a dash cinnamon. Finally, tear apart remaining basil leaves and sprinkle over the top.

Prep time: 1¼ hours, 15 minutes of which you're actually busy
Delicious with: Crusty white bread and red wine—a winning combination for spicy dishes
Calories per serving: 270

# Pesce con salsa di rucola
## Fish with arugula sauce

Light, fresh and delizioso

Feeds 4 arugula lovers:

1 bunch green onions (5–6)

1 bunch arugula (about 1 cup leaves)

2 cloves garlic

1½ lbs. fish fillets (e.g. halibut, swordfish, salmon)

Salt, freshly ground black pepper

¼ cup olive oil

1 tablespoon butter

2 tablespoons pine nuts

⅓ cup fish stock (or vegetable stock or water)

¾ cup cherry tomatoes

1 tablespoon lemon juice

**1** Remove any wilted parts and the root end from green onions, then rinse and chop rest. Remove thick stems and any wilted leaves from arugula, submerge the rest in cold water and swish back and forth to rinse; drain. Save a few arugula leaves for garnishing, and chop the rest finely. Peel garlic and mince.

**2** Rinse fish fillets well; pat dry. Season on both sides with salt and pepper.

**3** Set oven to 150°F and warm an oven safe platter in it. In a large pan on the stove, heat 2 tablespoons of the oil and the butter.

**4** Sauté fish fillets in the pan over medium heat for 1–2 minutes on each side or until opaque throughout. Transfer to the platter in the oven, covered with foil or a large oven-safe bowl.

**5** Pour pine nuts into the previously-used pan and toast over medium heat until golden-brown. Add remaining oil, green onions and garlic and sauté for a couple minutes, stirring occasionally. Add finely chopped arugula and fish stock and simmer on low for a few more minutes.

**6** In the meantime, rinse cherry tomatoes and quarter (to use as a garnish). Finely purée the arugula sauce with a hand blender (or blender) and season with lemon juice, salt and pepper to taste. Remove warmed fish fillets from the oven; pour arugula sauce over the top and garnish with tomatoes and reserved arugula. Serve immediately.

Prep time: 40 minutes
Delicious with: Italian bread or rosemary potatoes (page 110)
Calories per serving: 300

# Pesce con salsa di zafferano
## Fish with a bell pepper-saffron sauce

Yellow and green and good!

Feeds 4 colorful types:

1 yellow bell pepper

1 tomato

2 cloves garlic

¾ cup fresh basil sprigs

⅓ cup olive oil

½ cup fish stock (or vegetable stock)

1½ lbs. fish fillets (e.g. sole, cod or halibut)

Salt, freshly ground black pepper

Several threads saffron

2 teaspoons fresh lemon juice

**1** Rinse bell pepper, cut in half and remove stem and contents; dice rest. Rinse tomato and dice finely (discard stem/core). Peel garlic and mince. Rinse basil, pull off leaves and set aside. Coarsely chop stems.

**2** In a pot, heat 2 tablespoons of the oil. Sauté bell pepper, basil stems and garlic for a couple minutes, stirring. Add diced tomato and stock. Reduce heat to medium-low and simmer uncovered for about 10 minutes. Bell pepper should be soft rather than crisp-tender.

**3** In the meantime, rinse and pat dry fish fillets. Sprinkle both sides with salt and pepper.

**4** When the bell pepper cubes are soft, purée the sauce finely with a hand blender (or blender). Stir saffron into a little hot tap water and add mixture into the sauce. Season to taste with salt, pepper and lemon juice. Strain to discard pepper skins if desired.

**5** In a large pan, heat remaining oil. Add fish fillets and sauté for one minute, then turn (with a metal or hard melamine spatula so they won't fall apart) and sauté the other side for 1 minute (longer for thicker fillets— until opaque throughout).

**6** Cut basil leaves into strips and stir into the sauce or use as a garnish. Transfer fish fillets to four plates (preferably pre-warmed in a 150°F oven), top with sauce and serve.

Prep time: 35 minutes
Delicious with: Crusty Italian bread and spinach with butter and garlic
Calories per serving: 260

# Pesce alla siciliana
## Fresh tuna with an orange-lemon sauce

Imparts a tart flavor

This flavorful and hearty sauce goes well with any hearty fish.

Feeds 4 Sicily lovers:

2 oranges

1 1/2 lemons

4 fresh tuna steaks (about 6 oz. each)

Salt, freshly ground black pepper

3 tablespoons olive oil

1/3 cup dry Marsala wine

(may substitute white wine)

3 tablespoons cold butter

**1** Rinse oranges and lemons and dry. Zest 1 orange and both lemons and mince zest. Make sure you don't remove the white part with the zest—it imparts a bitter taste. Squeeze out juice from all the oranges and from 1 1/2 lemons.

**2** Season tuna generously with salt and pepper on both sides. Set oven to 150°F and heat a platter or large plate (oven-safe type).

**3** In a large pan, heat olive oil. Add fish fillets and sauté over medium heat for about 3 minutes. Then turn and sauté another 3 minutes or until opaque throughout. (Less time if fillets are less thick.) Transfer from the pan to the platter in the oven, covered with tinfoil, to keep warm.

**4** Pour orange juice, lemon juice and Marsala into the pan, turn up the heat to medium-high and reduce sauce slightly, stirring. Cut butter into small bits and whisk into the sauce. Stir in lemon and orange zest and season sauce to taste with salt and pepper. Pour over the fish—don't wait too long because fish tastes best when very hot!

Prep time: 30 minutes
Delicious with: Italian bread and caponata (page 109), plus white wine
Calories per serving: 580

# Fritto misto
## Mixed deep-fried fish

### Not so heavy because there's no batter

And with a few vegetables to give it even more variety.

Feeds 6 as a full meal:

3/4 lb. squid

(preferably small tubes and tentacles)

Salt

3/4 lb. raw, peeled and cleaned shrimp

1 lb. fresh sardines

1 1/4 lb. other small fish or fillets

(e.g. red mullet or small fillets of sole

or other white fish)

6 baby onions (can also be green onions)

6 small fresh Italian artichokes

or 6 marinated artichoke hearts

3 stalks celery or cardoon (a type of thistle

that looks similar to celery stalks and can

sometimes be found at farmer's markets)

Freshly ground black pepper

Flour for coating

4 1/2 cups olive oil (NOT extra virgin)

3 lemons

1 Rinse squid. To keep it from getting tough when you fry it, immerse for 30 seconds into a pot of boiling salted water. In a colander, rinse with cold water and drain; pat dry.

2 Rinse shrimp and fish. You can leave the heads and fins on sardines and other tiny whole fish. Rinse and pat dry fish fillets.

3 Peel baby onions and leave whole. Remove artichoke hearts from the jar and drain. If you managed to find fresh small ones, prepare them exactly as described on page 111. Rinse celery or cardoon, trim off ends and cut stalks crosswise into pieces about 1 1/2" long.

4 Season all fish and vegetables with salt and pepper. Spread flour on a large plate and lay fish on top. Using two forks, turn until fish are evenly coated on all sides with a thin layer of flour. Then do the same with the vegetables on a separate plate with flour.

5 Pour oil into the largest pot you have. Heat till very hot (use an oil thermometer and keep oil around 350–375 degrees, no higher). Set oven to 150ºF and place a large oven-safe platter in it.

6 Now for the finale: With a slotted metal spoon or skimmer, add as much fish and vegetables to the hot oil as can fit side by side. Squid and shrimp take 2–3 minutes, fresh sardines about 3, large red mullets take 4 minutes and thicker fish fillets about 5. Deep-fry the vegetables until they take on a nice color. Remove anything that's done with the metal utensil and let it drain for a moment over the pot. Put paper towels on top of the platter in the oven and transfer the fried fish and vegetables to it. When all has been fried, cut a lemon into 8 wedges and serve it up with the fritto misto!

Prep time: 70–90 minutes
Delicious with: A lot of crusty bread and a dry white wine
Calories per serving: 490

## Basic Tip

Deep-frying is easy, provided the oil is at the right temperature. Otherwise the fish and vegetables will soak up the oil instead of fry. To find out whether the oil is hot enough, lower the handle of a wooden mixing spoon into it. A lot of tiny bubbles should rise around the handle. If there are only a few bubbles, it's still too early. Or throw in a cube of white bread (on second thought, drop it gently so you don't splash the oil). If it turns brown in 1 minute, you can start. Or for the conscientious, use an oil thermometer—it's ready when it reads between 350-375 degrees.

# Carne

Mamma Mia! Where's the meat?

# etcetera

## [Meat and so on]

And God created Italy. With a wave of his finger, God piled up the Apennines in the Mediterranean, surrounded them with beaches, scattered around a few cities that immediately began to spread like wildfire, and made the rest into soccer fields.

But just as God made the Italians, they began to complain. "Dio! What are we supposed to eat?" So God tossed a rainbow of fish into the sea, planted durum wheat and firewood for pizza ovens and sent Columbus to the Americas to bring back tomatoes. "Mamma mia!" exclaimed the Italians, "Where's the meat?" So God made livestock and poultry rain down from the sky. "Now we don't have enough room!" called the Italians. That made God frustrated: "From now on, you'll have to work it out for yourselves and I'm just going to sit back and watch."

Since then, Italians prefer eating either animals when they're small (veal and lamb) or animals that never get too big (chickens or rabbits). Only pigs are allowed to reach their full size but then the sausage or ham is hung in the air where there's more room. And God? He's still standing back, because there's nothing more entertaining than watching the world's champion improvisers in action—they always take something simple and make it into something even better. Even if it takes forever to cure prosciutto.

Aunt Edna's Bavarian Tryst Chicken

# Truffle Chicken without the Truffles

Let me tell you about Xaver, an intriguing man from Lower Bavaria who once upon a time, having had a spiritual awakening in Turin, disappeared into deepest Piedmont in Italy where he stoked ovens in an abandoned trattoria. He's still there today acting Italian for his guests with such grandezza that you can't help but love him for it. But I love him most for his magnificent mock truffle chicken: To serve 2, peel 1 clove garlic, chop, sprinkle with salt and crush into a paste with the flat part of a chef's knife. Mix garlic paste with 1 tablespoon minced parsley and ¼ cup softened butter. Wipe off 6 flavorful mushrooms with a cloth (e.g. cremini, shiitake, porcini). Remove stems and chop them finely; mix with the herb-garlic butter. Slice mushroom tops thinly. Spread 1 teaspoon herb butter in the bottom of a baking dish and distribute mushroom slices on top. Spread remaining herb butter on 4 chicken breast fillets (skin-on; Xaver also slides a little under the skin); arrange on top of mushrooms. Bake at 375°F for 15 minutes or until chicken is no longer pink. Halfway through, add a little cream to the mushrooms if desired. Tastes great with polenta!

Five Tips for Using Leftovers:

# Meat & Poultry

Was your spaghetti so good that everyone stuffed themselves and couldn't find room for the roasted meat, no matter how delicious? Don't worry, tomorrow is another day, without pasta but not without leftovers. Here we go:

### Reinvented cutlets

Chop some zucchini, mushrooms or a leek and sauté in oil or butter. Add a liquid such as tomato sauce, cream, stock, wine, etc. and bring to a boil. Meanwhile cut leftover cutlets, steaks, or fillets into strips. Season sauce with salt, pepper, lemon and whatever herbs you want. Heat up the meat or poultry in the sauce without boiling. Done!

### Chops au gratin

Place breaded chops (lamb, veal, or pork) or cutlets from the previous day in a buttered baking dish, and sprinkle with Parmesan. Cover each piece of meat with 1 slice proscuitto, 2 slices tomato, basil leaves and sliced fresh mozzarella. Sprinkle with Parmesan, salt and pepper and bits of butter and bake at 350°F for 10–12 minutes.

### Breaded roast

Spread pesto or mustard on slices of roast and dredge in flour, then dip in egg, then into a mixture of: bread crumbs, freshly grated Parmesan and chopped herbs. In a pan, sauté slices in a generous amount of oil and butter until crispy and heated through.

### Sauce for pasta

Take leftover cooked meat and cut into small cubes—sauté in olive oil with some chopped garlic and onions. Add chopped canned tomatoes along with their juice. Also add a bit of tomato sauce, plus salt, pepper and herbs. If desired, add chopped pitted black olives, crushed dried red chiles or crushed red pepper flakes or mushrooms. Simmer for 15–30 minutes or more. Presto! Toss with your favorite cooked pasta.

### Pasta salad with chicken

Chop cooked chicken without the skin and combine with rinsed and quartered cherry tomatoes, basil leaves, fresh mozzarella cubes and leftover cooked pasta. Dress with lemon or vinegar and olive oil. Add your favorite spices and salt and pepper. You can also add olives, anchovies or capers.

## Our Favorite
## Cut of Meat
# The Cutlet

Cutlets are:
• Thin cuts of tender meat that cook quickly
  Usually veal, traditionally from the round
  (leg) but rump works, too
  Sometimes pork (di maiale) or chicken
  (di pollo)
• Hard to give a single name: Scaloppine
  is the most common name. Prepared with
  Marsala and lemon, they're called piccata.
  Sometimes cutlets are also called cotoletta
  or cotolettina. Note: In Italian, a chop is a
  costoletta

Cutlets need:
• To be sliced thinly ($\frac{1}{8}$–$\frac{1}{4}$"), and if that's
  not possible, pounded in a freezer bag or
  between layers of plastic wrap
• Sometimes to be marinated in wine or
  lemon juice with garlic or herbs
• To be dredged in flour, especially if a sauce
  is to be made from the pan juices (flour
  ultimately thickens the sauce)
• To be sautéed in oil and butter and then
  set aside, kept warm

Cutlets love:
• Balsamic vinegar, white wine, lemon juice,
  Marsala, cream, tomato sauce—mixed with
  pan juices
• Basil, oregano, parsley, sage, thyme
• Garlic, nutmeg, paprika, cinnamon
• Anchovies, capers, olives, prosciutto, bacon
• Fresh mozzarella, Parmesan, or cheeses
  that melt
• Broccoli, peas, carrots, mushrooms,
  spinach, zucchini
• Bread, potatoes, rice

# The Dish
# on Sauce

Italian sauces for meats are typically simple in nature.

Often a cutlet is served only with pan drippings that have been dislodged with a bit of wine, lemon juice or cream. You'll never find an Italian chef dedicating hours to what is to them obviously a side issue the way a French sauce-chef would.

But it is a different story when the sauce is the centerpiece, as in the case of pasta. Then chefs will simmer a bolognese for half a day, will painstakingly subject tomatoes to boiling water, cold water and peeling to make a genuine tomato sauce, and will patiently concoct a homemade pesto using a mortar. Those who love sauces and are smart will arrange their meals so that the pasta sauces can also accompany the meat dishes.

The Neapolitans, of world-wide pizza fame (see Pizza Saga, page 81), have already demonstrated this principle with their costoletta alla pizzaiola (page 134).

# Scaloppine al limone
## Veal cutlets with lemon sauce

### A true basic

Feeds 4 lovers of tradition:

4 thin veal cutlets (about 5 oz. each)

Salt, freshly ground black pepper

$\frac{1}{4}$ cup flour or more as needed

2 tablespoons butter

2 tablespoons olive oil

3 tablespoons fresh lemon juice

**1** First set the oven to 150°F and warm up an oven-safe platter. Later, this will be to keep the veal warm while you finish the sauce.

**2** Halve cutlets and press the pieces a little flatter with the heel of your hand. Salt and pepper both sides of cutlets. Spread flour on a plate and dredge cutlets in it, but make sure only a thin layer sticks to them. Knock off the excess.

**3** In a large pan, heat 1 tablespoon butter and the oil until very hot. Add cutlets and sauté 1 minute on each side. Then transfer to the platter in the oven.

**4** Add lemon juice and 1 tablespoon water (or more if needed) to the pan and stir well with a wooden spoon until all the residue from the bottom of the pan is mixed into the liquid. Cut remaining butter into bits, add and stir. Season sauce with salt and pepper, additional fresh lemon juice to taste; pour over cutlets and serve.

Prep time: 30 minutes
Delicious with: Spinach or salad and Italian bread
Calories per serving: 250

# Saltimbocca
## Veal cutlets with prosciutto

### They jump into your mouth!

Feeds 4 adventurous types:

8 small, thin veal cutlets (about 3 oz. each)

1 tender baby zucchini

4 slices prosciutto (or other raw-cured ham)

16 fresh sage leaves

¼ cup butter

6 tablespoons dry white wine

Salt, freshly ground black pepper

**1** Set oven to 150°F and warm up an oven safe plate or platter. Later you'll transfer the meat to the platter to keep warm. Press cutlets flatter with the heel of your hand.

**2** Rinse zucchini, trim ends and slice thinly lengthwise. Trim slices to the length of the cutlets. Cut prosciutto slices in half.

**3** Top each cutlet first with 1 zucchini slice, then 1 prosciutto slice and 2 sage leaves and fasten the prosciutto and zucchini to the meat by threading a toothpick through.

**4** In a large pan, melt 2 tablespoons of the butter but don't let it turn brown. Add 4 cutlets with the topped side down and let cook over medium heat for 2 minutes. Turn and cook for 1 minute more or till cutlet is just cooked throughout. Transfer to the platter in the oven. In the rest of the butter, sauté the rest of the cutlets in the same way.

**5** Pour wine into the pan and stir with a wooden spoon to loosen the particles stuck to the bottom of the pan; simmer briefly. Season cautiously with salt and pepper (the prosciutto on the cutlets is already salty). Top cutlets with sauce and serve immediately.

Prep time: 20 minutes
Delicious with: Crusty white bread
Calories per serving: 260

## Variations:

### Scaloppine al marsala
Substitute ⅓ cup dry Marsala for lemon juice in recipe "veal cutlets with lemon juice" (p. 132).

### Scaloppine al vino bianco
Substitute ⅓ cup dry white wine for lemon juice in recipe "veal cutlets with lemon juice" (p. 132).

### Scaloppine al radicchio
After sautéing the cutlets, sauté ¾ cup radicchio in the pan for 2–3 minutes. Add white wine and season to taste with lemon juice.

133

## Costolette alla milanese
### Breaded veal chops

Served Sundays
at Mamma's

Feeds 4 as a secondo:

4 veal chops (about 5 oz. each; best
to order ahead from your butcher—
in an emergency, use pork chops)

1 shallot

$1/2$ cup fresh parsley sprigs

$1/2$ cup fresh basil sprigs

A little fresh thyme

2 tablespoons butter

$1/2$ cup white wine vinegar
(preferably white balsamic)

1 bay leaf

Salt, freshly ground black pepper

2 eggs

$1/4$ cup flour or more as needed

$1^1/3$ cups bread crumbs

$1/4$ cup olive oil

1 large lemon

**1** Pat veal chops dry and arrange side by side in a dish (for marinating). Peel shallots and mince. Rinse herbs and shake dry. Pull leaves off parsley and basil, strip off thyme leaves and chop herbs very finely.

**2** In a pot, melt 1 tablespoon of the butter. Stir in shallots and sauté over medium heat for a couple minutes, stirring occasionally. Add herbs, vinegar and bay leaf; season with salt and pepper and pour over chops. Marinate chops for at least 1 hour, refrigerated.

**3** Then drain chops but leave as many herbs on them as possible. Season on both sides with salt and pepper. In a shallow bowl, whisk eggs briefly. Spread flour on one plate and bread crumbs on another.

**4** First dredge chops in flour, then dip in egg and finally in bread crumbs. Turn until nicely coated on both sides.

**5** In a large pan, heat remaining butter and the oil. Reduce heat to medium and sauté chops for 8 minutes on each side or till cooked through.

**6** Quarter lemon. Transfer sautéed chops to plates and drizzle with pan juices. Place a lemon quarter next to each chop and serve.

Prep time: $1^1/2$ hours, 40 minutes
of which you're actually busy
Delicious with: Rosemary potatoes (page 110)
Calories per serving: 480

## Costolette alla pizzaiola
### Pork chops with tomato sauce

Those clever
Neapolitans!

What the pizzaiola (the pizza baker) makes when he's not making pizza—he just can't make anything without tomatoes!

Feeds 4 as a full meal:

4 pork chops, not too thick
(cutlets will also work)

Salt, freshly ground black pepper

4 sprigs fresh marjoram or oregano

4 cloves garlic

1 (14 oz.) can peeled tomatoes

$1/4$ cup olive oil

$1/2$ cup red wine

1 tablespoon tomato paste

1 tablespoon capers (optional)

**1** Pat chops dry and season on both sides with salt and pepper. Rinse and dry herbs, strip off leaves and tear in half any large leaves. Peel garlic, cut in half and then slice thinly. Chop tomatoes (reserve juice from can).

**2** In a pan, heat 3 tablespoons of the oil. Sauté chops on both sides at high heat until lightly browned; remove and transfer to a plate.

**3** Pour remaining oil into pan. Stir in garlic and sauté briefly. Add herbs, tomatoes (and their juice), wine and tomato paste; season with salt and pepper and simmer uncovered for about 5 minutes to reduce the sauce a bit.

**4** Place chops in the sauce and spoon a little sauce over the top. Reduce heat, cover and simmer for about 15 minutes. Garnish with capers if desired, and serve.

Prep time: 50 minutes, 20 of which you're actually busy
Delicious with: Rosemary potatoes (page 110)
Calories per serving: 310

# Involtini di vitello
## Veal spirals

So small but so good

Feeds 4:

2 oz. pitted green olives

2 green onions

2 cloves garlic

1/2 cup fresh parsley sprigs

1 dried red chile or 1/2 teaspoon crushed red pepper flakes

4 oz. freshly grated young pecorino cheese

Salt, freshly ground black pepper

8 thin veal cutlets (3 oz. each)

1/4 cup flour or as needed

3 tablespoons olive oil

2/3 cup dry white wine or meat stock

1/2 lemon (zest and juice)

**1** Chop olives very finely. Rinse green onions, remove roots, dark greens and wilted parts; chop rest finely. Peel garlic and squeeze through a press. Rinse parsley and shake dry. Remove leaves, set a few aside for garnishing and finely chop the rest (set

aside). Pulverize chile in a mortar or crumble it between your fingers (wear gloves, or wash your hands well but be cautious and don't touch your face)—or use flakes.

**2** Combine olives, green onions, parsley, red chile and pecorino with garlic in a bowl; season with salt and pepper and mix well.

**3** Press cutlets flatter with the heel of your hand. Gently press olive-chile mixture (but not all the way to the edges) onto the top of each. Roll up cutlets and fasten with toothpicks. Season outsides of rolls with salt and pepper. Spread flour on a plate and dredge rolls in it to coat lightly with flour.

**4** In a large pan, heat oil. Sauté rolls until lightly browned on all sides. Add wine, reduce heat to low, cover and simmer for 10 minutes.

**5** In the meantime, rinse lemon and dry; then remove zest from half, halve and then squeeze out juice from half. Add lemon zest, juice and chopped parsley to the pan; season to taste with salt and pepper, garnish with reserved parsley leaves and enjoy!

Prep time: 35 minutes
Delicious with: Crusty Italian bread and a dry white wine, plus peperonata (page 108) or stewed mushrooms (page 110)
Calories per serving: 380

# Salsicce con lenticchie
## Pork sausages with balsamic lentils

### Substantial and hearty and typically Italian

Feeds 4 as a full meal:

1 carrot

1 stalk celery

1 bunch green onions (5–6)

2–3 cloves garlic

1 dried red chile or ½ teaspoon crushed red pepper flakes

¾ cup fresh parsley sprigs

¼ cup olive oil

2 cups dry brown lentils

1 cup stock + maybe a little extra for adding

1 cup dry red wine

1 tablespoon tomato paste

8 fresh salsicce (fresh, smoked pork sausages, about 1½ lbs. total; substitute other coarse, raw, smoked sausages but not those with non-Italian seasonings)

Salt, freshly ground black pepper

2 tablespoons balsamic vinegar

**1** Peel carrot. Rinse celery and green onions. Remove roots and any wilted greens from onions. Peel garlic. Chop all these ingredients together very finely along with dried red chile on a large board (wear gloves when working with chiles and don't touch your face—or use flakes instead). Rinse parsley, remove leaves and chop very finely (set aside).

**2** In a wide pot heat 2 tablespoons of the oil and sauté green onions, garlic, chiles, and parsley for 1-2 minutes. Stir in lentils. Add stock, wine and tomato paste. Stir, reduce to medium heat and cook lentils (covered) for about 30 minutes. Check once in a while to make sure there's enough liquid. Stir occasionally and add stock as needed.

**3** Just before the lentils are done, heat remaining oil in a pan and brown sausages well on all sides. Season lentils to taste with salt, pepper and balsamic vinegar. Place sausages on top, cover and cook for about 10 more minutes until the sausages are cooked through and lentils are tender but still firm. You may need to add a little more vinegar or salt and pepper to taste; serve.

Prep time: 1 hour, 30 minutes of which you're actually busy
Calories per serving: 890

# Polpettine al vino rosso
## Meatballs in red wine

### Costs very little

Makes enough for 4:

4 slices sandwich bread

½ cup milk

2 oz. prosciutto

¾ cup fresh parsley or basil sprigs

1⅓ lbs. ground meat (preferably have butcher freshly grind half beef, half veal)

1 tablespoon capers (optional)

2 tablespoons freshly grated Parmesan

Salt, freshly ground black pepper

1 medium onion

1 carrot

1 stalk celery

3 tablespoons olive oil

1 (14 oz.) can peeled tomatoes

¾ cup + 2 tablespoons dry red wine

About 10 sage leaves

**1** Remove and discard crust from bread, place rest in a shallow bowl with milk. Chop prosciutto finely. Rinse parsley or basil and chop leaves finely.

**2** Squeeze out bread with your hands and break into small pieces. Combine in a bowl with ground meat, prosciutto, herbs, capers and Parmesan. Season with salt and pepper and mix until the mixture holds together. Roll bits of the meat mixture between your hands to form meatballs about the size of golf balls.

**3** Peel onion and chop finely. Peel carrot, rinse celery and dice both finely. In a large pan, heat oil. Sauté onion, carrot, and celery briefly, then push to the side and add meatballs. Sauté balls until brown on all sides.

**4** Purée tomatoes along with their juice and the red wine (with blender or hand blender); add to the pan. Stir in sage, reduce to low heat, cover and simmer for about 30 minutes. Season sauce to taste with salt and pepper—serve meatballs with sauce at the table!

Prep time: At least 1 hour, 35 minutes of which you're actually busy
Delicious with: Polenta or risotto alla milanese (page 82)
Calories per serving: 600

# Arista
## Roast pork

### Dolce vita comfort food

Feeds 6 Tuscany lovers:

4 sprigs fresh rosemary

1 large lemon

4 cloves garlic

1–2 teaspoons fennel seeds

Salt, freshly ground black pepper

Freshly grated nutmeg

6 tablespoons olive oil

2 1/2 lb. pork roast (boneless, fat trimmed, preferably tied into shape by butcher)

1 cup dry white wine

**1** Rinse rosemary. Remove needles from 2 of the sprigs. Rinse lemon, dry and remove a thin layer of zest. Peel garlic.

**2** Pile rosemary needles, garlic, lemon zest and fennel seeds on a board and chop all finely. Combine that mixture in a small bowl with salt, pepper, pinch of nutmeg and 2 tablespoons of the oil. Pat meat dry and rub mixture into it on all sides. Now you can either cook the roast immediately or let stand for a couple hours (refrigerated).

**3** Preheat oven to 350°F. Take out a large roasting pan, preferably cast-iron.

**4** Heat roasting pan on the stove. Add remaining oil and brown roast well on all sides. Then place the roasting pan in the oven on the bottom rack. Add whole rosemary sprigs. Roast for 45 minutes (uncovered), then pour wine into the roasting pan. Cook another 1 1/4 hours or a bit longer for a larger roast, occasionally turning and basting with wine. Check the internal temperature of the roast with a meat thermometer if there's a question as to doneness (pork should be cooked to 170 degrees). In any case, let stand 10 minutes before slicing.

Prep time: 2 1/2 hours, 15 minutes of which you're actually busy
Delicious with: Rosemary potatoes (page 110)
Calories per serving: 615

137

# Brasato al vino rosso
## Beef pot roast in red wine

**It cooks itself!**

Feeds 6 sauce lovers:

1¼ lb. beef roast (bottom round, leg or rump)

Salt, freshly ground black pepper

2 carrots

2 stalks celery

1 onion

3 cloves garlic

Several sprigs fresh rosemary

¾ cup fresh basil sprigs

4 tomatoes

2 tablespoons butter

3 tablespoons olive oil

1⅔ cups good red wine

½ cup meat stock

2 whole cloves

1 stick cinnamon

1 bay leaf

1–2 tablespoons honey

**1** Briefly rinse beef roast under cold running water and pat dry with paper towels. Rub salt and pepper thoroughly into the meat on all sides.

**2** Peel carrots and cut off top ends. Rinse celery and pull off any noticeable threads. Leave tender celery greens, but cut off any wilted parts. Cut carrots and celery into strips, then dice. Peel onion and garlic and chop finely. Strip rosemary needles from stem and chop. Remove some sprigs from basil and set aside for garnish (refrigerate); coarsely chop the rest of the leaves and stems.

**3** Rinse tomatoes and dice very finely. Do we hear a gasp? Not peeling them for so fine a roast? No, not necessary because after stewing, the sauce gets strained and the peels will be caught by the fine mesh.

**4** Take out a dutch oven or other stovetop pan/pot that has a cover, that will work for roasting—preferably cast-iron. Heat butter and oil in it. Add the roast and sear on all sides so that it is brown and crusty.

**5** Now remove the roast briefly. Stir in vegetables, onion, garlic and herbs and sauté until onions soften a bit. Add tomatoes, wine and stock plus whole cloves, cinnamon and bay leaf. Season sauce with salt and pepper. Return roast to pan.

**6** Now reduce the heat to low and cover. Stew roast for about 3 hours—the liquid should be simmering slightly but never boiling, otherwise the roast won't be tender. Remove the cover to check on it periodically.

**7** After 3 hours, remove the roast and let stand 10 minutes before slicing. Remove and discard bay leaf. Pour sauce through a fine mesh strainer and back into the pan. Then turn up the heat and let the sauce reduce for a couple minutes. Finish up with salt, pepper and honey to taste. Slice roast, place slices in the sauce and garnish with basil sprigs. Serve in the roasting pan on the table.

Prep time: 3½ hours, only 30 minutes of which you're actually busy
Delicious with: Rosemary potatoes (page 110) or crusty white bread and the red wine you used to make the sauce
Calories per serving: 425

# Ossobuco
## Stewed veal shank slices

### Unbeatable

Feeds 4 lovers of tradition:

**For the meat and sauce:**

4 slices veal shank (with marrow bone
in the center, each about 7 oz.)

3 carrots

2 onions

3 cloves garlic

3 stalks celery

1/2 cup fresh parsley sprigs

2 tablespoons butter

2 tablespoons olive oil

Salt, freshly ground black pepper

1 (14 oz.) can peeled tomatoes

About 1 cup meat stock

**For the gremolata:**

1 lemon

3/4 cup fresh Italian parsley sprigs

2 cloves garlic

**1** Rinse meat slices briefly under cold running water to remove any bone splinters. Dry well with a thick layer of paper towels.

**2** Peel carrots, onions and garlic. Rinse celery and chop all these ingredients very finely. Rinse parsley, shake dry, remove leaves and chop.

**3** In a large casserole, dutch oven or roasting pan, heat butter and oil. Brown meat slices on high heat so that they stick slightly—then the crust is brown enough and the pores are sealed. Repeat on all sides. Remove and season with salt and pepper.

**4** Stir chopped vegetables and parsley into the pot and sauté briefly. Chop tomatoes and pour along with juice from the can into the pot along with the stock. Turn heat down to medium and reduce liquid slightly, for about 20 minutes.

**5** Now return the meat slices to the pot, preferably laying them side by side and spooning a little sauce over the top. Cover and simmer over low heat for about 1 1/2 hours until tender. Just before serving, season with salt and pepper to taste. Meanwhile:

**6** While the roast is simmering, prepare the highlight of the dish—the gremolata. Start by rinsing the lemon; pat dry. Remove a thin layer of zest, avoiding the white bitter part. Rinse parsley and pull off leaves. Peel garlic. Chop zest, parsley, and garlic together on the cutting board very finely, using a large chef's knife. Transfer to a small bowl and place on the table as a condiment. Sprinkle it over the meat slices when served to make the dish wonderfully refreshing!

Prep time: 2 1/2 hours, only about
30 minutes of which you're actually busy
Delicious with: Fried polenta slices (using polenta recipe on page 89; then slice polenta and sauté in a pan with oil and butter until browned) or with fresh Italian bread
Calories per serving: 310

# Bollito misto
## Mixed meat stew

### Satisfies a large group

All you need is a very large pot, a variety of meats and vegetables. Recipe is served with a fruit mustard but also tastes delicious with the salsa verde on p. 41.

Feeds 8 as a full meal:

1³/₄ lbs. beef for stewing

1 lb. veal for stewing

1 chicken cut into 8 pieces (about 2¹/₄ lbs.)

2 rabbit legs (or equivalent of other cut of rabbit)

4–5 fresh salsicce (raw, smoked sausage with Italian-type seasoning)

1 onion

2 cloves garlic

4 sprigs fresh marjoram + some for garnishing

2–3 bay leaves (preferably fresh)

1 teaspoon juniper berries

1 teaspoon whole cloves

1 teaspoon peppercorns

Salt

4 carrots

4 stalks celery

Also needed: cheesecloth and kitchen string

**For the fruit mustard:**

1 lemon

1 orange

1 large apple

1 large pear

1 cup white grape juice

1 cup dry white wine

¹/₃ cup Vin Santo

(optional, or other sweet wine)

2 tablespoons spicy deli mustard

Salt, freshly ground black pepper

1 pinch cinnamon

1 Briefly rinse all meat & poultry under running water. Pat dry.

2 Take out your largest pot. Place stewing beef in it, pour in 4 quarts water and heat slowly. Just before it starts to boil, turn down the heat. Meanwhile: peel and halve onion and garlic. Rinse marjoram and shake dry. Add onion, garlic and marjoram to the pot. Tie bay leaves, juniper berries, cloves and peppercorns into a double-layer cheesecloth pouch with kitchen string and add to pot. Add a little salt.

3 Cover pot halfway and keep it at a simmer (do not allow to boil). Stew the beef for 1 hour.

4 Peel carrots and halve lengthwise. Then cut in half crosswise. Wash celery, trim and discard ends and cut stalks into 2" sections.

5 Add carrots, celery, chicken and veal to the pot and simmer another 30 minutes. Then add rabbit and sausages and simmer yet another 30 minutes.

6 During this long cooking time, you'll have plenty of time to make the fruit mustard: Rinse lemon and orange and dry. Remove lemon zest and squeeze out juice. Set orange aside. Peel apple and pear; remove core and cut rest into wedges.

7 In a pot, combine apple and pear wedges, lemon juice, lemon zest, white grape juice, wine, and Vin Santo and heat. Cover, reduce heat to low and simmer fruit for about 20 minutes until soft.

8 Remove lid and simmer another 20 minutes, uncovered, then purée. Now zest the orange and add it to the purée along with mustard, salt, pepper and cinnamon. Transfer to a small bowl and let cool. You can also make this sauce a day ahead of time.

9 Remove meat from the pot and cut into serving-size portions. Transfer to a bowl or large platter along with the vegetables. Ladle a little cooking liquid over the top and garnish with fresh marjoram; serve. Use the fruit mustard as a condiment.

Prep time: 2¹/₂ hours, about 1 hour of which you're actually busy
Delicious with: Crusty Italian bread or boiled or roasted potatoes
Calories per serving: 580

# Coniglio al finocchio
## Rabbit with fennel

### The fennel makes this dish

Feeds 3 guests and 1 host:

1 whole rabbit (purchase from a butcher—have it cut into 8 pieces)

Salt, freshly ground black pepper

2 fennel bulbs

2 oz. pancetta or streaky bacon

1 onion

2 cloves garlic

A couple sprigs of fresh sage

3 tablespoons olive oil

1/2 cup pitted black olives (e.g. kalamata)

1 cup dry white wine

**1** If the rabbit is whole, cut it up with a sharp knife and poultry shears: cut the legs to the joint and separate. Cut the back in half. Cut the breast (the meatier side) into four pieces. Better yet, have the butcher cut it for you. Rub salt and pepper into all pieces.

**2** Rinse fennel and remove wilted layers and thick stems. Cut bulbs lengthwise into quarters or eighths—cut wedges through the core so the layers stay together. Save the fennel greens. Chop pancetta. Peel onion and garlic and chop both finely. Rinse sage, remove leaves and cut most of them into strips; reserve a few.

**3** Heat oil in a large stockpot. Add rabbit pieces (no more than you can lay side by side) and brown well. Remove rabbit from pan.

**4** Stir in pancetta, onion, garlic and sage. Then add fennel and sauté slightly. Return rabbit pieces to the pot and add olives and wine. Reduce heat to low; simmer covered 45 minutes. Before serving, sprinkle with reserved fennel greens and sage leaves.

Prep time: 1 1/4 hours, 30 minutes of which you're actually busy
Delicious with: Rosemary potatoes (page 110) or bread and caponata (page 109) or peperonata (page 108)
Calories per serving: 800

# Pollo alla cacciatora
## Hunter's chicken

### Free-range are happiest!

Makes enough for 4:

1 chicken (about 3 lbs.), cut into 8 pieces

1 large onion

2 cloves garlic

1 carrot

1 stalk celery

3/4 cup fresh parsley sprigs

4–6 sage leaves

1 2/3 cups dry white wine

1/4 cup white wine vinegar (preferably white balsamic)

Salt, freshly ground black pepper

2 oz. pancetta

2 cups mushrooms

1/4 cup olive oil

1 (14 oz.) can peeled tomatoes

1 bunch basil

**1** Rinse chicken well inside and out under cold running water. Pat dry and cut into 8 pieces using a sharp knife and poultry shears (or purchase pre-cut). Place pieces in a bowl.

**2** Peel onion and garlic and chop both finely. Peel carrot, rinse celery and chop both. Rinse parsley and sage and chop finely.

**3** Combine onion, garlic, carrot, celery, parsley and sage with wine and vinegar and pour over chicken pieces. Marinate refrigerated for 6 hours or, even better, overnight.

**4** Afterwards, remove chicken pieces, drain (reserve marinade) and season with salt and pepper. Pour marinade through a fine mesh strainer (reserve both the vegetables and the liquid). Dice pancetta finely. Remove and discard ends of stems from mushrooms; wipe off mushrooms with a paper towel and quarter.

**5** In a large stockpot, heat oil. Stir in pancetta. Also add chicken pieces in batches and brown well on all sides, then remove.

**6** Add mushrooms to the pot and cook thoroughly with vegetables from the marinade. Chop tomatoes and pour with their juice into the pot along with ⅓ cup of the marinade (discard rest if any). Return chicken pieces to the pot, reduce heat to low, cover and stew chicken for about 35 minutes. Pierce chicken at the thickest point with a sharp knife. If it's done, the juice that runs out should be clear. Finely chop basil and sprinkle over the top to serve.

Prep time: 1½ hours, 1 hour of which you're actually busy (not including marinating time)
Calories per serving: 850

# Spezzatino di vitello
## Stewed veal with grapes

### For the fall

Grapes at reasonable prices are typically available in the fall. At other times of the year, use small onions or shallots and green olives.

Feeds 4 curious types:
1¾ lb. veal for stewing
(shoulder or blade roast)
1 onion
2 cloves garlic
Several sprigs fresh sage
¼ cup olive oil
⅔ cup Vin Santo (or other sweet wine)
Salt, freshly ground black pepper
2 cups white grapes, removed from stems
1 tablespoon butter
1 tablespoon fresh lemon juice

**1** Rinse veal under cold water and pat dry. Cut into bite-sized pieces and remove any significant fat and tough sinews.

**2** Peel onion and garlic and chop both finely. Rinse sage, remove leaves and cut into strips.

**3** In a large stockpot, heat oil and brown half the meat on medium high, stirring. When browned, remove cubes with a slotted spoon, add the second batch and brown.

**4** When this second batch is brown, return all meat to the pot and add onion, garlic and sage. Pour in Vin Santo and season with salt and pepper. Reduce heat to low, cover and simmer for 20 minutes.

**5** Rinse grapes and pat dry. In a small pan, heat butter and stir in grapes. Season to taste with salt, pepper and fresh lemon juice, then add to the meat. Simmer for another 10 minutes. Add salt and pepper to taste, then let the feast begin!

Prep time: 1 hour, 40 minutes of which you're actually busy
Delicious with: Fresh Italian bread or gnocchi (page 86) and a dry white wine
Calories per serving: 430

# Pollo alla diavola
## Spicy grilled chicken

### For grilling—but this can also be made in the oven

If you order pollo alla diavola in Italy, you might be disappointed—it isn't always spicy. Sometimes the devilishness in its name refers only to the dark color of the grilled meat. This version has a kick!

Feeds 4:

1 roasting chicken (about 2½ lbs. total), halved

Several sprigs fresh sage and rosemary

2 cloves garlic

1–2 dried red chile(s) or ½ teaspoon crushed red pepper flakes

3–4 tablespoons fresh lemon juice

⅓ cup olive oil

Salt

**1** Rinse chicken halves well inside and out under cold running water and pat dry.

**2** Rinse herbs, shake dry, remove leaves and needles and chop coarsely. Peel garlic and squeeze through a press. Crush dried red chiles in a mortar or chop finely on a board (best to wear gloves; omit seeds for less heat). Make sure you wash your hands well and don't rub your eyes for several hours afterwards. Otherwise they'll start burning like the devil! Or, use the crushed red pepper flakes.

**3** In a small mixing bowl, combine herbs, crushed chile, lemon juice, garlic, and oil; season generously with salt and stir until smooth.

**4** Pour this mixture over the chicken halves and spread on with a brush. Cover pieces with plastic wrap and marinate for at least 2 hours or even longer if possible.

**5** Now it's time to start grilling. Make a mound of charcoal in your grill; douse with charcoal starter fluid—light with a match. Let that heat until the coals start turning whitish. Spread them out with a tool and put the grate on top—now you're ready to get cookin'! (Never pour liquid starter on hot coals—very dangerous!) If you decide to cook it in the oven instead, heat to 375°F (or you can also do it under the broiler).

**6** Grill chicken halves on the charcoal grill (preferably on a rack covered with aluminum foil) OR on a baking sheet under the broiler for about 30 minutes OR bake for about 30 minutes. Then turn halves and grill or bake another 30 minutes. If using the broil or bake method, now set the oven to 425°F and cook another 10 minutes until the skin has a nice brown color. For any cooking method, pierce the thickest part of the thigh with a thin-bladed knife. If clear juice runs out, the chicken is done. If the juice is still reddish, cook longer until the juice runs out clear. Very important. Then it will taste devilishly good!

Prep time: 1½ hours, only 20 minutes of which you're actually busy (not including marinating time)
Delicious with: Crusty white bread, tossed salad and red wine
Calories per serving: 575

# Pollo al limone
## Lemon chicken

### Truly refreshing

Feeds 4 in the summer:

1 roasting chicken (about 2 ¾ lbs.)

3 lemons + 1 for garnish

3 cloves garlic

1 sprig fresh rosemary + more for garnish

Salt, freshly ground black pepper

2 tablespoons butter

**1** Rinse chicken well inside and out under cold running water and pat dry. Rinse 1 lemon and slice, then squeeze juice from the other two.

**2** Preheat oven to 375°F. Peel garlic, cut into slices then strips. Remove rosemary needles. Pierce chicken skin several times with the tip of a knife but don't cut into the meat! Insert garlic sticks and rosemary needles inside the holes and poke under the skin.

**3** Rub salt and pepper into chicken. Melt butter but don't let it turn brown. Combine with lemon juice and brush the lemon butter onto the chicken.

**4** Now place the chicken in the broiler pan (the bottom deep baking pan). Top with lemon slices and also place some lemon slices in the cavity; roast on the middle shelf for about 1 hour and 20 minutes, occasionally basting with more lemon butter. Toward the end, baste with the meat juice as well. Pierce the thigh and if juice runs clear, it's done. Let stand for a few minutes. Meanwhile, cut up the lemon and garnish the chicken with it and some fresh rosemary. Cut into pieces and enjoy.

Prep time: 1 hour and 40 minutes, only about 20 minutes of which you're actually busy
Delicious with: Crusty Italian bread or rosemary potatoes (page 110), fagioli all'uccelletto (page 108) and white wine
Calories per serving: 570

# Agnello spezzato
## Stewed lamb

### Simple and sophisticated

Feeds 4 with big appetites:

2¼ lbs. lamb (leg or lean boneless shoulder)

6 cloves garlic

2 onions

4 sprigs fresh rosemary

4 sprigs fresh thyme

4 sprigs fresh marjoram or oregano

2 tablespoons butter

2 tablespoons olive oil

¼ cup white wine vinegar
(preferably white balsamic)

½ cup dry white wine

Salt, freshly ground black pepper

**1** Trim any significant fat from lamb and remove any tough sinews. Then cut lamb into bite-sized pieces.

**2** Peel garlic and onions and chop both finely. Rinse herbs and shake dry. Remove leaves from stems and chop.

**3** Place the stockpot on the stove. Also have ready a plate covered with paper towels.

**4** In the pot, heat 1 tablespoon of the butter mixed with 1 tablespoon of the oil. On high, sauté half the meat while stirring until the pieces are brown on all sides. Remove with a slotted spoon and transfer to the plate. Heat remaining oil and butter in the pot, sauté the second batch of meat in exactly the same way and transfer to the plate.

**5** Add garlic and onions to the pot and sauté briefly (add more olive oil if necessary). Return meat to the pot and add vinegar, wine and most of the herbs (save some small sprigs for garnishing). Season meat lightly with salt and pepper.

**6** Reduce heat to low. Cover pot and simmer meat for 1 hour until nice and tender. Check on it and stir occasionally. Don't let all the liquid evaporate—pour in a little more wine or even water if necessary. Finally, season with salt and pepper, garnish with herbs, and serve.

Prep time: 1¾ hours, about 45 minutes of which you're actually busy
Delicious with: Crusty white bread or fried polenta, stuffed tomatoes and a light red wine
Calories per serving: 710

### Tip

Agnello spezzato is also delicious with pasta, in which case this recipe makes enough for 6-8. And if desired, you can also mix in a few chopped tomatoes.

# Agnello al forno
## Roast leg of lamb

### Comes with its own side dishes

Feeds 5–6 guests and 1 host:

2 lbs. ripe tomatoes

2 lbs. potatoes

6 tablespoons olive oil

4 sprigs fresh rosemary

Salt, freshly ground black pepper

1 onion

5 cloves garlic

1 lemon

$^3/_4$ cup fresh Italian parsley sprigs

1–2 dried red chiles or $^3/_4$ teaspoon crushed red pepper flakes

1 piece boneless leg of lamb (about 2 $^1/_2$ lbs.)

$^1/_2$ cup bread crumbs

2 oz. ($^1/_2$ cup) freshly grated Parmesan or pecorino

**1** Remove cores from tomatoes. Place tomatoes in a pot, pour boiling water over the top and leave for a minute or so. Rinse under cold water, slip off skins, squeeze out seeds and dice rest. Peel potatoes, rinse and cut into slices about $^1/_3$'" thick.

**2** Brush 1 tablespoon of the oil onto the oven broiler pan (the bottom deep baking pan) or other sturdy, deep baking pan. Fill with potato slices and sprinkle diced tomatoes over the top. Rinse rosemary, shake dry, remove needles and sprinkle over the top (reserve some rosemary for garnishing). Sprinkle on some salt and pepper.

**3** Peel onion and garlic and chop both finely. Rinse lemon and dry. Remove zest and squeeze out juice. Rinse parsley, shake dry and finely chop leaves. Crush dried red chiles in a mortar or chop finely on a board (wear gloves; in any case wash your hands well and don't touch your face)—or use flakes.

**4** Preheat oven to 350ºF. Rinse leg of lamb under cold water and pat dry. Cut off any significant fat and remove tough sinews. Mix onion, garlic, lemon zest, lemon juice, parsley and crushed chiles with 2 tablespoons of the oil. Season lamb with salt and rub mixture into the lamb on all sides. Place on top of the potatoes. Place broiler pan in the oven on bottom rack and cook meat for 1 $^1/_2$ hours. Turn lamb once halfway through.

**5** Increase temperature to 425ºF. Combine bread crumbs, Parmesan and remaining oil. Spread paste over the lamb and cook for another 15 minutes until crust becomes nicely browned.

**6** Remove broiler pan from oven, cover lamb with a large piece of aluminum foil and let stand for 10 minutes. This will allow the juices to evenly diffuse throughout the meat. Transfer the lamb to a board and slice. Garnish with fresh rosemary, and serve slices with the potatoes and tomatoes.

Prep time: 2 hours and 20 minutes,
45 minutes of which you're actually busy
Delicious with: Crusty Italian bread and
a full-bodied red wine
Calories per serving: 650

# Dolci

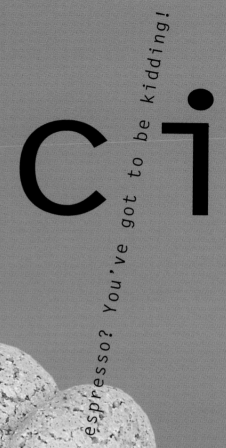

At most, an amaretti with the espresso? You've got to be kidding!

# [Something sweet]

So once more from the beginning: In Italy they eat salad with nothing but oil and vinegar, pasta is served only as an appetizer, the main dish is served without side dishes and fish is somewhat of a rarity. And this is supposed to be the gourmet's paradise? Isn't it at least the land of the dolce vita when it comes to dessert and coffee? You don't mean to tell me that Italians eat plain fruit after a meal! At most an amaretti cookie with the espresso? You've got to be kidding! Bake a decent cake instead. And why haven't we seen anything with chocolate? "Torta di cioccolata"? Now that's starting to sound a little better. And what is this, "Granita di caffè"? Now that also sounds interesting. Well, okay Italy, we trust you. Do whatever you want as long as it tastes good!

**Fruit is:**
- Stone fruit such as the apricot (albicocca), cherry (ciliegia), nectarine (pesca noce), peach (pesca), plum (prugna) or the round, yellow-to-dark-red Japanese plum (susina)
- Berries such as the strawberry (fragola), blueberry (mirtillo) and raspberry (lampone)
- Core fruit such as the apple (mela) and pear (pera)
- Citrus fruit such as the orange (arancia) and lemon (limone)
- Other fruits such as the fig (fico), grape (uva), watermelon (anguria), honeydew melon (melone) and cantaloupe (melone cantalupo)

**Fruit has:**
- Fructose and fruit acid which, depending on the distribution, can have an effect ranging from soothing to stimulating
- Vitamins, above all C, which is good for the immune system
- Potassium (for muscles) in the apricot, fig, honeydew melon and nectarine; manganese (sharpens the mind) in apricots and blueberries

**Fruit needs:**
- To be ripe and fresh, which is why it tastes best in season and harvested locally
- To be ripened. The following can be ripened after picking if necessary: pears, figs, nectarines, peaches, plums and honey-dew. But these should ripen before picking: berries, cherries, grapes, watermelon or citrus
- Preferably to be organically grown

**Fruit loves:**
- To be served alone after a meal as a simple treat
- To be made into fruit salad: Cut up three or four different types—sourness, sweetness, and textures should complement each other. If the fruit is perfect, no sugar, nor lemon juice, nor liqueur is needed. But if not, add to taste
- To be served slightly chilled but not as cold as refrigerator temperature
- To be frozen into sorbets and ice creams
- On rare occasions to make an appearance in baked goods

Tips for Using Leftovers
and Saving Time:

# Baked Goods

Maybe you have leftover baked goods and don't know what to do with them—a highly unlikely situation but if you ever do, see below.

## Gelato agli amaretti
Place amaretti cookies in a freezer bag and crush with a rolling pin but not too finely. Roll a slightly thawed block of vanilla gelato or ice cream in the crumbs and refreeze. Cut into slices—the amaretti form a crust (you can also roll scoops of ice cream).

## The new tiramisu
Remove and discard pits from 2 nectarines and dice rest. Break apart 1 handful almond biscotti. Grate 1 bar bittersweet chocolate. Fill 4 tall glasses with consecutive layers of a little mascarpone (mixed with some sugar and thinned with cream if desired), grated chocolate, almond biscotti pieces and nectarines. Then drizzle some Vin Santo (or Amaretto, Marsala or other sweet wine) on top and repeat layering—the last two layers should be mascarpone and chocolate. Refrigerate.

## Dolci di bruschetta
Dip 12 slices white bread (day-old works) briefly into 3 beaten eggs. Pan-fry in oil until crispy and layer in a shallow baking dish. Bring to a boil 1/2 cup white or red wine, 1 teaspoon vanilla, 3 tablespoons sugar and 1/4 cup raisins. Sprinkle bread with 1 teaspoon cinnamon and additional sugar. Drizzle wine-raisin mixture on top; bake at 350°F for 10 minutes.

## Individual bread puddings
With just a little prep time and a lot of baking time, this dessert leaves you time to make the primi & secundi: Cut up 5 oz. of the sweet baked good of your choice (cinnamon rolls work great). Bring to a boil 1/3 cup dessert wine with 1/3 cup chopped dried fruit of your choice. Drain fruit in a colander (reserve liquid). Whisk reserved liquid with 1/3 cup cream, 1 tablespoon sugar and 3 eggs. Combine baked good and fruit and transfer to 4 individual baking dishes buttered and sprinkled with sugar. Fill two-thirds full. Pour custard over the top and let stand 5 minutes; then stir each briefly. Place individual dishes on a cookie sheet on the middle rack of the oven. Bake at 325°F for 35–45 minutes or until set.

# The Gelato Story

Where does ice cream come from? No one knows for sure. But why would we need to? The Chinese, the Arabs and the Greeks may very well argue about which one was the first to mix mountain snow with fruit and honey, but it was the Italians who were the first to turn it into something splendid. Of course!

Look what fine frozen treats the Italians have made:

## Granita

As with pasta and pizza, southern Italy was also the birthplace of ice cream. Around Naples and on Sicily, the mixture of fruit, honey and snow was refined over the years into granita, a rich tasting sugar syrup (flavored, for example, with lemon) that is frozen and crushed. It's still made today in many bars in a granita machine.

## Gelato originale

The next step in ice cream's illustrious career brought it to Paris where in the 16th century, a Sicilian court confectioner made genuine gelato for the nobility—ice cream with puréed fruit or flavored milk that was stirred as it froze to keep it creamy. Even today, at ice cream counters, you have to choose between a fruity ice (sorbet) and creamy ice (ice cream or ice milk). Then you have to decide whether you want a "cono o coppo?" (cone or cup?) and if you want it "con panna" (with

whipped cream), although the latter in Italy typically applies to only chocolate ice cream. In Italy, they spread and smooth the gelato with a spatula rather than making balls with an ice-cream scoop.

## Sorbetto

In this more refined version of granita, puréed fruit and sugar syrup are frozen together and gently stirred during the process. Again, it was a Sicilian in Paris who first introduced it to the rest of the world. Since then, sorbet has become a classic item on French menus.

## Semifreddo

Here again, the French term "parfait" has come to be applied to this "half-frozen" concoction. Semifreddo is similar to gelato; cream that is high in fat is whipped and beaten into the basic cream so that it becomes very soft.

## Ice cream

In the U.S., it's mostly ice cream and only sometimes gelato. Ice cream freezes up much harder and gelato has a higher fat content so it won't stay as hard. In either case, it must be creamy, smooth, sweet and cold. Did you know that no one eats more ice cream than Americans? The eternal question remains whether the most popular flavor is vanilla or chocolate. Of course there are so many other flavors out there!

## Aunt Edna's Head-Over-Heels Cheese Course
## Parmesan Foam "Ice Cream" with Green Tomato

Just so you won't think I only cook boring, everyday fare, here's something that's very elegant and yet very simple because **it needs only six ingredients** that jazz it up all by themselves. Plus it combines the cheese and dessert courses in a single dish. A friend of mine weedled the recipe from a gourmet chef at Lake Garda.

The hardest part is getting **2 large or 3 medium bright-green tomatoes**. I recommend that you grow them or arrange ahead of time to purchase from your produce market or at the farmer's market. The rest is easy: Rinse tomatoes, chop and place in a pot with the zest from **1 lemon and 1 cup + 2 tablespoons sugar** (let sit). For the foam, heat **3/4 cup + 1 tablespoon cream** but don't let it boil. Gradu-

ally stir **5 oz. (1 1/4 cups) grated Parmesan and 2/3 cup ricotta** into the cream using a hand blender or hand mixer until dissolved. Pour cream mixture into a bowl. Fill your sink with ice water and immerse bowl down into the ice water. Occasionally mix the cream-Parmesan mixture with the mixer, especially as it becomes cold and more solid, which will also make it foamy. Then cover with plastic wrap and refrigerate for 2 hours. Bring tomatoes to a boil and boil for 5 minutes while stirring. Push through a sieve or food mill and let cool. Then scoop balls of cheese foam into ice cream dishes along with some tomato jam and grissini (Italian breadsticks). The first bite comes as a shock but the rest is pure joy. I just can't let this dish alone!

151

# Tiramisu
## "Pull me up"

An eternal favorite dessert of so many!
No Italian cookbook would be complete
without it.

Feeds 6–8 after a light meal:

1 2/3 cups strong espresso or coffee

1 large lemon

12 oz. (1 1/2 cups) mascarpone

6 oz. (3/4 cup) crème fraiche or sour cream

6 tablespoons milk

1/2 cup sugar or more to taste

1 teaspoon vanilla

5–7 oz. ladyfingers (Better from
a bakery than a supermarket; even
better, see *Basic Baking*, page 102)

2 tablespoons Grappa

1 teaspoon cocoa powder

1 pinch cinnamon

**1** First make the espresso/coffee and let
cool (boiling water and instant espresso
powder works well).

**2** Rinse lemon and dry—remove zest and
squeeze juice out of half. Spoon mascarpone
into a bowl and combine with crème fraiche,
milk, sugar and vanilla. Stir well with the
whisk attachment on a hand mixer until you
have a smooth, spreadable cream. Stir in
lemon zest and 1 tablespoon fresh lemon
juice. Adjust sugar to taste.

Take out a 9" square brownie pan that s 2" high sides. Cover the bottom with a ver of ladyfingers. Combine Espresso and appa and drizzle a little on the ladyfingers, brush on (or you can dip the ladyfingers efly, then put them in the pan). It's best uniformly soak the ladyfingers (if you ve a squeeze bottle, use that).

When the ladyfingers are nice and coffee-lored, spread on one-third of the creamy ixture. Cover with another layer of lady-gers and drizzle with liquid—then cream, en ladyfingers and liquid, then ending ith a layer of cream.

Finally, combine cocoa powder and cinna-on and dust the tiramisu using a fine mesh rainer. Refrigerate covered for at least 8 ours so it can all soak in well before it gets ten up!

ep time: 30 minutes plus cooling time r espresso and 8 hrs. refrigeration time alories per serving (8): 490

# Flan di caffé
Espresso flan

Impressive without a lot of effort

Feeds 6 for spooning:

1 cup + 1 tablespoon espresso

1 vanilla bean

1 cup + 1 tablespoon milk

¾ cup sugar

2 eggs

4 egg yolks

Cinnamon for sprinkling on top

**1** Start by making the espresso (or use instant espresso powder with boiling water). In the meantime, lay the vanilla bean on a board, slit open lengthwise and fold open the two halves. Scrape out the pulp (i.e. the tiny black seeds) with the back of a knife.

**2** Combine vanilla pulp and bean, espresso and milk in a pot and bring to a boil. Turn off burner and let stand.

**3** Preheat oven to 300°F. Take out six individual baking dishes (each with ⅔ cup capacity).

**4** Pour ⅓ cup of the sugar into a small pot. Over medium heat, stir constantly until the sugar liquefies and then turns golden-brown but not too dark. Add 6 tablespoons water and cook at a rolling boil until it becomes syrupy. Distribute this caramel in the baking dishes.

**5** Combine eggs, egg yolks and remaining sugar in a mixing bowl and whisk until nice and foamy. Remove the vanilla bean from the milk and gradually pour milk-espresso mixture into egg mixture while continuing to whisk. Now slowly pour the mixture into the baking dishes slowly so that the caramel remains on the bottom.

**6** Place the small baking dishes in a large baking dish with sides and pour in enough warm water around the small dishes to go at least halfway up the sides. Place on the bottom rack of the oven and cook for about 1 hour—it might take another 10 minutes—until the mixture becomes set and the middle doesn't jiggle. In the meantime it's okay if tiny bubbles are rising in the water around the dishes but don't let it boil. If it begins to boil, add a little cold water.

**7** Remove dishes from the water and let them cool. Run a knife blade around the edges to loosen the flan. Cover each dish with an upside-down plate, hold it tight and reverse quickly. The flan should slide out onto the plate. Then sprinkle with a tiny bit of cinnamon and live it up!

Prep time: 1½ hours, 20 minutes of which you're actually busy (not including cooling time)
Calories per serving: 215

# Frutta con crema di mascarpone
## Fruit with a mascarpone cream

### Tastes like summer

Feeds 4 as a dessert:

1 orange

1/2 lemon

8 oz. mascarpone

2/3 cup cream, more if needed

1 cup powdered sugar

About 1 1/3 lbs. mixed fresh fruit

(e.g. peaches, blackberries,

apricots and blueberries)

Almond biscotti

**1** Rinse orange and lemon; dry. Zest the orange and half a lemon. Squeeze juice from orange and from half of the lemon.

**2** In a bowl, combine mascarpone, cream, powdered sugar, and orange and lemon juices. Mix well with the whisk attachment of an electric mixer until the cream is so smooth and creamy that it slowly runs off a spoon (add cream if necessary).

**3** Rinse peaches and apricots. For berries, run water in the sink or a large bowl, swish the berries in it once; remove immediately, then drain in a colander. Cut peaches and apricots in half and remove the pits. Cut fruit into narrow wedges and distribute on plates along with berries.

**4** Pour mascarpone cream over the top or on the side and sprinkle citrus zest over the top. Lay some biscotti on the side and enjoy.

Prep time: 25 minutes
Calories per serving: 590

## Variation:

### Fragole all'aceto
Carefully rinse about a pound of strawberries (preferably smaller ones) and pinch off stems. Combine berries with 2 tablespoons balsamic vinegar and 2 tablespoons sugar; marinate for several hours. Serve with mascarpone cream (recipe at left). These berries can also be served alongside panna cotta (recipe at right).

# Panna cotta
## "Cooked cream"

Feeds 4 with sweet tooths:

1 vanilla bean

2 cups + 2 tablespoons cream

1/4 cup sugar

1 3/4 teaspoons powdered gelatin

Butter for greasing ramekins (unsalted)

3 ripe peaches

1 tablespoon powdered sugar

2 tablespoons Amaretto

1 tablespoon fresh lemon juice

**1** Slit open vanilla bean lengthwise and fold out the two halves. Scrape out black seeds with a small paring knife and place in a pot along with the vanilla bean, the 2 cups cream, and sugar.

**2** Heat cream mixture. When it starts to boil, reduce heat and simmer for about 10 minutes. Meanwhile, in a small cup or bowl, stir powdered gelatin into the 2 tablespoons of cream—allow to soften for about 3 minutes (the last 3 minutes that the cream is simmering). Whisk gelatin mixture into cream mixture and keep stirring until completely dissolved.

**3** Take out four individual ramekins or molds (each with ⅔ cup capacity) and grease them well with unsalted butter.

**4** Let cream cool slightly, and then pour into ramekins; let cool to room temperature (about an hour or more) and then refrigerate for about 6 hours so the cream will become firm enough for you to reverse it onto a plate.

**5** In the meantime, make the sauce. Rinse peaches and cut in half. Remove and discard pits and dice rest. In a pot, heat peaches along with powdered sugar and Amaretto. Cover, reduce heat to low and simmer for 10 minutes until soft. Let cool and purée with a hand blender or blender (or keep as is). Mix with fresh lemon juice.

**6** Run a thin knife blade around the edges of the panna cotta to loosen each from the ramekins. Cover with an upside-down plate and reverse quickly. The panna cotta slides out onto the plate. Pour peach sauce all around.

Prep time: 25 minutes plus 6 hours refrigeration time
Calories per serving: 480

# Pesche ripiene
## Stuffed peaches

### Worth the trouble!

Feeds 4 as a dessert:

4 large ripe peaches

2 oz. amaretti (almond cookies) or ladyfingers

2 teaspoons candied orange peel
(specialty store—or boil orange zest
in sugar water and let dry)

⅔ cup chopped almonds

⅓ cup powdered sugar

1 egg yolk

⅓ cup white wine or Marsala

**1** Peaches taste even better without the skin. Either peel with a sharp paring knife or pour boiling water over them as you would with tomatoes (cut a couple small slits in the skin first); wait a few minutes and then rinse under cold water. Now you can easily slip off the skins. Cut peaches in half and remove and discard pits. Hollow out the halves a little more with a spoon and mash the removed fruit with a fork or dice very finely.

**2** Preheat oven to 375°F. Grease a baking dish.

**3** Finely crumble amaretti. Chop candied orange peel finely. Combine both with mashed peach, almonds, half the powdered sugar and the egg yolk—mix well.

**4** Fill the hollowed out peach halves with the amaretti mixture. Arrange peaches side by side in the baking dish so they are stable and won't tip over. Trimming the bottoms of the peaches to be flatter helps.

**5** Combine wine or Marsala with remaining powdered sugar and pour into the baking dish around the peaches. Bake on middle rack for about 20 minutes. Let cool slightly or completely.

Prep time: 30 minutes of activity
and 20 minutes baking time
Calories per serving: 240

# Granita di caffè
## Espresso sorbet

### In the summer, rivals espresso after a meal

Feeds 4 as a light dessert:

2 cups + 2 tablespoons strong espresso

(or strong coffee)

⅓ cup sugar

½ teaspoon vanilla

3 teaspoons cocoa powder

1 tablespoon Sambuca liqueur

(optional, or other coffee-type liqueur)

1 pint strawberries

(as small and flavorful as possible)

1 tablespoon powdered sugar

**1** Make espresso (okay to use instant espresso powder and boiling water) and dissolve sugar and 1 teaspoon cocoa powder in it while still hot. Stir in vanilla and also the sambuca if desired.

**2** Let espresso mixture cool. Take out a metal bowl that fits in your freezer. Pour in espresso and freeze for about 4 hours, stirring well once per hour.

**3** Carefully rinse strawberries and pinch or cut off stems, and slice. Combine powdered sugar and remaining cocoa and sift over the top of the strawberries.

**4** Divide granita into portions and transfer to small cups, glasses, or bowls. Place strawberries on top or serve on the side. Time to enjoy!

Prep time: 25 minutes plus 4 hours freezing time with short stirring times
Calories per serving: 100

# Cappuccino ghiacciato
## Iced cappuccino

### ...or cappuccino ice cream, depending on how much time you have

Feeds 4 who don't mind waiting

or 4 in a hurry:

½ cup strong cold espresso

⅔ cup cream

⅓ cup sugar

20 ice cubes

1 pinch cinnamon

1 tablespoon grated chocolate

**1** Make espresso (okay to use powdered instant espresso and boiling water) and chil Combine chilled espresso, cream, sugar and ice cubes in a blender and blend until smooth—but no longer than that or the mixture will become warm.

**2** Either: Pour immediately into glasses—and mix cinnamon and grated chocolate and sprinkle on top. Then serve ice cappuccino with straws and spoons.

**3** Or: Place ice-cold blended espresso mixture in the freezer for at least 1 hour (stir once midway through). Then serve as ice cream in dessert bowls garnished with cinnamon and grated chocolate.

Prep time: 5 minutes
(and possibly 1 hour freezing time)
Calories per serving: 160

# Gelato di limone
## Lemon ice

### Fresh and fruity

Feeds 4 summer vacationers:

1 cup sugar

4 lemons

Small mint leaves

**1** Pour sugar into a pot with 1 cup water. Slowly bring to a boil while stirring constantly. Simmer liquid over medium heat for about 10–12 minutes until it becomes syrupy and a very pale golden color, to create a syrup. Let cool.

**2** In the meantime, rinse lemons, dry and remove zest. Squeeze out lemon juice. Take out a metal bowl that fits in your freezer.

**3** Stir lemon juice and zest into cooled syrup and pour into metal bowl. Place bowl in the freezer and freeze for about 4 hours. The more often you stir the lemon ice during this period (vigorously!), the smoother it will be. Try to at least stir once per hour.

**4** Distribute lemon ice in glasses and garnish with mint leaves, and maybe additional lemon slices as well. Enjoy before it melts!

Prep time: 25 minutes plus cooling time and 4 hours freezing time with short stirring times
Delicious with: Whipped cream
Calories per serving: 210

# Zabaglione

### The cream is a dream!

Feeds 4 in a hurry:

$1/2$ lemon

4 very fresh egg yolks

$1/4$ cup sugar

6 tablespoons Marsala or white wine

A little cocoa powder

**1** For zabaglione, either use a double boiler or create one: you need a stainless steel bowl that you can set on top of a pot. Fill the pot with a couple inches of water and bring to a gentle boil (don't put the bowl on top yet).

**2** In the meantime, rinse lemon half, dry, remove zest and squeeze out juice. Have four nice glasses or small bowls ready.

**3** Place egg yolks and sugar in the bowl (not on the stove yet) and beat or whisk until foamy. Mix in Marsala or wine and lemon zest (but not the juice yet).

**4** Move bowl on top of the pot of gently boiling water and continue whisking mixture until it becomes foamy and thick and warm—this takes about 3–5 minutes. Season to taste with 1–2 teaspoons of the fresh lemon juice, then transfer zabaglione to the glasses/bowls, dust with a little cocoa powder and serve immediately. Otherwise the foam will no longer be foam, which would really be a shame!

Prep time: 15 minutes
Calories per serving: 130

# Zuppa inglese
## Italian trifle

### Nothing English about it!

Feeds 6 after a light meal:

3 very fresh egg yolks

½ cup sugar + 2 tablespoons

½ teaspoon vanilla

¼ cup flour

2¼ cups milk

⅓ lb. candied dried fruit
(apricots, pineapple, etc.)

5–6 oz. ladyfingers (from a good baker
or see *Basic Baking*, page 102)

Sambuca liqueur and marsala
for trickling over the top

¾ cup + 2 tablespoons cream

**1** Separate eggs for making the custard: tap each egg against the edge of a bowl, break apart the shell into two halves and pour yolk back and forth between the halves until all the egg white runs out (discard egg whites or use for something else).

**2** Then combine egg yolks, the ½ cup sugar, vanilla, flour and milk in a pot and stir well. Slowly heat egg yolk mixture over medium-low heat, stirring constantly so that it cooks only long enough for the mixture to become creamy (about 10 minutes). Don't let it boil. Instead, occasionally remove the pot from the burner if necessary. Transfer the custard to a bowl and let cool.

**3** Dice candied fruit very finely. Stir two-thirds of it into the custard. Take out a square pan. Arrange a layer of ladyfingers on the bottom and drizzle with a little liqueur. Spread a layer of custard on top, then another layer of ladyfingers, soak with liqueur, and so on. Finally, beat cream with remaining 2 tablespoons sugar until stiff and spread on top. Sprinkle with remaining candied fruit. Let zuppa inglese stand in the refrigerator (covered) for at least 2 hours.

Prep time: 1½ hours plus 2 hours
refrigeration time
Calories per serving: 420

### Tips

This zuppa is easy to modify. In Tuscany, they like to include a layer of stewed fruit. It's especially delicious with grapes, peaches or apricots.

In southern Italy, the zuppa is very fancy: The cream is cooked as described and then supplemented with 2 oz. grated or finely chopped chocolate and 2 cups (rounded) of ricotta. This type has no candied fruit but does have a golden-brown topping instead: Beat 1 egg white, 1 tablespoon sugar and a little fresh lemon juice until stiff, cool and spread on top of the zuppa. In a very hot oven (475°F), bake only for about 5 minutes until the topping is browned. Serve immediately.

# Torta di cioccolata
## Chocolate cake

Pure sin...

Fills a 10" round cake pan:

7 oz. dark chocolate couverture
(specialty baking store)

$2/3$ cup pine nuts

$1/2$ cup butter + 2 teaspoons butter for the pan

4 eggs

$3/4$ cup sugar

1 teaspoon vanilla

$1/3$ cup flour

Powdered sugar and cocoa powder
for dusting

1 Cut up couverture and melt over a double boiler (or a stainless steel bowl set on top of a pot of 2" deep of boiling water), stirring frequently. Remove from heat and let cool to room temperature.

2 Pour pine nuts onto a large board and chop very finely with a large, heavy knife.

3 Preheat oven to 300°F. Brush butter onto the cake pan.

4 Separate eggs: Tap each egg against the edge of a bowl and break apart the shell into two halves. Part of the egg white will already run into the bowl. Pour yolk back and forth between the halves until almost all the egg white runs out into the bowl. Place the egg yolk in another small bowl and set aside.

5 Place butter in a mixing bowl. Add sugar and vanilla and beat until nice and creamy (use electric mixer). Add egg yolks one by one and beat only until incorporated. Mix in melted chocolate a little bit at a time and then do the same with the flour (sift it in) and then the pine nuts.

6 Now beat the egg whites with the whisk attachment or an electric mixer until slightly stiff (make sure beaters/whisk are exceptionally clean and dry).

7 Fold a bit of the egg whites into the batter to soften it. Then pile the rest of the egg whites on top and fold them in gently until incorporated.

8 Pour the mixture into the pan, using a rubber spatula to scrape the bowl clean. Bake on the middle shelf for 45–50 minutes, or until a toothpick inserted near the middle of the cake comes out clean. Let cake stand in the pan for about 15 minutes, then take it out and let cool on a cake rack before cutting it. Pour powdered sugar and/or cocoa into a small strainer and sift it over the cake. Cut and serve.

Prep time: 30 minutes of activity,
45–50 minutes baking time
Calories per piece (16 pieces): 230

# Crostata di ciliegie
## Crispy cherry tart

**Mamma's favorite**

Fills a 10"–11" round cake pan:

**For the dough:**

2 cups flour or more if necessary

²⁄₃ cup finely chopped almonds

1 pinch salt

¹⁄₃ cup sugar

¹⁄₂ cup + 1 tablespoon cold butter

1 egg

1 egg yolk

**For the filling:**

1 ³⁄₄ lbs. fresh cherries, pitted

¹⁄₂ cup sugar

1 pinch ground cloves

1 lemon

**For brushing on:**

1 egg yolk

1 tablespoon milk

1 For the dough, combine flour, almonds, salt and sugar in a bowl. Cut butter into small cubes and add to the bowl along with 1 egg and 1 egg yolk.

2 First mix the contents of the bowl until it holds together a little, then continue kneading it on a work surface until it looks a little smooth (add a bit of flour if sticky) and you no longer see bits of butter. Form the dough into a ball, wrap in waxed paper and refrigerate for 1 hour.

3 In the meantime, make the filling. Rinse fresh cherries and pull off stems. Remove pits with a cherry pitter.

4 Heat fresh cherries with sugar and cloves. Then simmer over medium-low heat for about 15 minutes uncovered to allow the mixture to thicken. Rinse lemon and dry. Grate off zest and add to cherries.

5 Preheat oven to 350°F. Take out a pan and leave ungreased.

6 Divide dough into thirds and set aside one-third. Knead the other two-thirds together and form into a ball. Lay a sheet of plastic wrap or waxed paper on the table.

Place the ball of dough (the two-thirds) in the center and lay another sheet of plastic on top. Between the plastic sheets, roll out the dough into a thin circle that's slightly larger than the pan. Remove the top sheet of plastic, reverse the dough into the pan and remove the other sheet of plastic. Press dough into the pan, pierce several times with a fork and form an edge all around about 1" high.

7 Roll out the rest of the dough on a floured surface (or between plastic) and cut into strips. Spread stewed cherries on the dough in the pan. Lay dough strips on top of the cherries, about 1" apart. Then turn the pan and lay out another set of strips to form a grid. Mix together egg yolk and milk and brush onto the strips of dough. Bake tart on the middle shelf for about 45 minutes until top crust looks golden brown. Let stand for 10 minutes in the pan, then place on a cake rack and let cool.

Prep time: 2 ¹⁄₂ hours, 45 minutes
of which is baking time
Calories per serving (for 14 servings): 245

# The Communicating-with Your-Whole-Body Glossary

If there was a Dolce Vita School these tips would be part of the curriculum:

"Mano e piede! Our ever popular body language course for conversing with Italians. You will learn how to kiss when saying hello, gesticulate with a full glass of red wine, hold a cell phone (telefonino) while simultaneously twirling spaghetti, shrug your shoulders energetically, heartily pound on someone's shoulder, give powerful hugs, and kiss when saying good-bye."

Okay, we could do that. But we also want to talk like the Italians. What should we talk about? About food? No, we've heard enough about that already. So now what? Maybe this:

## Affari — Business

For Italians, doing business is like breathing—and who ruins a fine meal by talking about breathing? But once your mouth has been rinsed out and the caffè corretto has arrived, it's time to start talking business, if only to give the lunch break the appearance of having a purpose.
Good opener: "Lunch is on me, of course!"
Bad opener: "Lunch is on you, of course!"

## Amici — Friends

Friends are as sacred as family: Better because you choose them yourself but worse because you're not allowed to treat them as badly as your siblings. In Italy, both women and men are proud of their friends and maintain friendships with kisses on the cheek (baci).
Good: "Who do you want me to clobber for you?"
Bad: "Sounds like your problem to me."

## Amore — Love

Amore rhymes with "lavore" (work) but it's mainly only in the beginning that love requires work. The secret to the Italians' success is they've mastered the fine art of talking and listening—must be all that extra time they have for pranzo, caffè, aperitivo and such. Couples who still demonstrate this skill after marriage and after kids are highly regarded, where even in Italy, they are a rare find.
Good: "I could listen to you for hours!"
Bad: "Oh, what did you just say? Were you still talking?"

## Automobile

When the Germans invented the car, God said, "Very nice, but you'll never win a race with that." So he gave the auto to the Italians who worked their magic and invented the Fiat 500 (called Topolino or "Mickey Mouse") as well as the horn, running red lights and parking across four lanes. "Va bene," said God, "but what about winning that auto race?" "Subito," the Italians replied, and invented the Formula 1 Ferrari. But since it was good neither for honking, nor for running red lights nor for parking badly, they weren't sure what to do with it. So God called in a man who came from a land where auto races were officially sanctioned every day, without speed limits, without traffic lights and without stopping. Since then, the Italian automobile found its niche and everybody's happy.
Good: Shoomee, Shoomee, Shoomee!
Bad: "I'm so sick of hearing about Schumacher!"

## Bambini — Kids

Why don't real Italian restaurants have highchairs or crayons? Because a real Italian kid doesn't like to sit quietly at the table but would rather run to the antipasti counter and entertain people with shrieks of joy, teach the waiters to slalom, and take lobsters out of the aquarium to play with their pinchers. When the food comes, they sit down and enjoy their pizza, risotto, mussels, saltimbocca and tiramisu—meaning you won't find a children's menu at real Italian restaurants. But why aren't there any children pictured in this Italian cookbook? Well, um, because, well...
Good: "Just like your papa!"
Bad: "Isn't it past your bedtime?"

## Calcio — Soccer

"I think the Italians are the most peace-loving people in the world." Then you've never stood in the stands at an Italian soccer game! "Yes I have, that's why I say it!" How's that? "What I mean is, anyone who puts that much energy into a game has no strength or energy left to start a war." Okay, I get it.
Good: "As I was saying to my pal, Franz Beckenbauer..."
Bad: "So does Milan have two teams?"

## Dottore!

This is how pizzeria owners address their foreign guests, usually accompanied by an arm thrown wildly in the air that then settles gently and briefly around their shoulder. The following responses have been observed:
Good: "Ciao, maestro" (but without returning the shoulder pounding).
Bad: "Did we go to school together?"

## Famiglia — Family

It starts with your mamma and never stops, whether there are two of you or 10, and whether you want it or not—like working in the family business, like true love. It's always there for you and sticks with you through thick and thin. It knows a lot…it knows better…it wants to know everything, or it doesn't want to know a thing about it. It makes you strong and builds you up. It can make you weep, laugh, scream, fall silent, fight, hug…It's never boring, especially during a meal.
Good: "I love my mamma!"
Bad: "I want to take your sister out for a date and keep her past curfew"

## Loren, Sophia

The most desirable woman in the world, according to a survey conducted in 1999. And the same will be true in 2099. Dream woman, dream lover, dream wife, dream mamma, dream nonna, dream daughter, dream sister, dream colleague of every Italian male aged 0 to 100. She should have done the fountain scene in Fellini's "La Dolce Vita" but she refused to bleach her hair blond.
Good: "Sophia? She comes over and cooks me spaghetti once in a while."
Bad: "Loren, Loren…Isn't that a Swedish name?"

## Mare mediterraneo — The Mediterranean

The sea with gentle waves and eternal sunshine surrounded by three continents, whose European center is, naturalmente, Italy. To the health-conscious outside Italy, it's the paradoxical paradise where people run around full of olive oil, red wine and caffè but don't suffer heart attacks. A lovely theory, say the Italians, but don't forget how healthy it is to watch soccer!
Good: "Would you also like a glass of olive oil?"
Bad: "I'm on a fat-free diet."

## Occhiali da sole — Sunglasses

They make you look cool and mysterious, and they let you stare shamelessly. If you wear them all the time, they prove the sun always shines in Italy. Oh, right, and they also protect you from the sun.
Good: "Could I have your autograph?"
Bad: "Excuse me, sir, the sun isn't even shining."

## Rumore — Noise

If you consider the hissing of a cappuccino maker, choir practice, soccer cheers, the ringing of cell phones, children's laughter, a chef cursing, plates clashing, radios blaring, Vespa horns blaring and raucous greetings to be noise, you probably also like to listen to quiet boring music during dinner. How sweet!
Good: "And now, everybody, SALUTE!"
Bad: "Does your wife have to laugh so loud?"

## Toscana — Tuscany

This region is like an open-air museum in the heart of Italy, with considerable resources. Duty: Visiting the statues and structures of Florence, Siena, Pisa and Lucca, then touring the olive groves and red wine vineyards and daily demonstrations of everyday farm life by the natives. Pleasure: Simply eating and drinking in Tuscany (or anywhere in Italy for that matter).
Good: "Cypresses always make me so introspective."
Bad: "Y'all have strange trees here!"

## Ufficio — Office

Offices divide the country more than the conflicts between the North and South, men and women, or AC Milan and Inter Milan. The Italian people are divided fairly equally into civil servants who sit behind counters and do nothing and petitioners who wait in front of counters and can't do anything about it. Depending on which side of the counter you occupy, it can be very calming or very upsetting. So make sure of the positions of your individual guests before you bring this up at the table. Notice I didn't say "Don't bring it up!"
Good (if none are civil servants): "Recently I was at the tax office and…"
Bad (if one or more are civil servants): "Recently I was at the tax office and…"
Very good: (if all are civil servants but don't work for the tax office): Recently I was at the tax office and…"

## Vacanza — Vacation

Ciao bella, ciao bello, see you in our next book! We've had a good time but now we really need to take some time off. And when we come back, we'll throw a huge party, we promise!

# Index

# Credits

## The Authors:

**Sebastian Dickhaut**, text pages

**Cornelia Schinharl**, recipe pages

**Kelsey Lane**, American team editor

## Photography
### Germany and U.S. teams

Food photographs: Barbara Bonisolli, Lisa Keenan
Recipe Stylist: Hans Gerlach
Photographer's Assistants: Kristina Babics, Norbert Hellinger
People photographs: Alexander Walter
Requisitioning, styling & food for people photos: Sigrid Burghard, Sabine Sälzer, Christa Schmedes

**Tomato on title page:** Studio Eising / Martina Görlach

**Barbara Bonisolli:**
Food photos, product photos pages 8–9, Souvenirs pages 28–29: music, bar sign
Feature product photos pages 41, 55, 74, 76, 84, 85, 90, 92, 119, 140, 143, 147, 148

**Lisa Keenan:**
People photos pages 63, 75, 82, 89, 103, 107, 111, 123 (photo on right), 135, 155 (photo on right)

**Alexander Walter:**
People photos of basic models (except those on pages indicated above), still-life feature photos pages 3, 7, 16, 22, 42, 62, 64, 65, 69, 135, 157

**Stock Food Photos**
Studio Bonisolli: pages 14, 78, 82, 114, 130, 158
Studio Eising: page 36
S. & P. Eising: pages 81, 112
Susie Eising: page 24
Bernard Grilly: page 29 (ice cream man)
Lehmann, Joerg: page 28 (table and chair)
Halsey Creativ Serv.: page 34
Harry Bischof: pages 56, 96
Maximilian Stock: pages 12, 128
Studio Eising / Martina Görlach: pages 28–29 (8 motifs: bag, newspaper, oil & vinegar, espresso cup, cell phone, spaghetti, water carafe, Averna), 50, 151
Image Bank / Sean Justice: page 28 (man with roses)
F Ruggeri: page 29 (sea)
Franz Marc Frei: page 29 (general store), 115, 150
Roberto Simoni: pages 13 (2), 18, 58, 59, 80, 98

The dolce vita models: Janna Sälzer, Pina Sälzer, Gabie Schnitzlein, Markus Röleke, Christian Finger, Alexander Klingholz

## German Team:
Editing and production: Sabine Sälzer
Layout and design: Sybille Engels, Thomas Jankov
Production: Susanne Mühldorfer
Reader: Susanne Bodensteiner
Final corrections: Mischa Gallé, Fiorella de Lotto
Recipe testing: Ursula Eicher, Dorothea Henghuber, Ulla Thomsen, Redaktion Kochen
Set: Filmsatz Schröter, Munich
Repro: w & co
Printing and binding: Druckhaus Kaufmann

## U.S. Team:
Editing: Kelsey Lane
Translation: Christie Tam
Production: Patty Holden
Photography: Lisa Keenan
Reader: Randy Mann

A special thank you to Bob Lane for helping with the index preparation.

Published originally under the title ITALIAN BASICS: Alles, was man braucht für das dolce vita zu Hause
© 2001 Gräfe und Unzer Verlag, GmbH, Munich

English translation copyright: © 2002 Silverback Books

ISBN: 1-930603-96-7

Printed in Singapore